A Priest in Hell

GANGS, MURDERERS, AND
SNITCHING IN A CALIFORNIA JAIL

RANDALL RADIC

ECW Press

Published by ECW Press, 2120 Queen Street East, Suite 200,
Toronto, Ontario, Canada M4E 1E2
416.694.3348 / info@ecwpress.com

LIBRARY AND ARCHIVES CANADA CATALOGUING IN PUBLICATION

Radic, Randall
A priest in hell : gangs, murderers, and snitching
in a California jail / Randall Radic.

ISBN-13: 978-1-55022-869-4
ISBN-10: 1-55022-869-2

1. Radic, Randall. 2. Prisoners—California—Biography.
3. Criminals—California—Biography. 4. Clergy—California--
Ripon—Biography. I. Title.

HV9468.R35A3 2009   365′.44092   C2008-905430-X

Cover design: Brett Miller
Cover image: © Christian Schmidt / Zefa / Corbis
Text design: Tania Craan
Typesetting: Mary Bowness
Printing: Thomson-Shore

To my Dad,
who is probably rolling
over in his grave.

ACKNOWLEDGEMENTS

This book wouldn't exist without three women: my mother and my sister, who paid my attorney and came up with a big chunk of restitution money for my initial plea bargain. Once I got out of jail, Sharla paid my attorney and went to work to earn the money to pay the bills and buy the bread. She told me to "go write."

I love all three of them. They are wonderful, honest people.

My publisher, Jack David, is a handsome, talented Canuck, who recognizes superlative talent when he sees it. My dictionary tells me that "Canuck" is "often used disparagingly." I'm using it favorably, as a compliment. He has my gratitude. My editor, Emily Schultz, is a flat-out genius. She waved her magic wand and improved my meager efforts. Thank you, thank you very much.

Chloe decorated my office, the lair in which the Crazy Croat writes. Without her festive, artistic creations, I would have been too bored to do anything.

Boh Gay, Mike Wilson, Matt Berg, Josh Ordonez, Jefferson Stillwell III, Todd Hayford, Porky, Mikey, and Jimbo — thanks dogs.

Mike Babitzke has my undying gratitude. Not only is he a superb attorney, he has soul and a sense of humor. "I wanna be like Mike." I sing paeans to the office of the District Attorney in San Joaquin County. Their integrity shines. To the COs who treated me with respect, I say thanks for protecting me.

LET'S MAKE A DEAL

The echoing sound of metal on metal again, the key turns in the lock, the door opens. The Hispanic bailiff stands all buff in the doorway. "Mr. Radic," he says, motioning me out. "Your attorney wants to speak with you."

Dragging my chains, which sound like gravel crunching down a metal chute, I walk ten feet, turn left, stand at the "bubble" door, waiting for the bailiff to unlock it. The bubble is a four-foot by eight-foot room, divided in half by a low wall topped by chain-link that has a hole cut in it. The hole is for passing legal documents. The chain-link fence is so you can see and talk to your attorney in privacy. There is one chair on each side of the fence.

The piss-yellow door is unlocked by the guard. "Thank you," I say as I enter and seat myself. The door is locked behind me. My side of the fence is yellow on the inside. The other side of the fence is pastel green. It is warmer in here than in the holding tank.

The rival door opens, a plump man enters. His hair is graying, balding; as he seats himself across from me, I note facial hairs his razor missed, most of them just under his nose, like vines in front of a dark cave.

"Good morning, Randall," he says, placing a folder, one of those old-fashioned attorney-kind folders (the ones that are a dried-shit-brown color with the funky metal clasp), on the small ledge between us, just in front of the paper pass hole. "How are you?"

"Nervous," I say, "but otherwise good."

"Okay." He gets right to the point. "Two gentlemen, the district attorney and his investigator, will join us in just a few moments. They will ask you some questions. Be sure to answer fully, providing precise details." His voice is steady, musical, with a hint of nasality.

Michael F. Babitzke is his name; attorney at law is his vocation. Criminal law is his specialty. According to one of his hyped, high-priced peers, he is "an honest, hard-working attorney who has a wonderful presence in the courtroom." He is my attorney. And I am thankful for him because he is smart as God.

"How long will it take?" I ask, sitting slumped in my chair, hands clasped in my lap.

"Probably thirty to forty minutes," he says. "Why?"

"I just like to know how long things are going to take." I pause, afraid to ask what I want to ask. Taking a deep breath, I exhale, trying to eject my inner fear in a puff of carbon dioxide. It doesn't work. I am still afraid. "Do you think they'll make a deal?"

"I think they're very interested. And if they attach importance to what they hear, they will probably deal. But remember, nothing is guaranteed."

He is hedging his bets, I know. He doesn't like to be pinned down, make guarantees. He's been around too long, seen too much, to do that.

"I understand that," I say. "But if they do make a deal, how soon will I get out?" I need hope, something I can lessen my fear with.

"Within a week, I would anticipate," he says as he stands.

"You'll be here when they're questioning me, right?"

"Yes." He leaves the bubble. I wait, trying to project myself into the immediate future, running through the many, various scenarios of the coming interrogation. In my mind, the conclusion of each version is thus: I answer their questions, my answers are good, but they are not good enough. And having gleaned what I own, they will abandon me to finish my time in jail. I will go to DVI, which is Deuel Vocational Institute. It sounds like a kind of trade school where they teach you how to be a car mechanic or how to repair crunched fenders. Wrong. DVI is the processing center for inmates. They give you psych tests, interview you, decide if you are "prison material." Then after six weeks they assign you to one of California's thirty-two prisons and ship you off.

If I can't make a deal, since my remaining time is so short, I will be in DVI for the next nine weeks; after that, I will be released. Then they will subpoena me to appear anyway. And if I fail to appear, or refuse to testify, they will imprison me for obstruction of justice.

It's a sick way of thinking, one I have acquired through the past six months of being in jail. The disease of incarceration: trust no one, because no one is to be trusted.

If you think of jail as some freakish system of education, the most important course is Survival 101: basic, dynamic techniques for continued existence that include seminars on the following subjects: don't barter, don't trade, don't owe anyone anything, never socialize outside your race. Hate everyone who is not the same color you are, act tough, look mean and supercool, and remember that violence is always better than passivity.

The cumulative effect: detached, vigilant distrust.

All this thinking results in only more fear. The BIG dog of fear, noshing on an eight-hundred-ton bone of fear. I wipe my palms on my orange-clad thighs, but they're still moist with sweat. I sympathize with Lady Macbeth. Sliding my tongue over my lips doesn't moisten them because my tongue feels like tree bark, dry, brown, highly texturized. My breathing is shallow, one notch on the hysteria gauge from hyperventilation.

Babitzke returns through the pastel green door, leads two men into their half of the bubble. Which is two too many. It's crowded on their side.

Silk Cut brand of cigarette, already lit. That's what the DA looks like: trim, with incandescent eyes, à la mode presentation.

A mustachioed maduro cigar sits down in the sole chair on the "white hats'" side — the investigator. I mislay his name as he introduces himself, because I'm undergoing a type of self-inflicted mental X-ray, attempting to isolate and photograph the single growing tumor of my anxiety.

Silk Cut says, "I'm Robert Himelblaugh, the district attorney." The Man — wired into the power, and the power flows through him and his office.

I nod, unable to respond due to paralysis of my larynx.

"We're going to ask you some questions," says the DA. "Take your time. Answer as clearly as you can, be as specific as you can." He favors me with a small smile. This small, human gesture thaws my vocal cords. I don't say anything but feel safe knowing that the capacity for speech is mine once more.

"Mr. Radic," says the investigator, "or may I call you Randall?"

"Randall is fine," I say.

"Randall, I'm going to ask you some questions concerning Roy Gerald Smith. But first," he glances down at his spiral notepad, "has anyone made any promises or representations to you regarding the outcome of this conversation?"

"No, sir."

"And you requested this meeting, did you not?"

"Yes, sir."

"Why do you feel compelled by this case?" says the investigator, staring at me.

"I don't think I understand the question," I say, looking to Babitzke for help, for clarification. He says nothing, stands still as an insect.

"You obviously are compelled by Roy Smith," says the DA,

coming to my rescue. "Why are you willing to provide us with information concerning this case?"

"For two reasons: one, I'd like to get out earlier, even though I only have two months to go. Two, and most importantly, Roy is . . ." I look down at my orange-clad legs, like trying to see the bottom of the lake before I jump in. "He's a monster. If he gets out, the same thing will happen all over again. Some other poor woman will end up dead."

I glance from the investigator to Himelblaugh, look for acceptance in their eyes. I mean what I just said.

"Does Roy ever make any sexual references?" says the investigator.

My eyebrows come together, providing the expression of "whaddaya mean?"

"In other words," says Himelblaugh, starting to twist his body, "does Mr. Smith ever speak of sexual interludes or of sexual preferences?"

"Yes," I say. "He does. In fact, almost every remark that I have made to him, he has twisted it somehow . . . into something nasty."

The investigator: "Can you give us an example?"

"Sure. We were walking one day, Bob and I, and Roy jumped in behind me — which gives me a creepy feeling, knowing he is behind me — and Bob made a joke about the spicy hot dogs we had for lunch. Roy perverted it into some kind of penis analogy. I can't remember exactly what he said. But it was sick and totally out of place."

"So he contorts statements, said in innocence, into bizarre sexual innuendos?" says the DA, again half-twisting his body while wringing out an invisible wet towel with his hands.

"Yes. He also made the statement to me, once, that the police had seized his computer when they arrested him. I told him they had seized mine too. Then he added, very quickly, even though I didn't ask, 'I look at porno, but it's not kiddie porn.'"

I gaze straight at the DA. He looks back.

"I know that he's been twice convicted of child molestation," I say.

The DA nods.

"Randall, how many conversations have you had with Mr. Smith?" says the investigator.

"Many," I say. "Too many to count."

"Does Mr. Smith know you are a priest?"

"Yes."

"Did he at any time believe that you were functioning as a priest in these conversations or that he was confessing to you in your capacity as a priest?"

"No."

"How do you know that?"

"Because he often made jokes about taking up a collection for me. Told me he was making some Styrofoam collection plates for me. He knew what I'd done because he got the paper, read it. I made the statement to him that I 'used' to be a pastor but was not anymore."

"So these were nothing more than simple conversations?"

"Yes."

"Did he have conversations with other people?"

"Some, I'm sure. But not many because he rarely comes out of his cell, even during rec time. And then just to smoke or get a book."

"But he would have conversations with you?"

"Yes, and with Bob."

"Why do you think that was? That he talked primarily to you and Bob?"

"Probably because we're all 'old guys,'" I say, which causes the DA to smile. "And because I'm from Ripon, and Roy worked in that area, at Franzia Winery. And because Bob is in for murder also."

"So it was compatibility of age as much as anything?" says the investigator.

"Yes. There are very few inmates over twenty-one or twenty-two."

He glances at his notes again, turns a page, then back again. "In any of your conversations . . . did Mr. Smith tell you the whereabouts of the body of Mary Starkey?"

Boom. Right between the eyes — the Granddaddy Question: do I know where the body is?

"No, sir."

I stare at his face, seeking some kind of sign. Disappointment, disbelief, anger. I can't read anything from his features.

"Did Mr. Smith make any reference to Mary Starkey at all?"

"Yes, sir."

"In what manner? And please make your explanation as detailed as possible."

"There were three what I call 'damning conversations,'" I say. "Should I go through them as they happened?"

"Please," says the DA.

"Okay," I say, marshaling my retentive powers. "My attorney has copies of all three of the pertinent conversations. All are dated, and I noted the time."

"Did you say both dated and the time?" says the investigator, jotting something in his spiral notepad.

"Yes, sir. And my fiancée has the original copies."

"How long after the conversations occurred and when you wrote them down?" says the investigator.

"About ten to twenty minutes," I say.

"Why did you write them down?" the investigator says.

"Because I knew they were important, and because I knew that if I didn't I'd start to forget the details," I say.

"Like we all do," says the DA, nodding in agreement and what I hope is approval.

"Please relate the first conversation," says the investigator.

Six eyes peer at me. My attorney exudes an aura of complete confidence. The district attorney, all suave and stylish, is attentive, alert, pensive, a three-in-one special effect.

Pen poised over his notepad, like Moses on Mount Sinai, the investigator looks puffy with expectancy, an oblique leaning aspect that speaks of heightened interest.

BEGINNINGS

I'm trying to make a deal to get out of jail. I am here because I embezzled, forged, and committed fraud. I had this really, really good idea. At least it seemed so at the time. Now, of course, it seems like a really, really bad idea. The mother of all bad ideas.

The church, my church, where I was the pastor, let me live in a house called a parsonage. The church owned the house; it sat one block over from the church itself, in what I called "the slums of Ripon." All the houses were small, boxy projections of the early 1950s. No cars in front yards were up on cinder blocks yet, but it was coming. They were already parking their cars on their front lawns. The parsonage was small and boxy, with three bedrooms and two bathrooms; it was adequate but in dire need of some maintenance. It needed a new roof, new flooring, new plumbing, a new fence, and grass in the yard. Not new grass, grass. Oh, and gallons of paint inside and out, preferably in anything other than high-gloss hospital white, which was its inaugural color.

But it was free.

Pastors of my church were expected to be spiritual and poor, emphasis on the poor. Because poor is spiritual. And the way the church guaranteed spirituality was to pay poorly.

I was tired of sucking on the shriveled teat of poverty, barely able to make my car payments and buy food. I wanted to be somebody. I wanted people to like me. And most of all, I wanted someone to love me. If I had a plump car, trendy clothes, and money to spend in nice restaurants, then people would like me. Some of them might even love me.

I did it for love. I know that sounds ludicrous and crazy, but think about it. What would you do to feel loved, to have someone to love? Probably — if you're human and normal and unafraid to admit that you *crave* love — just about anything.

So I forged a deed of trust, which stated that the house had been sold to me, that I owned it free and clear. I got the deed notarized and took out a first and second mortgage on the house for $200,000.

I made the mortgage payments with the money the mortgage companies had loaned me. The rest of the money I spent. I got a new car, a silver BMW 330. And I started painting because I'd always been interested in art but couldn't afford ten-dollar tubes of oil paints and hundred-dollar canvases. I got a giant easel, set the four-foot by five-foot canvas on it, and started painting. Although it was more like scraping paint than brushing it on. I even stretched two giant canvases. First I built frames for them. Then yanked and pulled and stapled the cloth. Then applied gallons of gesso. In the end, I had two BIG BOY canvases. One was eight feet by eight feet, the other eight feet by ten feet. I hung them on the walls in the garage. Then I began painting on them. Whole tubes of paint were applied with drywall spatulas, great thick swaths of paint.

I ate out all the time at expensive restaurants, where they serve risotto instead of rice. My favorite was Christopaolo's. Every afternoon I'd arrive for lunch. Caesar salad with anchovies to clean the palate. Then sea bass grilled to perfection in some exotic nectar. All of it washed down with ZD Chardonnay. When Christopaolo's got boring, I drove the Beemer to Oceana's, where I dined on swordfish floating daintily in raspberry sauce. The waitress didn't "serve" it. She delivered it with religious solemnity, like High Mass. For dessert, there were only two choices really: Cherries jubilee or the chocolat éclair that was so light it hovered over the plate. I'd leave a fifty percent tip.

Other times I would drive over to San Francisco and dine at Bin 38. They advertised an "ambitious and interesting menu." And it was. The spareribs melted in my mouth, and the Kobe-style flank steak made me want to kiss a cow. They also served a Madeira-laced braised salmon with white asparagus, which I devoured with pleasure. Definitely haute cuisine.

After dinner, a short drive to La Dolce Vita Wine Lounge. It was ground zero for posses of sophisticated, intelligent techies from Silicon Valley. It offered thirty-seven different wines by the glass, and I indulged in taste flights from the best wineries in the world. They even had cupcakes to snack on.

I bought furniture for my house from David's, an exclusive designer boutique. A down-filled couch and matching ottoman for ten grand, and they were on sale. I ordered them in this unbelievable burnt-orange color. A new bed with 1,200-thread-count eggshell sheets. Like sleeping on a cloud.

I smoked ten-dollar Hoyas, sometimes five a day. And I looked good while I puffed away because I wore dark Chicago relax fit jeans ($158), a Henningsvaer wool sweater ($269), and a Laxenburg coat with buttons made from horn ($2,200). When I preached on Sundays, I wore black gabardine wool slacks ($300) and black Drexler wingtips.

And I took a couple of nice vacations. One to La Jolla, and one to Lake Tahoe. I rented Jet Skis, worked on my tan, and ate at restaurants where cordon bleu chefs concocted food that I'd never heard of, like paella and escabeche. And a decent wine cost $300. The next night I'd eat at Joe's Crab Shack on Pacific Beach, drinking green margaritas from a plastic cup while watching surfers silhouetted against a setting sun. Later I'd sit on the verandah of the house I'd rented and smoke a cigar as I listened to the ocean breathe in great, wet sighs.

It was great because people liked me. I had a fiancée, and she loved me. We were planning on getting married after my divorce from my second wife, who lived in Modesto.

Then the money ran out, and I couldn't make the mortgage payments anymore. I needed more money to pay back the money that wasn't mine in the first place. If I didn't get a lot of money fast, there'd be the devil to pay. There was only one thing left to sell. So I sold my church, even though it wasn't mine to sell. Got a commercial real estate agent who had it appraised, then showed it to potential buyers. Some guy made an offer. Inspections were performed, the money went into escrow, I signed a bunch of papers, the title was transferred, and the deal was done.

I opened a new bank account in Modesto, depositing $500,000. Then somebody flushed the toilet. The bank got suspicious and froze my accounts before I could transfer the money down south to San Diego, which was where I planned to move. I had already resigned from the church, effective October 30.

October 20, 2005, I was walking over to the local gym for my morning workout. Out of the corner of my eye, I saw one of the directors of the church driving down Main Street in his red Nissan. He saw me and whipped a hard left turn so he wouldn't have to wave to me. Totally out of character for him. A feeling hit me like someone dumped a bucket of ice water over me. I knew that they knew.

I raced back home, changed clothes, and grabbed the clothes from the closet in the spare bedroom. This was my getaway closet. I knew it was coming sooner or later, so I had everything I planned to take with me in it. Dumping it all in the trunk of my brand-new black 2006 BMW 750i, I drove to Modesto. Arriving at my new bank, I attempted to withdraw $5,000. The teller, with a smug look blazing from her face, told me my account had been frozen.

I left immediately, headed for Colorado, where my family

lived. Out of $500,000, I had $1,000 in my wallet. The rest of the money was in the bank, except for the $100,000 I'd spent on the car.

Looking back on it now, I maintain I was temporarily insane, because it was just so stupidly wrong.

Near Reno, I called Sharla, my fiancée, and told her the truth about what I'd done. She was at work. "Sharla," I said into my cell phone.

"Hi," she said. "What's going on?"

"Well, I'm driving to Colorado to see my mom."

"What?"

"Yeah," I said. "Time for me to visit her. Listen, I have to tell you something, and I don't think you're going to like it."

"What? What's going on?" Panic in her voice.

"You know all that money I told you my mom gave me?"

"Yeah."

"Well, she didn't. I mortgaged the parsonage and then sold the church."

Stunned silence.

"You what?" she said. Then added, "I can't believe this."

"Well, it's true. Finally," I said, "I can tell the truth. And it feels so good. The guilt has been killing me."

"I knew it," she shouted into the phone. "I knew something was wrong. You've been losing weight and looking all pale and everything."

"Yeah," I said. "I can't sleep, can't eat. I just feel sick with guilt and shame. I can barely look anyone in the face anymore." I paused. "I don't know what to do."

"Well, going to Colorado is not going to make it go away," she said. "Does anybody else know?"

"I'm assuming the police are in on it even as we speak," I said. "I went to my bank to get some cash, but the account is frozen."

"Oh, my God."

"Yeah, and I do not want to go to jail. So I'm leaving."

"Randy," she said. "That won't help. They'll catch you anyway."

"I know," I said.

"Listen," she said. "I've got to get back to work. I want you to turn around and come back. Turn yourself in."

"No. I'm too scared."

"I . . . I . . . don't know what to say," she said. "Except this: I'm glad it wasn't another woman. That's what I was afraid of."

I laughed. "Well, lucky you. It's certainly not another woman." Then my voice grew somber. Self-pity settled on me. "I doubt you'll ever want to talk to me again. And I understand."

"Don't be an idiot," she sparked. "I love you, you know that. But you have to come back and turn yourself in."

"I'll think about it, but it scares me too much," I said.

"I've got to get back to work," she said. "Call me. I'll be home by three."

"Okay," I said. "I'll call. Bye."

I felt a relief, the relief of telling the truth. I'd been depressed and nauseous for the past six months. I thought the money from the sale of the church would make it all go away. But it didn't. All it did was pull the knot in my stomach tighter.

The next day, late at night, I got to my mom's house. I'd already called her and told her what was going on.

Her comment was a doozy: "Oh, Randy."

She then informed me that I could stay the night, but then I would have to leave. She would not harbor a fugitive. This stunned me. I had nowhere to go. If I continued running, I would never see anyone I loved again, never see anyone I cared about or who cared for me. The thought hummed like a flawed tuning fork in my brain.

After about four hours of restless sleep in her spare bedroom, I made up my mind that I would have to turn myself in. The idea curdled my inner organs, left me gasping for breath. But it was the only way to get rid of the guilt, which was like swimming under ice. No way out and drowning fast.

Sharla called and told me to get an attorney. She gave me three names and numbers. She got them from her sister, Maureen.

"Whatever you do," she said, her voice stern, "do not turn yourself in to the police and confess to them."

"Why not?" I asked, oozing naïveté. I didn't understand.

"'Cuz they'll bury you with it," she said. "Maureen talked to a friend of hers. He's a criminal defense attorney. He said don't do it. Only talk to your attorney." She paused, then added for emphasis, "Is that clear? Only to your attorney."

"Yeah, I understand." A wave of dizziness washed over me.

I dialed the first number and talked to Michael F. Babitzke in Stockton, California. He told me not to worry, just drive back and come to his office.

Three hours later I kissed my mom and sister good-bye and returned the way I'd just come. I felt separated from the world as I drove, like I was an ant in a glass ant farm. I was running down a tunnel inside my own little world. People watched me, and I watched them watching me through my glass window looking out on this other world. From my perspective, I was outside looking in.

Back in California, I drove to Stockton. Sitting down in Babitzke's office, I told him about my crime. I was still scared, though, so I did not tell him about the forged deed on the parsonage. I only mentioned the church. Lying had become such a way of life that I couldn't stop it — not yet.

Babitzke arranged for me to turn myself in. Three days later I drove to Manteca, walked into the courthouse. Sixty seconds later the judge released me on my own recognizance. My next court date was one month away. I had to turn the BMW over to the police. It was parked on a side street near the courthouse. One of their officers, Detective Sauer, drove it away. Sharla picked me up in front of the courthouse.

With no place to go, I stayed with Sharla, sleeping in her spare bedroom. My picture was on the front page of the newspapers every day. And I was the lead story on all the evening newscasts. Seeing myself on television, hearing the newscasters describe my crimes, alarmed me. Upset and queasy, I switched off the television, believing that would make the nightmare go away.

At night, lying in Sharla's spare bedroom, guilt, shame, and fear pricked me from all angles, like poisoned darts. Crying silently, I stared at the ceiling fan whirling slowly above me. The pulsating shush-shush sound it made sounded like felon-felon, liar-liar, loser-loser.

After a week, the authorities knew about the house too. Four more felonies were added to my charges; a warrant was issued for my arrest. I was about to learn — the hard way — that lying was like quicksand, it sucks you down and suffocates you.

ARREST

November 4, 2005

I back the VW Jetta out of the garage. Next to me, in the passenger's seat, sits Sharla. In the back, his seat belt on, sits Andrew, her eight-year-old son. Next to him sits his huge black backpack. In it reside schoolbooks, tablets, pencils, toys, anything and everything. I will drop him at the school bus stop at the end of the block, then drive my fiancée to work. From there, I will go to the gym and then over to my ex-wife's house to watch the girls.

A gold Lincoln Town Car is parked fifty yards from the house. In it is Detective Danny Sauer of the Ripon Police Department. I do not notice it or him.

At the corner, I pull the car over. Andrew and his black backpack emerge from the back seat.

"Bye, Andrew," says his mom.

"See ya, Andrew," I say.

"Bye," says Andrew.

I turn left at the stop sign, travel fifty yards to another stop sign, and prepare to turn left again. A white Ripon police car appears in my rearview mirror, its lights flashing. A sense of foreboding fills me; a chill runs up my spine to my mouth, leaving the sour, metallic taste of fear. Completing the left turn, I pull over.

The white police car parks behind me, while the gold Lincoln Town Car parks in front of me. Effectively sandwiched, I sit stunned.

A black-uniformed officer approaches my side window. I lower the window. A bull-faced man, thick and squat, like a fireplug, looks at me from underneath reddish eyebrows.

"Mr. Radic?" he asks.

"Yes, sir."

"I'm going to ask you to step out of the car, sir." He steps back from the car door.

"Okay." I climb out of the car. My mouth tastes coppery, the corrosive metallic tang of fear and consequences. My right hand begins to tremble.

Detective Sauer joins our little society. Twenty something, he is tall, dark, and handsome, dressed in tan slacks and a sport shirt. He turns me around to face the car, begins patting me down. It's an easy search because I am wearing a T-shirt, a sweatshirt, gym shorts, athletic shoes.

"You got anything on you?" asks Detective Sauer.

"Just my wallet and my cell phone," I reply. "Am I under arrest?"

"Yes," states Detective Sauer. His voice is mechanical, as are his movements. A practiced professional. He confiscates my wallet and cell phone, places them in a plastic baggie, which he seals.

Sharla gets out of the car as Detective Sauer cuffs my hands behind my back. He walks me around to the passenger side of the Jetta.

"Call Traci —" I start to say to Sharla.

"Sorry. You're under arrest. No talking to anyone other than police personnel," declares Detective Sauer.

"What's going on?" asks my fiancée.

"Your boyfriend is under arrest," Detective Sauer tells her.

The uniformed officer stands beside his car, speaking into a microphone.

"Excuse me, officer," I say to the detective. "Can I say something to my fiancée? I'm supposed to be going to my ex-wife's to babysit."

"Sure," says Detective Sauer. "But keep it short. And no touching or passing anything between you. Stand five feet apart."

"Call Traci," I tell her. "Explain what's going on. That I won't be able to make it. Tell her I'm sorry."

"Okay," she says.

"And call Babitzke," I add. "First thing, call him. Tell him I've been arrested. He's got to get me out."

"Okay."

"Right," says Detective Sauer. "Time to go." He passes me over to the officer, who leads me to his car, opens the door, presses me inside. His hand protects my head just like on TV.

I've never been in a police car before. The seat is hard, made of washable, solid plastic. My cuffed hands dig into my lower back. A lattice of steel divides me from the front.

The officer gets in, speaks into his microphone. "Unit 32, en route," he says.

He drives to the police station, which is about half a mile away. A chain-link gate rolls aside as we approach. We drive through the gap, and the gate rolls closed. Around a corner and he parks the car. The back of the police station.

The officer opens my door, takes my arm as I clamber out.

"Stand here for a minute," he orders. Then he goes inside the station, through a gray steel door.

I stand mute. Looking around, I note my BMW 750i. It is parked one row behind me, facing the opposite direction. Its pearlescent black finish is coated with dust.

The officer returns. "Right," he says. "This way."

Holding my cuffs with one hand, he accompanies me through the gray steel door. Inside is gray cement, some type of vestibule with steel doors leading out to different rooms.

"Have a seat," he says, pointing to a metal bench.

I sit, feeling the goosebumps rise on my legs. My emotions want to be moved but can find nothing familiar on the stark, scorched wasteland before them. I breathe, but my lungs feel tight like I'm holding my breath.

He empties the plastic baggie, which contains my wallet and cell phone. Taking my driver's license, he begins entering information from it into a computer. The room is spartan: a wall phone, gray cabinets above a shelf whereupon resides the computer.

Finished, he turns to me. "Right," he says. "This way."

We pass through a steel door to my right.

"In here," he says, pointing to a holding cell.

I enter. He shuts the door, which is barred, just like on TV.

My holding cell has one stainless steel bench, upon which I drop my cold haunches. There is a stainless steel toilet, a stainless steel sink. No mirror. It is five feet by eight feet, composed of gray cement.

The officer stands at another shelf, his back to me. He is keying another computer.

"Am I allowed a phone call?" I ask.

"Yes," he says, not turning. "But not right now. Detective Sauer will handle that."

He leaves.

I sit, cold and alone.

Two other officers wander in, pretend to do something at the computer. They are just sightseeing. Look at the criminal.

An hour later Detective Sauer enters the room, drops his keys and his cell phone on the shelf. He looks at me. "You okay?"

"I'm cold," I say. "And I'm thirsty."

He stares at me, thinking. Then moves to the cell door. "You're not going to do anything to harm yourself, are you?" he asks.

"What?" I don't understand the question.

"I mean you're not suicidal, are you?"

"No," I laugh. "I'm too much of a coward for anything like that."

He smiles. "Right," he says. "I'm not supposed to, but I'll take your cuffs off. Step over to the door."

I back myself to the cell door. Reaching between the bars, he unlocks my cuffs.

"We have to be sure that you're not going to hurt yourself," he explains. "We're liable if you do."

"Thanks," I say, rubbing my wrists.

I sit down on my bench.

"Am I allowed a phone call?" I ask.

"Yes," he replies. "In fact, you're allowed three phone calls. We'll do that in a few minutes. I have some paperwork to take care of first."

He leaves.

Three minutes later another officer enters the room. He carries a bright yellow package. Pulling it open, he unfolds a yellow rubbery blanket.

"Here," he says. "Detective Sauer said you might be cold." He stuffs the blanket through the bars.

"Thanks," I say. I wrap the blanket around myself. Numb with fear, I am on autopilot. When I speak, it is as if I am reading my lines from a script, like a machine, without feeling.

He leaves.

Detective Sauer returns about fifteen minutes later.

"One more thing to do," he tells me, "then you can make your phone calls."

"Okay."

He leaves again, carrying the baggie with my wallet and cell phone.

Another officer enters the room, his pistol prominent on his Sam Browne belt. "You okay?" he says.

"Okay, considering the circumstances," I say.

"You need anything, just yell out," he says.

It hits me: they are keeping a close watch on me. I wonder why. And shouldn't someone, like on TV, read me my rights?

Detective Sauer enters. "Right," he says. "Let's make your phone calls." He unlocks the cell door. "Over here first."

I walk to the shelf, where a clipboard sits.

"Sign here and here," he indicates with a finger. He hands me a pen.

"What am I signing?" I ask, hesitating.

"Just that we have your property. Cell phone and wallet," he says.

I sign.

He points to the phone on the wall. "Right," he says. "Now you can make your calls. You are allowed three."

He hands me the handset. I move to dial, but he stops me.

"I'll dial for you," he states. "Just tell me the number."

I give him Sharla's cell number.

"Hello?" she says. Anxiety fills her voice.

"Hey," I say.

"Where are you? Are you all right?" she asks.

"I'm fine. I'm in the Ripon jail."

"Are you sure you're all right?"

"Yes, I'm good. Did you call Traci?"

"Yes. She will make other arrangements for the girls."

"What about my attorney?" I ask.

"I called him. He's in court. He'll get back to me as soon as he can."

"Okay. Thanks, sweet girl. Remember, I love you," I say. "Oh, call my mom."

"I love you," she replies.

"Okay, I need to go."

"Can I come see you in there?"

I turn to Detective Sauer. "Can she come see me here?"

"No."

"No, you can't," I say.

"I love you, Randy." She is crying now.

"I love you. I'm counting on you," I tell her. The words come out of my mouth without any sensation behind them.

"I know," she says.

"Bye, sweet girl." I hand the handset to Detective Sauer.

"You still have two more calls," he says in his official tone.

"There's no one else to call."

"What about your attorney?" he asks.

"She called him already. He's not in right now."

"Right," he says, hangs up the handset.

I move toward the holding cell.

"No," he says. "Wait just a second while I drop this off." He holds up the plastic baggie. "Then we'll go."

"Where?" I ask.

"I'll transport you to the county facility."

I shrug. Indifference is the only emotion I can muster.

He picks up some papers, the plastic baggie, and walks into the outer vestibule. Fifteen seconds later he is back.

"Sorry," he says, "but the cuffs have to be on during transport."

I turn, and he cuffs my hands behind my back.

"Right," he says, taking my arm. "Let's go."

Out the steel gray doors to his gold Lincoln Town Car. He places me in the back seat.

We drive out the rolling gate, through Ripon, then onto Highway 99.

I sit mute, afraid, numb.

"Sharla told me you wrote some religious books," he says.

"Yes."

"What about?"

"Love and the fruit of the Spirit."

"I'd like to read one sometime." Then he makes a pronouncement: "I'm a Christian."

"Yeah? What church do you attend?" I ask.

"Sequoia Baptist."

"Oh."

"We like it," he says.

"How long have you been a police officer?" I ask.

"Three years."

"Aren't you kind of young to be a detective?"

"Yeah," he smiles. "I got lucky when one of the detectives

retired. They asked me to take his place. I'm the youngest detective in the history of the Ripon Police Department."

"You must be good," I say. I can't believe I am having this conversation, as if we're on our way to the country club to play tennis, then have a drink. I scream a silent scream.

"I try," he says, his voice full of pride and self-satisfaction.

"What's going to happen to me now?" I ask. My fear wants to know how afraid it should be.

"At the jail, you'll be booked, then assigned a unit." He glances at me in his rearview mirror.

"I'm scared."

"Yes, I would imagine so. I'd be scared too."

"Will they treat me the way you have? You've been very professional, I mean. You didn't maltreat me."

"They'll treat you the way you treat them," he says, glancing in his mirror. He looks away. "It's not a nice place."

"No, I wouldn't imagine so." A horror ignites in my stomach, begins to burn white hot.

"But you'll be all right," he says. "Just do what they tell you to do."

"Will I be able to get out on bail?"

"Maybe." There's a funny quality to his voice.

"Why maybe?" I ask.

"Well," he says, shifting in his seat. "Your bail is pretty high." He doesn't look at me in the mirror.

"How high is pretty high?"

"One point five million," he states.

My eyes widen. "What? Why so high?"

"I don't really know," he says. "Usually, if it's that high, you're a murderer." There is a confessional note in his voice.

"I don't understand. What am I charged with?"

"Embezzlement, fraud, forgery," he recites.

"Well, that seems pretty tame compared to murder. A million and a half?" My voice stumbles over the amount as my tongue swells in my mouth.

"That's what it says. A judge signed it when we got the search warrants," he says.

"What search warrants?"

"To search Sharla's house," he says.

"For what? She didn't do anything."

"I know," he agrees. "But they searched it, seized your computer and some other things you had there. They're also going to search your house."

"What for?" I laugh. "There's nothing in it. Literally, nothing in it."

"It's procedure," he says in a mechanical voice.

"A million and a half?" I echo. "How much of that do I have to come up with to get out?"

"Normally, ten percent. But when it's that high, the bondsmen want more, as a kind of security blanket."

"How much more?"

"Probably the entire sum," he says. "Of course, I'm not a bondsman or an attorney." He glances at me in his mirror. "Maybe your attorney can get the bail reduced."

We enter the jail compound, driving through a massive pale green steel gate. Detective Sauer parks the car, lets me out. Then he leads me to gray steel double doors. An inset paper pass opens in the double doors. Detective Sauer inserts the papers and the baggie into the opening.

"This is as far as I go," he tells me.

The double doors open. A black-clad correction officer stands there, holding the inserted papers

"Radic?" she asks.

Detective Sauer nods. "Good luck," he says. "Remember, do as you're told, and you'll be all right."

I pass through the doors. They slam shut behind me. Inside is a large waiting area, like in a hospital. Before me and to my right stands a bank of computers. The CO points to two yellow feet painted on the floor.

"Stand there," she orders.

I step on the yellow footprints. Disassociated, that's how I feel. Like I'm sitting in a theater watching a movie, a movie about me, starring me. Yet I sit quiescent, beholding myself, aware of what is happening on the screen, to me, yet none of it is real. Like it's make-believe.

But it's not.

"Ever been in jail before?" rasps the CO. Her back is to me as she enters my data into the computer. She gleans the data from the official forms before her.

"No, ma'am," I say, hoping to God that is the correct form of address.

"Never?" she asks, as if she doesn't believe me. She glances at me for a moment.

"No, ma'am," I repeat.

"In the chair," she commands, pointing to a black plastic chair at the end of the counter. She wears white latex surgical gloves on both hands. The contrast between the white gloves and the black uniform captivates me.

I take three paces to the chair, sit. Gazing up, I see a camera, like the ones they use at the DMV.

"Look at the camera," the CO orders.

I comply, not even trying to smile. This is my booking picture. It will be splashed over all the local newspapers, across television screens. It portrays a gaunt, soulless zombie that generally resembles me.

"Okay," says the CO. "Stand up and turn around. I'll take those cuffs off." She jerks at the steel handcuffs, which fall free. I massage my wrists.

"Take a seat over there. Wait to be called," she instructs me. She turns to some other task.

I walk into the waiting room, which boasts thirty black plastic chairs. And a large-screen television mounted on the far wall. The television seems completely out of place, especially since it is on. Some news program.

Five other zombies inhabit the waiting room. Two females

who look as if their very breath carries AIDS or VD microbes. I move to a chair as far from them as possible. Sitting down, I notice my nearest neighbor: a mean-looking black guy dressed in filthy blue jeans and a gray T-shirt. He lounges in his chair, almost sitting on his back, watching the television screen.

Three chairs to his left leans a stupefied Mexican with long, greasy hair. He is mumbling to himself.

In the back row, near the podium behind which stand two male COs, sits a blond, moist, fat guy. His legs are crossed, and his "up" foot bounces a frenetic cadence. Every ten seconds he wipes the back of his left hand across his forehead. Then mops his hand on his black jeans, which have a large, growing wet spot where he keeps wiping.

Moving to a bank of telephones, the black guy selects one, punches in a series of numbers. He waits. Then slams the handset down onto its rocker.

"Fucking shit!" he says loudly. Striding over to the podium, he says something to one of the black-clad COs, who doesn't even look up as the black guy complains to him.

"I don't give a fuck," says the CO. His voice is loud but not angry.

He glances up from his computer monitor, looks at the black guy. "Have a seat," he says, then looks back at the monitor.

The black guy says something else.

The CO stares at him. "Have a fucking seat. Now!" barks the CO.

The black guy walks back over to the same phone, dials, waits. He slams the phone down. "God damn fucking fuck," he says. Reaching for the handset, he pounds it against the phone's steel box.

"Cut that shit out, asshole!" yells the same CO. "Sit the fuck down, or you're in a holding cell!" He stares at the black guy, who takes a seat, talking to himself.

"Radic!" screams a female voice.

Looking over to my right, I see an obese woman standing in a doorway. She wears white pants, white shoes, a loose purple top.

Jumping up, I walk over to her.

"Radic?" she asks.

"Yes, ma'am," I reply.

"In here," she says. She walks to a desk in the office and sits down. Rolling her chair forward, she rests her elbows on the desk. "Sit down," she says, nodding to a chair across from her.

I sit. The desk is pale yellow with an army green rubber bumper around its edge. The walls and the woman's skin are the same shade of yellow.

"I'm the duty nurse," she says in a voice like tearing paper. She studies some form in front of her. "I'm going to ask you some questions. If you lie to me, it's a felony." She looks at me. "Understood?"

"Yes, ma'am," I say.

"Age?"

"Fifty-two."

"Are you presently taking any medications?" she asks in a bored tone. Her matted hair is short, lacking any styling or vanity.

"No, ma'am."

"None?" she asks, as if I'm lying.

"No, ma'am."

"Any health problems? Like diabetes, TB, AIDS, VD, high blood pressure?"

"No, ma'am."

She makes a notation on her form.

"Any other medical problems?" She gives me a warning look.

"I have periodic familial paralysis," I say.

"What? Say that again."

"Periodic familial paralysis," I repeat.

"What's that?" she asks, glaring at me. She makes a notation on her form.

"It's also called hypokalemia," I say. "It's kind of rare. I become paralyzed, but I can still feel. It's a muscular paralysis."

"Ccuhh!" she ejaculates, like she's coughing and hissing at the same time. She stares at me hard. Reaching for her phone, she punches in three numbers.

"Wait outside," she says to me.

I jump up, walk outside, watching her through the glass windows of her office. She speaks into the phone, listens, tapping her pen on the desk. She writes three sentences on the form, then hangs up the phone.

Waving me back into the office, she glares at me.

"You have to have a TB test," she declares. "Pull up your right sleeve."

Struggling to her feet, she lumbers to a counter to her right, picks up a plastic syringe. Uncapping it with her teeth, she grasps my right arm, inserts the pudgy needle just under my skin, injects a clear liquid. A small bubble of flesh appears on the inside of my forearm where the fluid was introduced.

"They'll check that in a few days," she says, tossing the syringe into a receptacle.

Back behind her desk, she looks over my shoulder as she thinks. Tapping her pen on the desk, she says to herself, "Where to put you?" Looking at me now, she says, "I can't put you on the farm with the animals." She thinks some more, then says, "Okay, the Med Unit." She makes a notation on her form.

"Back outside," she says. "Have a seat."

As I walk back to my former spot, I notice that the stupefied Mexican has taken my chair. He leans against the arm of the chair, slumped over. I select one near him, careful to leave one empty chair between us.

"Hey," he mumbles to me.

"What?" I say, surprised he is conscious. He has not moved.

"Hey. Got anything to eat?"

"No, I don't. Sorry."

"Hey," he says. "Got anything to eat?"

"No. Sorry, nothing to eat on me." I pat the pockets of my jacket, my shorts, to demonstrate the truth of the matter.

"Hey," he says. "Got anything to eat?"

"No," I reply loudly. I get up, move three rows back, and sit down. I hear the Mexican ask again, "Hey. Got anything to eat?"

Glancing over to my left, I see the fat blond guy wipe his forehead. His foot still jerking.

Getting up from my chair, I walk over to the phone the black guy tried to use. A small plastic placard above the phone states "All calls are collect. Dial the area code first, then the number. The connection process may take up to one minute."

I pick up the handset, dial Sharla's number. A recorded female voice announces, "That number is restricted."

I dial my attorney's number. "State your name," instructs the recorded tinny voice.

"Randall Radic," I say.

"Please wait while Evercom connects you," directs the voice.

Three rings. "Law offices, this is Toni," says a real voice, female.

"This is Randall Radic," I say.

"Yes, Mr. Radic. What can I do for you?"

"I've been arrested, and I'm in jail," I say. "Is the counselor in?"

"I'm sorry, Mr. Radic, he's in court. Can I take a message?"

"Tell him I'm in jail, and I'm counting on him to get me out," I say.

"Certainly," says Toni. "I'll be sure he gets the message. Anything else?"

"No. Just that I'm in jail," I say, wanting to scream.

"I'll see he gets your message. Thank you." She hangs up.

I replace the handset, wondering if I really just had that conversation.

"Radic!" yells a voice from the podium.

I walk rapidly toward the podium. "Yes, sir," I say, stopping five feet from the podium.

"Whaddaya got?" the CO asks.

"Sir?" I don't understand the question.

He is tall and wide, with close-cropped blond hair.

"Property," he snarls. "What property do you have?" He leans forward, looks over the podium at me.

"Athletic shoes, red and blue," he says. "Blue shorts, black T-shirt, blue sweat jacket. Glasses." Leaning back, he keys the information into his computer. "Do you need the glasses?" he asks.

"I can't see without them," I reply.

Looking up at me, he asks, "You got underwear on?"

"Yes, sir."

"What color?"

"Black, sir," I respond.

"Boxers? Or jock style?" he asks.

"Boxers, sir," I say.

He opens a plastic baggie, dumps the contents on the podium. "Wallet, DL, SS card, Medi-Cal card," he recites. "One blue cell phone." He picks up my cell phone, examines it, then tosses it back on the podium. "No brand name," he recites. He opens my wallet. "Twenty dollars." He looks at me. "Correct?"

"Yes, sir."

"That'll go on your books," he says.

I don't know what he means, but he scares me, so I remain silent.

"Here. Look this over, then sign if it's correct," he says, pushing a printout toward me.

I read it, sign, hand it back to him.

"Have a seat," he growls.

Just as I'm about to sit down, I hear, "Radic!"

I return to the podium. Another blond CO stares at me.

"Over here," he says. He points to another counter next to the podium.

Taking my right hand, he places it on a clear plastic pad. The pad has finger-like indentations on it. I smell his cologne. Old Spice.

"Hold your hand there," he says. "Don't move."

Stepping behind the counter, he presses a button. A bar of light moves under the pad, like a copy machine. He studies a monitor in front of him. "Okay," he says. "You can drop your hand."

I take my hand off the pad, stand waiting.

Glancing up, he scowls at me. "You're done. Have a seat."

I sit down, four seats away from the fat guy. He is still jerking and mopping sweat from his forehead.

I look at the television screen. Some news show, or the same one, I don't know. I look but do not watch. Nothing registers. Only my ears function. They are tuned to hear my name.

Bored, I wait. Even waiting is tedious, adding to the thick sense of monotony. No magazines, no books, no pamphlets to read. Conversation is out of the question since my fellow bookees appear to be less than intellectually endowed; half of them have achieved altered states of consciousness, and the other half carry exotic communicable diseases. There is only television, which, when examined from my new vantage, projects superficial redundancies about nonsense. In a word, television is boring and appeals only to already bored minds.

There is nothing to do but wait.

An hour later a female voice says, "Randall Radic?"

I turn and see a petite woman, thirty something. She wears an official polo shirt, which is either light gray or off-white. I can't decide. Official blue slacks, black shoes. She holds a clipboard.

I walk over to her.

"Randall Radic?" she asks.

"Yes, ma'am."

"This way, please."

I follow her around a corner to another section of the waiting room. This section is smaller and has four tables with folding chairs at each table. She takes a seat at one of the tables. I sit across from her.

"I'm PO Ruiz," she says, looking at her clipboard. She looks up at me. "I'm a probation officer, assigned to ask you some questions regarding your status. Anything you say or reveal to me may be used against you. So if you don't want to answer, you don't have to." She looks at me expectantly.

"Why wouldn't I want to answer?" I ask. "I mean, what kind of questions are you going to ask me?"

"General background questions," she replies.

"About my charges?" I ask. I don't get it.

"No," she says. "I'm not an investigator. The questions are about your job, your family, things like that. However, any information you give me may be used against you, if it pertains to your charges."

She looks bored, indifferent. Her dark eyes look right through me, like I'm a bug that splatted on her car's windshield.

"I doubt anything I say will be of any significance," I say.

"You may request that your attorney be present, if you wish," she recites in a monotone.

"No, go ahead. Ask away."

She pushes a piece of paper and a pen toward me. "This states that I advised you that anything you say may be used against you and, further, that you have of your own free will decided to answer my questions."

"Okay," I say. I sign.

She reads from her clipboard. "What is your profession?"

"I *was* a pastor," I say.

"Were you fired, laid off? What?"

"I resigned," I say.

"Are you presently employed?" she reads from the clipboard. Even though the progression of questions makes no sense, she reads them.

"No."

"Do you have medical insurance?"

"I did have Medi-Cal. However, I'm assuming it's been canceled as of about this morning when I was arrested," I answer.

"Are you married?"

"Separated," I say.

"Any children?"

"Yes. One daughter," I reply.

"And how old is the child?"

"Four years old. She'll be five in March."

"Where is the child residing?"

"With her mother."

"The mother's name and address?"

I tell her. She writes it down. She writes it all down, placing checks in some boxes on her forms, x-ing out other boxes.

"Is the child's mother able to care for her?"

I am amazed at the question. "Yes," I reply slowly.

"Has the child's mother ever been arrested for a felony or for any drug- or alcohol-related offense?"

I flinch back. "No. Nothing like that. Ever."

"Has the child's mother ever been charged with or arrested for child abuse?"

"Of course not," I say adamantly.

"Do you have a checking account?" she reads from the clipboard.

"I did," I say, "until October 20th. It was seized, along with my car and my house."

She writes on her clipboard with a blue Bic pen.

"Do you have a savings account, IRA, annuity, or any other type of retirement account?"

"No. I have no job, no house, no car, and no money."

"Do you have a private attorney, or will you be requesting a public defender?"

"I have an attorney," I reply.

She looks at me, asks, "Are you a member of any gang?"

"No, ma'am."

"Have you ever been a member of a gang?"

"No, ma'am."

"Do you have any gang-related tattoos?"

"I don't have *any* tattoos," I answer.

"Are you aware of the charges against you?" she reads from her clipboard.

"Vaguely," I reply. "No one told me exactly why I was being arrested."

"Are you guilty of the charges against you?" she reads.

"I thought you weren't an investigator?" I ask, narrowing my eyes at her.

"Please answer the question as I read it," she says, staring at me.

"Not without consulting my attorney," I say. I'm catching on.

She sniffs, reads the next question. "Is there anyone in jail that knows you or that might wish to harm you physically?"

I think about this. And I realize I'm just a thing to her. I'm not even shit, because shit would cause her to wrinkle her nose. She knows nothing about me, cares nothing about me. The realization stuns me.

"No," I respond.

She glances up at me. "You're sure?"

"Yes, I'm sure. I don't know anyone in here," I say.

She writes a few sentences on her clipboard. Looking through me, she says, "You can go back and have a seat."

I leave her sitting at the table with her clipboard.

Back in the waiting room, I note the two females have moved. They are now sitting by the phones. One of them is sobbing uncontrollably. The other sits next to her, looking apathetic.

A loud banging noise erupts behind me. I turn to locate the disturbance and see a black face peering out from a small window in a gray steel door. The steel door is over near the nurse's office.

The two COs behind the podium walk over to the steel door. Their postures are menacing.

One of the COs pounds his fist on the door. "Shut the fuck up!" he shouts.

In reply, the banging gets louder. A voice spits out something from within the cell.

One CO steps back two paces, his hand on a fat capsule attached to his Sam Browne belt; the other CO unlocks the steel door, swings it open. "Shut the fuck up, asshole!" he bellows into the cell.

"Fuck you!" says the black figure inside the cell. He wears a shiny orange jumpsuit. A short Afro haircut puffs from his head.

"Outside!" yells the CO.

The orange jumpsuit pimp rolls out of the cell. His hands are cuffed in front. Tall, he looks around sixteen or seventeen. Snide arrogance spills from his face.

"Whatcha fuckin' want?" shouts the black guy.

"I want you to fuckin' shut up," snarls the CO.

The other CO unsnaps the capsule on his belt, removes a canister from it.

"I need to stretch my fuckin' legs," shouts the black guy.

"Look, asshole," says the CO, "you don't tell us what you want. Get it?" He points into the cell. "Now get the fuck back in there and shut the fuck up!"

Laughing, the black kid struts back into his cell. He has thongs on his feet, white socks, and the bottoms of his orange jumpsuit are tucked into the socks.

The CO slams the cell door shut with a booming sound. He locks it. Then he pounds his fist on the door. "Now keep the fuck quiet!"

Both COs walk back to the podium. They smile and joke with one another.

The black kid's face appears in the window. He is laughing.

I heave a huge breath. I move to the front row of chairs and sit down. My mind spins in my head like a top. This place is insane, I tell myself. I need to get out of here. And right now.

About an hour later one of the COs steps out from behind the podium. He holds a piece of paper in his hands. He reads out five names, one of which is mine. "If I read your name, get your ass over here!" he barks.

I move quickly to obey. Four others gather slowly near me, forming a semicircle with the CO in the middle. The black guy in the gray T-shirt, the fat blond guy, the staggering Mexican, whose white T-shirt I now see is stained with vomit, and two other guys dressed in orange pajamas that have JAIL stenciled on them.

"You two," snaps the CO, indicating the two orange-clad guys, "take a seat over there." He points to a bench.

"You three," he says, "one each in those rooms there. Take off your clothes, put 'em in the green bag on the floor. Then wait."

There are five rooms to choose from. Each has a gray steel door with a two-foot black number on it. I enter room 2. It is ten feet by ten feet, with a gray cement floor. The floor is stained with dark blobs. The walls are yellow cinderblock. On the far wall is a sliding glass window, which looks into a room full of green mesh bags.

I take off all my clothes, shove them in the bag. There is a side pocket in the bag for my shoes. I jam them in the pocket.

The window slides open. "Hand me the green bag," says a voice. I see only arms and a chest encased in a black uniform through the window.

I hand him the bag. Orange clothing, white underwear, a white T-shirt, white socks, and a pair of rubber slippers are tossed through the window into my room. The window slides shut with a final thunk.

Naked, I stand shivering, wondering if I should put the clothes on.

The door swings open. The blond CO who wears Old Spice stands in the doorway. "Over in the corner," he commands.

I obey, moving to the far corner.

"Turn and face the corner," he snaps.

I obey, shivering with the cold and fear.

"Bend over, spread your ass cheeks," he says.

I obey. Grabbing my ass cheeks, I spread them wide. My asshole looks back at the CO like a cyclops.

"Cough," he says.

"What?" I ask.

"Cough! Three times, hard!" he yells.

I cough.

"Stand up and turn around," he says.

I obey.

"Lift up your balls, let me see your crotch," says the CO.

I look at him as I obey. His face is an indifferent mask. How many assholes a day does he get to view? I wonder.

"Drop 'em," he says. "Now lift up your arms, turn around slowly."

I obey, pirouetting slowly before him. I feel like a stripper at a titty club must feel.

"Okay. Put on those clothes. T-shirt tucked in, with the top over it." The door slams shut.

I dress, making sure to tuck my T-shirt in. Sliding my feet into the rubber slippers, I stand waiting.

The door opens. "Outside," commands the CO. "Have a seat," he says, pointing at a bench with his white-latex-gloved finger.

I sit. Three of the five are already there, all dressed in orange. Then the stupefied Mexican emerges from door number three. He, too, is dressed in jail orange.

"Tuck in your fucking T-shirt," barks the CO.

The Mexican responds with erratic shoving motions as he attempts to tuck in his T-shirt. He gets the front in, but the rear hangs out below his top. He gives up and drops to the bench.

The CO doesn't notice the errant T-shirt; he is now distributing ID tags. Made of white plastic, they are the size of a credit card and depict a one-inch-square color photo, full name and birth date, sex (a big black M on the right edge), and, most importantly, a booking number.

Once they are distributed, the CO says, "Do not lose your ID tag. Wear it on your top at all times, except when in your cell. You must have your ID to eat, to receive medical care, to use the library, for everything." He clears his throat. "Your escort will be here in a minute. He will take you to your assigned units."

A heavy popping noise announces our escort's arrival. He enters through a heavy, wide door composed of steel cross-bars and Plexiglas. He is about sixty years old, has white hair, and jingles when he walks. The jingling is caused by the many sets of handcuffs he carries or wears on his Sam Browne belt.

"On your feet," snaps the young blond CO, the one who gets to look at assholes all day long.

I stand.

The Mexican cannot rise to his feet. He appears to be barely conscious. One of the other inmates tries to help him.

"Don't touch him!" snarls the blond CO. He walks over to the bench, stands with his white Playtex hands on his hips in front of the Mexican. "Look, fuckhead," he says, "get up or go to the hole." The CO kicks the bench leg. "Get up, mother-fucker!" he roars. He glances over at the white-haired CO. "Goddamnit," he says. "I can't believe the shit we get in here."

He pauses to think for a moment, then he looks at the older CO. "Okay," he says. "You take them to their units. I'll take care of this asshole." His distaste for his task floats in the air. He stares at the Mexican asshole slumped over on the bench.

"Okay, gentlemen," says the older CO, "follow me in a single file. Keep tight but don't walk on the guy in front of you. Keep to my right down the hall."

He pauses at the door as a camera scrutinizes him. The door pops. He pushes it open and waits for us to file out. I am last in the four-man procession.

We walk down an empty, long hall with pale green walls and cancer green linoleum on the floor. The CO is to our left, leading the group. He walks slowly, jingling, unconcerned, relaxed. In his right hand he carries a computer printout.

One hundred yards down the hall we stop at a heavy door. Another camera examines our CO. The door pops, and we enter GP (general population).

Ten feet inside the door the CO stops. We stop. Consulting his printout, he reads out three names. "Grant, Ruiz, Gonzalez," he intones. "Step forward two paces."

I stand alone, segregated by two paces.

The CO consults his printout once more, then glances at me. "Radic?" he says.

"Yes, sir."

"Wait here," he says.

He leads the other three over to the podium. Behind it sit two black-clad COs. They look relaxed, happy.

I glance around GP. Waves of orange-clad bodies move to and fro, surging here and there, with no apparent pattern. I see males and females. Shouts, screeches, and laughter swim in the smell of disinfectant and sweat.

My escort returns. He stops at the heavy door as the camera eyes him. The door pops, and we are back in the hall. We walk twenty yards farther, turn left, walk up a ramp.

MED UNIT

As we approach another heavy steel and Plexiglas door, I note the sign above the door: MED UNIT, in three-inch white letters. Again the camera screens the CO, the door pops, and we enter.

Inside it is very quiet. The carpet is dark blue, not gray as in GP. The podium we approach is shaped like half a doughnut. One CO stands behind it. He is in his early twenties, with close-cropped blond hair, blue eyes.

As we approach him, I read his name tag: Palmer.

"Got one for ya," says my escort. He hands Palmer some papers.

Palmer glances at the papers. "Radic?" he asks.

"Yes, sir," I reply.

Palmer looks at the monitor on his counter. "Okay," he says, "over in nineteen." He points behind me. He doesn't wear white gloves.

I look over my shoulder. There it is, my new home. Cell 19. I look back at CO Palmer.

"Go," he says.

I turn and walk over to the door of cell 19. It pops as I approach. I open the door, enter, shut it softly behind me. The hydraulic lock snaps back into place. I push the door, testing it. Yes, it is locked.

I look at my cell. It is nine feet by twelve feet, with white walls and a gray cement floor. Single bunk already made.

White porcelain sink, with a mirror above it. Next to the sink and right by the large glass window is the toilet, which is also white porcelain. It looks clean.

There is a white towel hanging from a stainless steel hook to the right of the sink. At the far end of the cell sits a small dresser with two drawers.

I sit on the bunk. The mattress is three inches thick and hard.

Tears run down my face. I have nothing left. No energy, no thoughts, no possessions, no food, no personal items, no cup to drink from. No job, no house, no car, no money, no one I love. No book to read, no paper to write on, no pencil. All I have is the orange clothing I wear, and it is not even mine.

I rise and walk to the window. Across the way, I see other cells, most of them dark. Over to the right, I see one cell with lights on. A figure appears in the window, turns, and disappears. After a few seconds, he appears again, turns, and disappears. Whoever he is, he is walking, pacing back and forth in a diagonal line across his cell. His face is off-kilter somehow, asymmetrical.

Directly across from me, a figure stands at his window. He looks at me, smiles. He looks Arabian to me, plump with dark skin and a mustache. He makes gestures with his hands to me. Sign language. I shrug my incomprehension to him. He smiles, makes eating motions with his hands. Then points toward the podium. I shrug. I don't get it.

I sit back down on my bunk. I am numb, as if my emotions have been surgically removed. There is nothing left.

Fifteen minutes later Palmer walks by my window, glances in as he passes. I jump up and move to the window. I watch him circumnavigate the unit, checking each cell as he passes.

When he finishes his rounds, I see an orange-clad inmate wearing a plastic apron and a white plastic cap. He is pushing a cart heaped with plastic trays. Parking the cart, he begins rolling out collapsible tables, which he unfolds with a bang. He places four gray plastic chairs around each of the six tables.

He says something to Palmer at the podium. Palmer nods. I hear popping noises around the unit. My door pops. I push it, and it swings open.

"Chow time!" shouts CO Palmer. "Chow time! Get it now, or don't get it at all."

Cell doors open, and orange-clad bodies flow out. I walk slowly out of cell 19.

The other inmates line up near the cart, and I imitate them. Taking a tray from the cart, I move to another, smaller cart. Arrayed on it are white Styrofoam cups filled with coffee. I take one.

Turning, I look around for an empty chair at one of the tables. Seeing one, I walk toward it. I drop my tray on the table and sit in a chair.

Three faces stare at me. Across from me is a morbidly obese hulk of a man with dark hair and a goatee. He is stuffing his face with food, as if he hasn't eaten in a week. To my right sits the pacer, the guy I saw walking in his cell. He is small and thin, with a malformed jaw. I try not to stare at his distorted face. To my left sits a middle-aged man, average build, with hair graying around the temples.

Moments pass as they stare at me. Then, as if on cue, they all go back to eating.

I drink my coffee as I examine the dinner on my beige plastic tray. Cornbread, a dollop of margarine, a mass of vile-looking brown beans swimming in fecal brown liquid, an orange, and four slices of white bread. I peel the orange and eat it.

"I get back to GP," says the fat guy in a voice thick with menace, "I'm gonna kick Garth's ass and rule GP. I'll be a fuckin' god."

"Yeah," agrees the deformed jaw.

The middle-aged guy to my left laughs, takes a huge bite of cornbread.

"Thinks he tough shit," says the fat guy. "Well, he ain't."

"How soon they send you back?" asks the deformed jaw.

"Soon," says the fat guy. "The doc says my blood sugar is almost normal. So pretty soon."

The others nod.

"You gonna eat that?" the fat guy says, staring at my tray.

"No, I'm not hungry," I say.

"Here, I'll eat it." His chair creaks as he shifts his bulk forward.

"Okay," I say slowly.

All three of them gaze at me with owl eyes.

He pulls my tray across the table, shoves his empty tray toward me.

I watch as he breaks the bread into the beans then adds the cornbread and mixes it all together with his spork. He inhales the rubbery mass like a human vacuum.

"Okay, gentlemen," shouts CO Palmer from behind the podium. "Let's start wrapping it up."

Orange-clad bodies begin to rise from the tables, carrying their empty trays. They file past a large plastic trash can, dump their trash, stack their trays on the cart. I follow suit with the fat guy's empty tray.

I turn to walk back to cell 19.

"You guys have rec time until nine," shouts CO Palmer. "Keep it quiet!"

A small cheer goes up.

I stand where I am. I don't know what to do. Feeling like Ishmael — alone in a crowded world — I walk toward the phones. There are two hanging on the wall, and both are being used.

Another morbidly obese guy is on one phone; his hair is long and gray. He makes sucking noises between his front teeth as he holds the handset to his ear.

"This is John Stofft," says the guy on the second phone. Frustration gathers in his voice like dust on a table. He is fifty something, with short gray hair, which needs the services of a comb, and slender. "I'm trying to get hold of Martin. I'm in the jail, and I need a bail bondsman, someone to get me out. Is anyone there? Please pick up!"

A machine, I realize; he is talking to an answering machine. Hence his frustration. They cannot call him back, not in jail.

He hangs up the phone, turns, stops. Staring at a torn fragment of paper in his hand, he mumbles to himself. The plump Arabian guy from across the way comes over to John.

"Did you get 'em?" asks the Arab. He has no accent, so maybe he's not Arabian, I think to myself.

"No," moans John Stofft. "Just a machine. Why don't he pick up?"

"It's Friday," replies the Arab. "Busy night for bondsmen, ya gotta understand."

John nods, but his face, even his posture, grimaces. "I got the money," he says to the Arab. "I got the money. I can even put my house up if I need to."

"How much is your bail?" the Arab asks.

"Forty thousand," John says. "Can you believe that? Forty grand just 'cuz the bitch says I slapped her? That's fucking bullshit." John is not angry so much as stymied. His soft voice reveals bafflement.

"So you got the money?" asks the Arab.

"Yeah, yeah," John assures him. "I got it. I just got to talk to someone." He presses his fists to his temples, as if he has a migraine. "I can't get out if I can't talk to someone."

"Anyone you can call?" asks the Arab. "Any family?"

John's face brightens. "I got a brother," he says. "I could call him." He pauses to think. "But I don't have his number. It's in my cell phone." He looks at the carpet. "Lemme think, lemme think."

After a moment, he looks at the Arab. "I can't remember it," he says. Tears stream down his cheeks. "I can't remember it."

"Well, just keep trying Aladdin," says the Arab. "You'll get 'em sooner or later."

The Arab turns to me, sees me listening. He smiles. "Hey," he says to me, "you need a bail bondsman?"

"Sure," I say. "But I doubt they're going to want me." I smile to myself.

"Why you say that?" he asks.

"My bail's kind of high, and I don't have any money," I reply.

"Hey," he laughs, "you got a job, you make payments. No problem." He moves right in front of me.

Turning to John, he says, "You keep trying."

"How high is your bail?" he asks me.

"A million and a half," I say, cocking my head at him.

His eyes widen. "Whew! Who you kill?"

"No one," I say. "I'm charged with embezzlement and fraud. I don't know why it's so high."

"You some kinda flight risk?" he asks, giving me a sly look, tilting his head.

"I was," I confess. "But not now. I really don't know why it's so high."

"You got a house? A car? Any savings?" he asks me. "Because you can use that to put up your bail."

I smile at him. "No job, no house, no car, no money."

"Too bad," he says. He hands me a small piece of paper. "Anyway, you find any money, call my cousin. Ask for Martin. Tell him you know me. Belomar." He taps his chest with his fingers. "He'll take care of you."

I read the piece of paper. It is hand printed, in pencil: "Need bail? Call Aladdin Bail Bonds." Then it gives a phone number.

"If I find any money, I'll call him first thing," I say, wondering how come he's not out if his cousin is a bail bondsman. "Can anyone use the phones?"

"Sure, anyone," he says. "Who you going to call?"

I just look at him.

"No problem, no problem," he says, raising his hands. He

walks over to John Stofft, who is standing alone, fists pressed to his temples.

Picking up the handset, I dial Sharla's number.

"Please state your name at the beep," recites the female voice.

"Hello? Hello?" It's her! Then silence.

"Thank you for using Evercom," says the recorded voice.

"Hello?" I say.

"Hey," says Sharla. The word makes me melt.

We've known each other for five years. She is smart and loyal to a fault. No matter what anyone does, she forgives them because she sees only the good in people, the potential. That doesn't mean she doesn't get angry. She does. But she can't hold on to her anger. It vanishes, and all that's left is how she feels in her heart about you.

"Where are you?" she says.

"I'm in the Med Unit," I reply.

"Are you okay?"

"Yeah, I guess. I'm lonely and scared," I say.

"Don't be," she says. "I love you. And your mom loves you. I got ahold of her, and she will do anything for you. Anything."

"Thanks," I say, sighing from deep inside.

"And your attorney . . . I talked to him. He'll be out to see you in a couple of days."

"Okay," I say.

"He says don't worry. Just be careful of yourself, don't talk to anybody about your case until you talk to him. He's already contacting people to see what can be done."

"Okay," I say. "Are you going to come visit me?"

"Of course," she says. "I'll be there tomorrow. I don't know what time yet, but I'll call and find out the visiting hours, what it entails."

"Okay," I say. I hug the phone to my ear.

"I love you, Randy," she whispers.

"I love you too," I say. "I can hardly wait to see you."

"I know. Me too."

"Okay, there are others waiting to use the phone," I say, seeing orange-clad inmates standing behind me, glaring at me.

"You have to go already?" she asks.

"Well, other people are waiting," I explain. "I don't want to, I'd rather just stay on here with you until they tell me to get off."

"I understand," she says. "Remember, though, I love you. And I'll see you tomorrow."

"Okay, I love you too."

"Bye."

I hang up the handset, step aside. In an instant, the orange-clad body behind me has the phone to his mouth and ear. He coughs heavily, spraying germs all over the mouthpiece of the handset.

I step back, look at him. Then I look around me, scrutinizing all the inmates. Each one appears unhealthy. I walk to cell 19, my cell, glance around the sink. No soap. I want to wash my hands.

Back outside, I look for the Arab. I spot him over by the television; he is standing, talking to John Stofft. I walk right up to him.

"You finished your call?" he asks.

"Yeah," I reply. "Where can I get some soap?"

"Soap? You need soap? Didn't they give you any when you came in?"

"They didn't give me anything," I tell him. I grab the neck of my orange top, flap it. "Except these orange clothes."

"Well . . . ," says the Arab, pondering my dilemma.

"You need some soap?" says a voice.

I look down. The little guy with the deformed jaw is seated on a gray plastic chair in front of the TV. He is looking up at me.

"Yeah," I reply.

He gets up, motions me to follow him. As he walks in front

of me, I notice he limps, and he has shoes on, black cross-trainers, not rubber sandals. He leads me to his cell.

I start to enter, but he stops me. "Don't come in," he says, looking at me as he opens a drawer. "Don't ever enter another cell. If the guard sees you, he'll write you up. If another inmate sees you, he'll think you're trying to steal something."

I take a step back from the doorway. "Thanks," I say.

"How long you been here?" he asks, digging through a mass of stuff in the drawer.

Gazing around his cell, I see books, food, a toothbrush, a comb, all sorts of stuff. Even plastic bottles with lotions and shampoo balanced on the sink. This guy is living, I tell myself.

"Since today," I reply.

"I thought so," he says. "Here." He hands me a small bar of soap wrapped in paper, like in a cheap motel room.

"Thanks," I say. "Really, thanks a lot."

"Save it," he says. Then he gives me a funny look. "You want some coffee?"

"Yeah," I blurt out.

"Got a cup?" he asks me, holding up a white Styrofoam cup.

"No," I reply. "I don't have much of anything. How do I get a cup?"

He laughs, his deformed jaw angling off to the side. "Just take your cup from dinner," he says.

I nod. Looking at the bottles on his sink, I ask, "How'd you get all this stuff?"

He moves to the sink, presses the knob, holds it down with one hand, using the fingers of his other hand to test the water. "From commissary," he says.

"What's that?" I ask.

His jaw slants off as he laughs again. "Man, you are a new fish, huh?" He fills two Styrofoam cups with hot water, sets them on the sink's edge. Moving to his drawer, he removes a red package, peels it open. Taking a spork from another cup on top of his dresser, he spoons a lump of dark brown crystals from the red packet into each of the cups.

"Go see the guard later," he says. "They should have given you a new fish packet when you came in. Ask him for one."

"A new fish packet?" I repeat.

"Yeah, just ask the guard."

He stirs both cups with the spork. Handing me one of the cups, he says, "Once a week you get a commissary form, fill it out. Two days later your order shows up. They pass it out." He blows on the surface of his coffee, takes a sip. "Ahhh," he sighs. "That's good."

I take a sip. It is almost hot and tastes of chemicals. But it is coffee. "That's great. Thanks," I say.

"Save it," he says, takes another sip.

"You mean they just give you whatever you order?" I ask.

He laughs. "Well, you gotta pay for it. You got any money on your books?"

"I don't know," I say. "What are my books, and how do I get money on them?"

Shaking his head, laughing, he sits down on his bunk. "Sorry," he says, looking at me, "I'm not laughing at you, guy. It's just funny, is all."

"That's okay," I say. "I don't know anything about how any of this works."

"Your books are your account here at jail," he explains. "Like a bank account, kind of. You can spend up to fifty-five dollars a week, if you have that much money."

"How do I get the money?" I ask.

"Someone on the outside puts it there for you," he tells me. "They come in and tell them your name and give them the cash. No checks, has to be cash. The money is put into your account, and you can spend it on commissary."

"Oh," I say. "But what if I don't have anyone on the outside to put money on my books?"

"Then you're fucked," he says matter of factly. "They'll

feed you, but that's it." He looks up at me. "Did you have any money on you when you came in?"

"Twenty dollars," I say.

"Well, then," he says, "you have twenty dollars on your books, 'cuz they automatically put that money in your account."

"Oh. Okay." I smile.

He stands up. "Look, guy, be careful when you fill out your commissary form. Fill it out — all of it. Don't make any mistakes."

"Okay," I say. I don't get it, but I will remember it.

He gives me a quizzical look. "Why are you in here?"

"You mean in jail?" I ask.

"No," he says, "in here. In the Med Unit. And hey, guy," he adds, gazing at me over his cup as he takes another sip of coffee, "don't ever ask anyone why they're in jail. Not until you know them real good, okay?"

"Okay." I nod. I understand the warning. "I don't know why I'm in this unit."

"You sick?" he asks me. "'Cuz most of the guys in here're either diabetics or have bad hearts or are psych cases. But mostly they're diabetics. Like me."

"Oh." I nod. I think about this. "No, I'm not sick."

"Then you must be on suicide watch," he says, raising his eyebrows.

"I don't think so," I say. "I'm not suicidal. Not yet, anyway."

He nods, as if he believes me. "Well, they put you here for some reason."

"Yeah, I guess so," I say.

He moves toward me, so I step aside. He stops, thinks for a moment, says, "You need anything to read?"

"Sure," I say. "Anything to occupy my mind."

He limps to the small dresser. "Here," he says, tossing me a book. "I just finished it. It's not bad."

I read the title: *Death in the Valley of Horses*, by Max Evan. A western. "Thanks a lot," I say.

"Be sure to give it back to me," he cautions, walking out of his cell. "I'll trade it for others."

"Sure thing," I assure him.

"Lots of guys say they'll give 'em back, but they don't," he tells me, staring at me. There's a tightness in his stance.

"No, no," I tell him, "I'll be sure to give it back."

"Okay," he nods. "I'm gonna go finish my program." He walks away.

"Thanks again for the coffee," I say to his departing back.

He stops, turns. "Save it," he says.

I hurry to cell 19, place the book on top of my dresser. Then I head toward the podium.

CO Palmer stands behind it, gazing out at the orange-clad bodies. He gazes at me as I approach. I stop two feet from the podium, unsure of the protocol.

"Whaddaya need?" asks CO Palmer, both arms out, hands resting on the countertop.

"I'd like to request a new fish packet," I say.

His eyes tunnel into me for a brief instant, as if looking for a node of lies. "You didn't get one?" he asks.

"No, sir," I say.

"They should have given you one when you came in." His eyes balance on my face.

"I didn't get one," I say.

He reaches underneath the counter, pulls out a plastic bag, hands it to me. "You should've gotten one when you came in," he reiterates.

"Thank you, sir," I say. I walk away, examining the contents of my new fish packet: one six-inch black plastic comb, two small packets of Colgate toothpaste, a four-inch toothbrush, two white legal envelopes, one four-inch number two pencil, two small bars of soap in wrappers, and four sheets of white writing paper. I feel rich, civilized. Now I can brush my teeth, bathe, wash my hands, comb my hair.

The Arab, Belomar, walks up to me. "So, you got some soap?"

"Yeah," I reply, clutching the plastic bag.

"How come you're in here?" he asks. "You sick?"

"No, I'm not sick. I don't know why they put me in here."

"Probably got you on suicide watch," he says, as if he just got an official memo. He waves his hand at the unit. "Lots of these guys are on suicide watch."

"Yeah?"

"Many, many of them," he assures me. He makes a circular motion next to his ear. "Lots of whackos in here." He glances around.

"How long have you been in here?" I ask.

"In here," he says, jabbing his index finger toward the floor, "eight days. In jail," he laughs, "eight months."

I want to ask him what he did, but I don't.

He gives me a cryptic look, smiles, says, "You need anything, you talk to me, Belomar."

"Okay," I say, wondering what he means.

"And call Aladdin Bonds if you get some money," he reminds me as he walks away.

I walk to my cell, drop my new fish packet in the top drawer of my dresser. Sitting down on my bunk, I pick up the book, begin to read.

One hour later I hear CO Palmer shout, "Lockdown in twenty minutes! I will not give you any other warnings. Be in your cells by nine."

At nine o'clock precisely, the hydraulic locks clap into place. Sixty seconds later, CO Palmer passes by my cell. He returns almost immediately, taps on my window. Jumping up, I walk to the window.

"Name tag in the window," he yells, pointing to my ID, which hangs at my chest.

"Yes, sir," I say. I unclip my ID, shove it into the molding around the window.

Palmer nods at me, moves off.

Emotionally and nervously exhausted, I decide to sleep. Yet

I am afraid of sleep too. I am afraid of everything. Climbing under my one sheet and my one thin, blue blanket, I roll on my side, close my eyes. Despite the bright fluorescent lights in my cell, within seconds I fall asleep.

The next morning, 6:00 a.m., my cell door opens, startling me out of my sleep. In the doorway stands an orange-clad inmate. He wears a plastic cap on his head and a plastic apron. Clear plastic gloves cover his hands. Next to him, one hand on the cell door, stands the CO. It is not Palmer. This CO is taller, heavier, and has a sour look on his face.

"Breakfast," the trustee says, holding a tray out to me.

I leap out of my bunk, take the tray. Glancing over his shoulder, I see everyone else sitting at the tables, eating.

"That won't happen again," growls the CO.

"What?" I ask, bewildered.

"You won't be getting out again. To eat with the others," he snarls. "That was a mistake." He slams the cell door in my face.

A wave of fear hits me in the stomach. What did I do? Why won't they let me out of my cell?

I place the tray on top of the dresser. Watery oatmeal jiggles up at me, along with fried potatoes that have black spots on them, a dinner roll next to a blob of margarine, coffee, and milk.

I drink the coffee, wrap the dinner roll in my napkin, which is a coarse paper towel, and place it inside my dresser. If I get hungry enough, I will eat it. But not until then.

Thirty minutes later the trustee returns to pick up my tray. The sour CO accompanies him. The CO unlocks the cell door, opens it.

I hand the trustee my tray. "Thanks," I say.

"You're welcome." He gives me a secretive look.

"Sir?" I say to the CO.

"What?" he barks.

"Why wasn't I let out with the others? What did I do wrong?"

"You're PC," he snaps out. "You weren't supposed to get out for rec last night. I won't be making that mistake!" He bangs the door shut in my face.

"What's PC?" I ask through the glass.

He swings the door open again. "What?" he shouts. Anger spikes from his eyes.

"What's PC?" I ask.

"Protective Custody." The door slams shut. He locks it.

"Protective Custody," I mutter to myself, sitting down on my bunk. "What's that mean?"

After I brush my teeth, comb my hair, I settle on my bunk to read.

A few hours later the CO taps at my window. Jumping up, I walk to the glass.

"In about ten minutes, you're gonna have a visit," he says.

"Thank you, sir," I reply.

He walks off.

Fifteen minutes later the CO unlocks my cell door. He stands in the doorway. "You got a visit," he says, motioning me out.

I follow him down a short hall, which has four doors along one side. Each door leads into a three-foot by four-foot cubicle.

The CO halts, pointing at a door. "You have forty-five minutes," he growls.

I enter door number three, closing the door behind me. Inside, one white plastic chair sits in front of a six-inch counter. Mounted on the right wall is a handset. Beyond and above the counter is a thick pane of glass. The glass looks into another cubicle, which has two plastic chairs and a similar handset.

I sit down and wait. The CO stands outside the closed door behind me.

The door of the opposing cubicle opens, Sharla enters.

I smile.

Glancing over my shoulder, I see the CO scrutinizing her. After five seconds, he walks away.

She sits and picks up the handset. I pick up my handset. I stare at her through the heavy glass partition.

"Hey," she coos.

"Man, am I glad to see you," I say. Tears well up in my eyes.

"Let me look at you," she says, staring at me. We gaze at each other for five minutes, speaking only some mysterious language of the eyes.

"I got a question," I say. "How come you didn't dump me?"

She shakes her head. "I don't know," she explains. "Simply put, it's because I love you. I understand why you did what you did. And I forgive you for it. In fact, I knew all along that something was going on. What, I couldn't tell you, but something."

"You're sure you're not going to dump me?" I ask. "I mean, I would understand if you do. It would hurt, and I would cry, and I would never recover, but I would understand."

"Randy," she says. Her voice is a nail of intensity. "I'm never going to leave you. So don't even think about it."

"Okay," I say, relieved. "Thanks." I pause, swallowing the emotion pushing up from my stomach. "How come my bail is so high? Did my attorney have anything to say about that?"

"He says they maintain that you're a flight risk. But primarily, he says, it's because of politics. That and the fact of who you were and what you did. He's going to try to get it reduced. But he needs time."

"Whaddaya mean he needs time?" I squeak. "This place is horrifying. I'm scared to death. And he needs time?"

"He says it will all be over in sixty days," she says.

"Sixty days! I'll die if I have to be in here sixty days. What the hell is my mom paying him for? Tell him to get me out of here. I don't care how."

"He's doing everything he can," she says. "It's kind of complicated, Randy. You know? It's all over the papers and on TV. They even searched my house. And they impounded my car."

"What?" I ask. "Why would they impound *your* car? You had nothing to do with anything."

"Well, they did. They did because they could. Danny Sauer didn't have to. It was his decision, and he decided to do it. So they towed it. I had to go to Turlock to get it back and pay them 250 dollars." Bitterness flavors her words.

"Jesus, I'm sorry," I speak into the handset, pressing it against my ear. "And they searched your house? What for? You didn't do anything."

"Danny Sauer had a warrant," she says. "They came in and went through every room. They seized your laptop and were going to seize my computer . . . but they didn't. Then they took me down to the police station and asked me a bunch of questions. They threatened to arrest me if I didn't."

"What? That's bunk," I tell her. "You didn't do anything. You didn't know anything about anything. They're just hassling you."

"They seized your bank account. And," she leans forward, "they seized my bank account. I had 250 dollars left in it, and they took it."

"Why?"

"Because of those two checks you wrote me," she says. "I put stop payments on both of them. And they know it. All they have to do is check the bank's records."

"You better tell Babitzke," I urge her.

"I did," she says. "He's looking into it. He can't believe they impounded my car either." She shakes her head. "I knew Danny Sauer when he was growing up. Boy! Was I wrong about him."

"You know him?" I ask.

"Yeah," she says. "He went to First Church. This little kid running around."

"Great," I say, sarcasm melting on my tongue.

"Thank God they haven't put my name in the papers," she says. "They just refer to me as 'your fiancée.' My parents will die if they use my name."

"Speaking of your parents," I say, "what have they said? Anything?"

She grins at me through the glass. "My dad called and told me that after having read the numbers — how much money was involved — that I should just drop you. Never have anything to do with you again."

"Good old Morrie," I say. "Thanks for all the Christian support. What about your mom?"

"She told me to hold my head up high," she says. "Of course, she thinks I should dump you too. I told her I love you, and that's it."

"I'll bet that went over like a lead balloon," I say, smiling at her.

"It's funny in a way," she says. "Just having it all out in the open is such a relief." She stares at me. "You know, your getting caught is the best thing that ever happened to our relationship."

"Yeah, I know," I agree. "If I'd had one more week, I'd have been down in San Diego, living in a house on the beach. I already had one lined up."

"Yeah," she says, "and then I'd have come down, and then the whole thing would have blown up in our faces. They probably would have arrested me too."

"I know, I know," I say. I cannot meet her eyes. "Pretty dumb, huh?"

"Really dumb," she says. She laughs. "It'll all work out. I believe that more than ever."

I'm not sure I agree with that or not. I want to, but it's hard to from inside jail. "I hope so," I say. "God, this place scares me."

"Just be careful," she says. "Your attorney will do everything he can." She smiles again. "I like that man. I trust him too. He's very smart. And he's on your side. So you do what he tells you to do."

"Okay," I say. I look at her. I touch the glass separating us with my fingertips. "I wish I could touch you," I whisper into the handset.

She mirrors my fingers with her own. "I know. I want to hug you so bad."

"I'm so sorry," I say. "I'm so sorry for all this."

"I know," she says, moving her fingertips over the glass.

"How much time have I got left?" I ask. "I don't want to get in trouble." I look over my shoulder.

She checks her watch. "About five minutes," she says.

"Jesus," I say. "When can you come see me again?"

"You're only allowed two visits per week," she says.

"Only two?" I squeak.

"Only two," she states matter of factly. "So no one else better come visit you. 'Cuz they'll be using up my time with you."

"Who's gonna come visit me?" I scoff. "All the people from my church? Fat chance!"

"Certainly not David," she says. "He's such a creep. That man gives me the willies. You should read what he had to say about you in the paper. He told everyone on the council to absolutely make no statements to the media. And then he goes and blabs his big fat mouth." She shakes her head.

David is the president of the church council, the ruling body of the church.

"Forget David," I say. "I'm almost out of time with you." I look over my shoulder for the guard. But he's not in view

"I know," she says. "I love you, Randy. Never forget that — never doubt it. Not for an instant."

"Okay. I love you too," I say.

The guard taps on my door, startling me. He opens the door, taps his watch. "Three minutes," he growls. He shuts the door, walks away.

"Okay," I say, "I gotta go. I love you, sweet girl." I blow her a kiss.

"I love you," she says. She puckers her lips, kisses the air.

"Come see me soon," I say, pushing my chair back.

"I will," she says. "Call me whenever you can."

"Okay." I hang up my handset. Turning, I exit the cubicle, stand just outside, watching her leave.

She smiles at me one last time.

I walk back to the podium. The CO sits behind it, reading his newspaper. I pause in front of him. "Thank you, sir."

He looks up, checks his watch. "Back to your cell," he growls.

"Yes, sir," I say. I feel buoyed, like a drowning man who finds a plank of wood to grasp.

Back in cell 19, I sit Indian style on my bunk with my book in my lap. But I am not reading. I'm thinking about Sharla, how wonderful love is. All you need is love.

That evening, CO Palmer is back on duty. The shifts change at six in the morning and six in the evening, I now know.

At 7:00 p.m., he unlocks my door with his key. "Radic," he says, standing in the doorway, "you have one hour of rec time. Use it wisely."

I walk to the phones, dial Sharla's number. I tell her that I love her and that I have only a few minutes to talk. While I speak to her, I notice three other inmates are out of their cells: the Arab, Belomar, from across the unit; a long-haired man who is so grossly fat he can hardly walk; and a long-haired man with both hands and forearms wrapped in bandages. The fat guy waddles across the unit with a towel over his shoulder. He is going to shower, I realize. I tell Sharla that I love her, that I have to go.

Belomar sits in front of the television, watching some program. Next to him, singing, sits the guy with the bandages.

I walk over, stand beside Belomar's chair. His arms are crossed over his chest as he leans back. He looks content.

"Excuse me," I say.

They both look up at me. The singing halts.

"Welcome," says Belomar. "Have a seat."

"No, thanks," I say. "I just have a question. Are we allowed to shower?"

"Sure," he replies. He points to three dark gun-metal-blue doors. "Any one of those."

"Thanks," I say.

The guy with the bandages smiles at me, begins singing again in a high falsetto.

I nod to him, look back at Belomar. "Is there any way to request books to read?"

"Of course," says Belomar. "Just fill out a kite. The blue one. The white ones are for medical, work programs, that kind of shit."

"A kite?" I ask. "What's that?"

"An inmate request form," Belomar explains. "They're called kites."

"Well, where do I get one?"

"The co, usually," he says. "But they're out. I know, 'cuz I asked for some earlier."

I frown.

Belomar stands up, motions me to follow him. He walks to his cell. I tag along about ten feet behind.

He enters his cell, which is dark as his lights are off. Digging through a pile of paper on top of his dresser, he finds two white kites and two blue kites.

I peer through the doorway. His cell is a pig sty, food wrappers on the floor, articles of clothing on the floor.

"Here," he says. "You may have these." He hands me the kites. "Fill them out, then shove them through the door so the co can see them. He will pick them up."

"Okay," I say. "Thanks." I look at the kites. "Is this the only way to make requests?"

Belomar laughs. "You can ask the guards, but it won't get

you anywhere," he says. "'Cuz they don't give a shit about you. Also," he adds, "they can't do shit without permission. Everybody," he makes a sweeping gesture with his arm, indicating the entire jail, "thinks they can, but they can't. They do as they're told, just like we do."

"Okay," I drawl. "Then I guess I'll do it this way."

I look at him, curious. "How come you're in here — in the Med Unit? Where were you before?"

"GP," he says. "It's better over there. Out most of the time, lots of action, even girls." He grins at me.

I nod as if I know what he's talking about. "If it's so much better, how come you're over here?" I ask.

A sour smile flits across his mouth. His teeth, big and white, contrast in his dark face. "Some of the power assholes," he makes a fist in front of his chest, "think I dissed them," he says. He looks around, shrugs. "So I filled out a kite, got moved over here."

"Who?" I ask.

Belomar jerks his head back, looks at me like I'm some new species of insect. "White power assholes," he explains. "Skinhead fucks, you know?"

"Oh, yeah," I say.

"They're all about reputation, respect, and revenge," he says, spitting the words out. "Crackers, rednecks is what they are. Motherfucking stupid assholes. This whole place is nothing but gangland central." He gives his head a sad shake.

I nod, only half-comprehending what he is talking about.

"But, hey," he smiles, "you got a nice, private cell here. Kick back, relax, like a vacation, you know?"

I grimace, thinking about such a viewpoint. With a finger, I tap one of the kites. "If I fill this out and request a transfer, you think they'll move me to GP?" I like the idea of being "out most of the time."

Belomar shrugs. "Who knows, you know? Try it, see what happens." He tilts his head at me. "You got to be smart, though. Don't just request it, tell them why, you know? Give them a reason, do their thinking for them, you know?" He laughs. "They need a reason to move you. So give them one."

"Okay," I say, thinking about this statement.

Belomar crosses his arms over his chest, looks around the unit.

"You think I should go to GP?" I ask. "I mean, I don't want any trouble."

"GP is good," Belomar says. "But real political, you know? Lots of young guys on a power trip. Want you to follow their rules."

"That doesn't sound very appealing," I say.

"Fuck all, you know?" says Belomar. "You could go to the farm, but you haven't been sentenced yet, right?"

"No," I say. The word *sentenced* blows cold in my face.

"Well, then," Belomar says, "you got three choices: here, GP, or PC."

"What's PC like?" I ask.

"I don't know, you know? I never been there, but from what I hear I don't wanna find out neither, you know?"

"How come?" I ask.

"Very violent," Belomar explains. "Nothing but murderers and rapists, that kind of shit. Guys who don't know nothing about nothing — only violence."

"Well, then, I don't wanna go there," I say, looking at my kites. "I'll shoot for GP."

"Well, okay, you know? Still, it's nice here," he says, glancing around.

I nod. "I'm gonna go take a shower," I say.

"Okay, you know?" Belomar says. He heads for the television.

The next morning, after breakfast, my cell door pops. I jump up, walk to the door, peek my head out.

"Radic!" booms a voice. "See the nurse!"

I walk to the podium. The CO stands behind it. A large man

with short dark hair. He points to a chair next to the podium. I sit in the chair.

A small Asian woman in white pants and a floral top approaches my chair. She is carrying a blood pressure cuff and a clipboard. She sets her clipboard on the podium, turns to me. "Pull up your sleeve," she says.

I obey, pulling up the right sleeve of my sweatshirt.

She wraps the cuff around my bicep and pumps the sleeve up. Watching her digital readout, she finally announces, "Okay."

"Is it high?" I ask.

She looks at me, as if it's none of my business. Looking back at her clipboard, she makes a note. "Yes," she says. "We'll check it again this afternoon. You can talk to the doctor then." Looking over at me, she says, "That's all. You can go."

Back in my cell, I fill out a white kite. At the bottom of the kite are five blank lines for "comments." I write, "I don't know why I'm in the Med Unit. I haven't had an episode of PFP in more than a year. I would like to be transferred to GP." Pushing the kite through the door edge, I move to my bunk, sit down to finish my western book.

Fifteen minutes later the CO passes my door on his rounds. Snatching my kite from the door, where it hangs like a small white flag, he pauses, reading it. He looks at me, scowls, moves on.

After lunch, my cell door pops again. I push the door open, take one step out.

"Radic!" bellows the CO. "See the doctor."

I walk to the podium.

A fifty-something white guy sits in a chair at the end of the podium. He wears a stethoscope around his neck. His shirt is Hawaiian-ish, with large purple flowers on a yellow and green background. "Have a seat," he says, indicating a chair facing his position.

I sit down. He reads my file.

"Okay," he says. "Your blood pressure is high but seems to be coming down. You ever been on meds for it?" He looks at me.

"No, sir," I say.

"And you're fifty-two, right?"

"Yes, sir."

He looks at me. "Well, you're not overweight. In fact, just the opposite." He looks back at my file. "Any questions?"

"Should I be on medication?" I ask.

He leans back in his chair, gazes at me as he toys with his stethoscope. "Probably not," he says. "It's probably just from stress — the stress from this place." He smiles. "But we'll keep an eye on it."

"If it comes down," I ask, "would it be possible for me to be transferred out of here?"

He shrugs. "Maybe. I'm not the classification officer. I have no authority in that area." He leans forward to read another file.

"Yes, sir," I acknowledge, "but if you declared there was no medical reason to keep me in here, they'd be more likely to transfer me, wouldn't they?"

He leans back in his chair, putting his hands behind his head. "Probably," he concedes. A nod tips his head as he gazes at me. "We'll monitor it. If it comes down, I don't know why they wouldn't transfer you."

"Thank you, sir," I say.

"You can go," he says in an easy voice.

I walk back to my cell. A kernel of hope stirs in my mind; perhaps I will be moved to a different unit. One where the inmates are not locked down forty-seven of every forty-eight hours.

A nurse checks my blood pressure every morning and then again every evening. It improves daily, so that by Tuesday of the following week it is normal. On Wednesday, after lunch, my cell door pops. I jump up, open the door, take one step forward.

"Radic!" shouts the CO. "Roll up your stuff!"

I stand bewildered, ignorant of what "roll up your stuff" means. "Excuse me, sir?" I say.

The CO looks up at me. He is tall, blond, physically fit — the same CO who told me to bend over, spread my cheeks, and cough. There is a kind of freedom in that episode. It is difficult to be dishonest with a man who has gazed upon the cyclopean pucker of my asshole.

"Throw your stuff in a bag and bring it out here," he explains in a prickly tone. "Roll up your bedroll and throw it in one of these laundry barrels." He points to an army green plastic trash can upon which someone has scrawled "Laundry" in black magic marker.

"Yes, sir."

As I step back into my cell, he adds, "And hurry it up!"

Ten seconds later my bedroll is off the bed and rolled up. I grab my new fish packet from its perch above my white porcelain sink and walk out of cell 19. As instructed, I toss my bedroll into the "Laundry" barrel. Moving to the podium, I wonder, where am I going?

"Stand over there," the CO commands, pointing to a spot ten feet to the right of the podium.

I obey. Already, in just five days, fear has taught me the definition of blind obedience. The guards compel it; they have absolute power in their small universe. Do not question. Do not hesitate. Do not seek a reason. Do not speak unless necessary. Do not draw attention to yourself. Never get angry. Never threaten. Just obey.

I stand on my spot, looking around the unit.

"Radic?" says the CO, looking at me.

"Yes, sir?" I look by him, just inches to the right of his head. This shows respect; to meet eyes with a guard is disrespectful.

"You're the preacher, right?" he asks.

Startled by the question, by the appellation, I almost hesitate. "Yes, sir," I admit, wondering how he knows who I am or, for that matter, why he cares.

He nods and keeps nodding. "I read about you," he says. His voice is detached, as if he's noting that today is Wednesday.

"You read about me?" I ask, incredulous. I remind myself not to question.

"Yeah," he says, holding up a newspaper. "On the front page of today's paper."

"Yes, sir," I reply automatically.

"I guess you're famous," he says. A small smile plays around the corners of his mouth. He drops the paper on the counter.

I don't know how to reply without sounding like an asshole. So I don't speak.

He turns to his computer monitor. "Someone'll be here to pick you up soon," he says.

I think about the newspaper, being on the front page. In some indistinct way, I am humiliated and embarrassed, or should be. But the real world, outside, seems so remote that I am simply indifferent. Now my world is nine feet by twelve feet. In here, "out there" doesn't exist.

A heavy popping sound attacks my ears. I know the sound: the intake door is opening.

A CO rounds the corner. He carries a clipboard in his right hand and a smile on his face. Short and plump, he has two yellow stripes on his sleeves. A corporal. Nodding to the duty CO behind the podium, he walks over to me. "Radic?" he says. He reaches out and lifts my ID, matching name and number to those on his clipboard.

"Yes, sir."

"Let's go," he says, waving me toward the intake door, which lies at the end of a short hall around the corner.

As we near the intake door, he points at a spot on the floor. I stop on the spot. He continues forward six feet to the door and presses a button. A camera examines him, and in some remote control room another CO presses a button. The door locks pop. We pass through.

We are walking down the cancer green hallway. I am four feet off his right shoulder and three feet behind him.

The CO glances back at me. "Know where you're going?" he asks.

"No, sir," I say.

"Intake 2," he tells me. "Which is the PC unit."

"Yes, sir," I say as we keep walking.

The leather of his Sam Browne belt creaks. He hitches it up with his left hand. "Saw your picture in the paper today," he says. "Great big article on you on the front page."

"Yes, sir," I reply. "The CO in the Med Unit told me."

He turns his head to look at me. "You read it?" he asks.

"No, sir."

"Umm," he gargles. Then adds, "That's probably why they're putting you in PC."

I glance over at him. "Why's that, sir?"

"You being a preacher and all," he explains, motioning me to turn down a hallway to the right. "Probably concerned someone in GP would read it, decide to jump you."

"Why would anyone in GP care?" I ask.

He shakes his head. "Ohhh, they're kinda crazy in GP. Never know what's going to set them off." He smiles and shrugs. "You'll be better off in here anyway."

We stop at another massive door. Next to the door, painted in white eighteen-inch letters is I-2. The camera scrutinizes us, the door locks thud open.

The CO opens the door, waves me through. I keep to the right, looking around. We are in a keep. Another door, a mirror image of the one we just passed through, stands before us. Once more we are examined. The thud of the locks, and the CO pulls the heavy door open. I take two steps inside and stop.

Waving his clipboard to the left, the CO precedes me to the podium. Behind the podium, like a lithe and muscular Buddha, stands an Asian CO. Unlike Buddha, he is buff, and like Buddha his head is shaved clean.

"Got one for ya," says my CO. He releases the top few pages from his clipboard, hands them to the Asian CO.

"Oh, the preacher," says the Asian CO, reading the pages he holds. He gives me a curious glance, then stares at the monitor in front of him. "Okay," he says, clicking his mouse, "you'll be in cell 33 until Classification talks to you." He looks at me, nods at a huge laundry cart next to the podium. "Grab a bedroll and head on up to 33," he says, pointing at a flight of stairs to his right.

I lean deep into the cart, grab the last remaining bedroll. As I head for the stairs, my escort, the corporal, looks at me. "Good luck, preacher," he says.

"Thank you," I reply.

I climb the stairs to tier two. Passing three empty cells, I arrive at cell 33. I open the door, enter. The interior is similar to my cell in the Med Unit, only not as big. This one measures seven feet by twelve feet and has a thick shelf of wood, which functions as a desk rather than a small chest of drawers.

I make my bunk, which takes two minutes. Opening the metal drawers under the bunk, I discover a book, *Star Wars: Return of the Jedi.* This reminds me that I left the western book in my cell in the Med Unit. I shrug to myself. There is nothing I can do about it.

I spend the rest of the evening reading, halting only to accept my plastic dinner tray from two trustees, whom I later know as Chevy and Sleepy. Chicken and rice. It looks as if someone vomited on my tray. I drink the coffee, place the tray on the cell floor by the door, untouched.

Back on my bunk, I continue reading *Star Wars,* then fall asleep with the lights on.

The next morning, Chevy and Sleepy deliver my breakfast tray. The CO with them looks pissed off. He slams the cell door in my face as soon as I accept the tray from Sleepy.

As I sit on my bunk, sipping coffee, the door opens. A tall

man with a huge beer gut enters my cell and stands by the sink. He holds a clipboard.

"Stay seated," he says. He glances at his clipboard. "I'm Sergeant Conklin, the classification officer."

"Yes, sir," I say, wondering what "classification" means in this instance.

"I'm the one who assigns housing arrangements in the unit," he goes on. "I decide who bunks with who. Also," he stares at me, "if you have any problems with any of the cos, you come to me. If you have any problems with other inmates, you come to me. If you have any grievances, you come to me. Understand?"

"Yes, sir."

"If anyone threatens you or you feel threatened by anyone — anyone at all — you come to me." He looks at his clipboard. "This unit houses the Surenos. The Nortenos are segregated in other units. And the white power gangs are in mainline or mostly on the farm. For safety reasons, that's the way it has to be." He looks at me. "It's a mess, but that's the way it is. This unit also houses the more violent offenders and is a 'no contact' facility. Understand?"

"Yes, sir." I don't, but I wouldn't dream of saying so.

"You're the preacher," he says, eyeing me. "We have clergy that come in and minister to the inmates. I don't want to hear about you leading any prayer meetings or religious meetings or counseling any of the inmates. Understand?"

I sit paralyzed on my bunk. "Yes, sir."

He stares at me hard. "So you won't be doing any of that, right?"

"No, sir, I won't do any of that," I assure him.

"Good," he says. "I'm going to put you in cell 52. They'll pop your door after lunch, during rec, and you can move your property over to 52. Understand?"

"Yes, sir."

"Any questions?"

"Should I take my bedroll?" I ask, afraid to move.

"Yes," he says. "Anything that is yours, you take it."

I hesitate. "Why am I in PC?" I ask, looking up at his round face.

"Administration," he explains, gesturing at some remote, invisible entity, "decided that, because of you being a pastor, it would be safer for you in here."

"Should I be worried?" I ask.

He narrows his eyes at me. "As long as you keep to yourself and mind your own business, you'll be fine." He considers for a second, then adds, "Don't mingle with the young guys or the blacks. They're trouble."

I nod.

"Okay," says Conklin. "Remember, anyone threatens you or you even feel threatened, you come to me. Understand?"

"Yes, sir." His choice of words — *trouble, threatens, safer* — bothers me.

He reads his clipboard. "You'll be in with Ordonez. Josh Ordonez. He's scheduled for court this afternoon, so he won't be around when you get there. Take the empty bunk." He glances at me. "Any other questions?"

"No, sir."

"Okay," he says and leaves. He locks my cell door.

INTAKE 2

After lunch, my cell door pops. The CO opens my door. It is CO Palmer. He nods to me. "Okay," he says, "roll up your stuff and move it to cell 52." He walks off, leaving my cell door ajar.

I grab my bedroll, my new fish packet, and the *Star Wars* book. Descending the stairs, I enter a swirling vortex of orange-clad inmates. I remind myself of what CO Conklin said, "during rec." This is rec time.

Most of the inmates are young, scuzzy looking. Refraining from meeting anyone's eyes, I glance around, locate cell 52. Up another set of stairs and to the right. I enter the cell. The lower bunk wears a blue blanket. Tossing my bedroll onto the upper bunk, I begin making my bed as I look around.

It is evident that someone lives in here. Yet for all that, the room is tight, as if it wants to breathe but can't. There is no room in this room. It is just a little too little for one person, psychologically speaking. And now two people live here.

There are photographs around the mirror above the sink. Most of the photos depict young, pretty girls in various self-conscious poses. On the back edge of the desk squats a pile of paperback books, mysteries, thrillers, true crime. A white Styrofoam cup bristles with stubby yellow pencils. The edge of the sink holds a plastic tube of red Colgate toothpaste, a bottle of honey-gold Alberto VO5 shampoo, and a bottle of clear liquid, which is shaving lotion. In the cubby hole above the sink, a four-inch toothbrush butt-fucks a white Styrofoam cup in the upside-down position. A hole punched through the bottom of the cup makes this possible. The bristles on the brush are mangled and worn.

Bits of whisker stick to the bowl of the sink, and a brownish scum ring clings tenaciously to the toilet bowl's circumference, like some kind of disgusting birthmark. Half-dried yellow droplets of piss spot the toilet seat.

I leave my new fish packet on my bunk and march out the cell door, joining the mass of zoo animals. My mission: to locate cleaning supplies, especially disinfectant.

It is in here, in Intake 2, that my vocabulary increases willy-nilly. Living in jail is like living in a foreign country. The customs and culture are different, almost alien, and so is the language. Terms like PC, the hole, chilimos, chomos, DVI, snipe hunter, punk, rec time, Norteno, and Sureno imprint themselves on my brain, opening up whole new panoramas into the lives and lifestyles of human beings.

Here are some of the unique new words I learn and use.

PC is Protective Custody. In a PC unit, the inmates are locked in their cells most of the time, except during meals and rec time. The inmates in PC are either extremely violent, members of gangs, or in danger of being attacked by other inmates. In PC, any physical contact with another inmate is severely punished.

The hole is inmate slang for Administrative Segregation, sometimes simply "ad-seg," which is solitary confinement for forty-seven hours of every forty-eight-hour period. One hour out of every other day, during which the inmate is cuffed and shackled. Inmates in the hole are either royal fuckups or so violent they are deemed unsafe under any other circumstances.

Chilimo and chomo are inmate slang for child molestors, who are considered to be scum even by other inmates. Gang-bangers attack and try to kill chomos whenever possible.

Gangbangers are inmates who affiliate with gangs inside and outside jail. They are violent, usually young, into using and selling drugs and gunrunning. Gangs are based on race: Asian gangs, Hispanic gangs, white gangs, black gangs.

Hispanic gangs: Nortenos are from northern California. Their gang-sign/number is fourteen. Surenos are from southern California. Surenos are also called Mexican Mafia. Their gang-sign/number is thirteen. Because of territorial clashes, Nortenos and Surenos hate each other. Both gangs are so violent that they are rarely allowed to intermingle with any other inmates not affiliated with their gang.

White gangs: NLRs are Nazi Low Riders. They are racist, very violent, move drugs, especially meth, and there is no way out of the NLR other than death. NorCal Woods are a white supremacist gang from northern California, very violent, extremely racist. They refer to themselves as "the woodpile." Members of white supremacist gangs are sometimes called Pure Boys because of their insistence on racial purity.

Black gangs: primarily Crips and Bloods. Their business ventures include drugs and guns. Murder is esteemed as a badge of honor.

Paisas, or Pisas, are Hispanics who are not gang affiliated.

Snipe hunters are inmates who seek out and smoke discarded cigarette butts.

Punk is slang for scum, the lowest of the low. It is a horrible insult, and its use results in immediate violence.

OG is what I am: slang for an old guy, any inmate over thirty years of age. OG can also stand for old gangster, a gang member who is over thirty years old.

Homey, or sometimes homie, is a homeboy and refers to another member of one's gang.

Pimp roll is a way of walking, rolling from side to side while undulating the hips. It signifies supercool, toughness, arrogance, an attitude of "don't fuck with me."

Mainline, or sometimes called GP (general population), is

where the majority of inmates are housed. Their crimes are less violent and usually involve drug abuse, theft, car-jacking. Inmates in the general population are allowed more time out of their cells.

The farm is slang for the Honor Farm, a minimum-security facility for, supposedly, nonviolent offenders. They are allowed to work on the premises: laundry, kitchen, ground maintenance. Their privileges include daily commissary: cokes, hamburgers, milkshakes — all for a price, of course.

DVI stands for Deuel Vocational Institute. It is a processing facility where, after being sentenced, inmates are tested and classified according to a point system. The number of points determines which prison the inmate will be sent to. Prisons are minimum-, medium-, or maximum-security facilities. Some prisons have all three levels of security. DVI was built to house 1,700 inmates. It has 4,000 inmates sleeping in dorms, gyms, and hallways due to severe overcrowding. In reality, it is a zoo for violent animals, who are then shipped off to other zoos. The guards and staff call it "gladiator school" because there are so many savage fights.

Dog is inmate slang for another inmate, like "dude" or "man" or "pal" in the real world.

Lockdown is when inmates are locked in their cells.

Core-capping refers to early release from jail due to over-crowding. Less violent offenders may be released to make room for new arrivees.

Ninety-day op refers to a three-month period during which an inmate is tested and observed to determine if he is "prison material" or not. Basically, "prison material" means the inmate fits in with the other animals. He likes violence, drugs, and chaos. At the end of the ninety-day op, the inmate returns to court, where he may be released, resentenced to prison, or remanded to jail to finish his sentence.

Local time is when inmates serve their sentences in the county jail rather than prison. Any sentence over twelve months requires that the time be served in prison.

CDC is California Department of Corrections. CDC is the penal system in California. For the most part, they do the best they can. Recently, they changed the name to include the term "rehabilitation": California Department of Corrections and Rehabilitation. As yet, there is no money allocated for rehab.

CRC is California Rehabilitation Center, which is a prison facility for tweakers, euphemistically called "substance abusers."

Atascadero is the prison/mental hospital in California. A prison for the mentally ill, it is too small, understaffed, and underfunded.

Med Unit is a unit in jail for housing chronically ill inmates. For example, those with diabetes, TB, bad hearts, et cetera.

Sheltered Housing is a unit in jail for housing inmates recovering from injuries. It acts as a halfway house between hospitals and jail. When the criminal is released from the hospital, he is placed in this unit until well enough to be assigned regular housing in the jail.

Holding tanks are cells that temporarily hold inmates before and after loading them on buses, or at the courthouse, while the inmates await their scheduled time before the judge.

Level six is a jail-assigned security designation and denotes the highest level of security. Because they are either a threat to others, or because they have been threatened, level sixes are isolated from general population inmates at all times.

HUNGER STRIKE

November 14, 2005

Intake 2, Cell 52

11:00 p.m

Five minutes until lockdown. I am already in the cell when Josh enters. I've been here three days now, just transferred from the Med Unit, where I spent five days, so I'm still wary around Josh. His head is shaved. He is my height, weighs 220 pounds to my 165 pounds.

His surname, Ordonez, resides on his forearm in Cloister font and black ink, I guess, so he won't forget his name. Later I find out it's there because he's proud of his name, his father, who is dead. One time he showed me his dad's photo: young guy, about thirty-five when he died. He died from a drug overdose; he sold them, used them, lived for them. Because of this, Josh will have nothing to do with drugs, so he says.

But that's a lie, because Josh's uncle, who is twenty-eight, is four cells down, in 56. He is here for drug charges incurred while in prison. So he's in prison because of drugs, and while there he obtains and uses illicit drugs, gets caught, and now faces more prison time.

Not exactly a genius. In fact, he is a twenty-eight-year-old garbage sack of junk, junk food, and junk ideas. In the end, after three months, his case is tossed out, and they release him rather than send him back to prison for the few weeks remaining on his original sentence.

I know it's a lie because one day I come into the cell, and Josh is hunched over the desk, acting all fractal and weird;

obviously, he doesn't want me to see what he's doing or has on the desk. I leave.

Later on I come back for lockdown, and he's already on his bunk. Bizarre, because he is usually the last one in — if you're cool, that's what you do.

The hydraulic locks close with a Kellogg's SNAP, CRACKLE, POP. Only there are not cute elves running around, only COs dressed à la Darth Vader.

Josh is chattering, talking about his former job, he was a cook at Red Lobster, babbling on about some chicks, his girl-friend (former), his mom, his little brothers, the chomos down the way, Tommy the chomo in 58. How he'd kill anyone who touched his little brothers. On and never-ending on about chomos. He hates them so much I suspect he has latent homosexual tendencies.

I just listen. Next morning it comes out that he was smok-ing marijuana that his uncle brought in from prison. His uncle keystered it. Translation: he jammed a condom full of mari-juana up his ass. And Josh tried some last night, just for fun. That's why he was talking so much.

To proceed: Josh comes into the cell, just prior to lock-down, and Sleepy is with him. Sleepy is a trustee, Mexican, a Sureno. Surenos are Mexican Mafia. Their number/logo/sign is thirteen, the numerical position of M in the alphabet. M is for Mexican Mafia. They're into drugs, guns, turf, racketeer-ing, and pussy.

Sleepy and Josh exchange fists: knuckles against knuckles, accompanied by the word *dog*. It means they are friends, pals, buddies. And more, it means they will back each other up under certain circumstances. Those circumstances are loosely defined, and I can't delineate them with any accuracy.

As Sleepy leaves, he says, "Tell all the white brothers." Cryptic, to say the least.

The door locks snap into place. Locked down.

"What's going on?" I say.

"Nothing," says Josh, looking out the window, which he does a lot. Usually, he's talking to the guys in cell 66, across the way, talking with sign language, which most of the professional criminals utilize.

"Well, what was Sleepy talking about?" I've already learned to be forthright with Josh. Just come out and say it.

"There's going to be a hunger strike."

"What? Why?"

"The Surenos are striking over the rec time," Josh says. "The fucking guards just keep getting lazier and lazier. Never let us out. So the Surenos are going to go on strike. They're not eating until the guards come up with a schedule that gives us more time out."

"And they think that will work?" I say. I am shocked and afraid: afraid of the ramifications.

"Fuck," says Josh, "there's nothing to lose. They can't toss one hundred people in the hole. They haven't got room."

"Yeah, but isn't striking against the rules?" I ask.

"Rules? Fuck the rules," says Josh. "The fucking punk guards just use Intake 2 as rest time. They don't fucking let us out. Just eat and watch television. They don't do anything anyway."

"They protect us," I state.

"Fucking pussy," says Josh, staring at me hard. He means it too.

"Well, they do," I protest.

"Fuck!" he ejaculates. "They don't do shit. They're all punks." Punk in Josh's dictionary is the ultimate insult, so that's what he calls the guards.

I think about this hunger strike idea. I come to one conclusion: fear. Fear of the guards' retaliation, fear of the inmates' retaliation. If I go along with it, the guards will abuse me; if I don't, the inmates will hate me and physically threaten me.

"Are you going to go along with it?" I ask, lying on my top bunk rigid with dread. Besides which, I'm already losing weight. I don't want to not eat; of course, the food is inedible anyway. How much commissary do I have on hand? A few bags of Planter's peanuts, some precooked rice. I guess I won't starve.

"Fuck, yeah," says Josh.

"Do you think I should?" I ask and at once realize it is a pussy question. It's me asking someone else to make my decision for me.

"Do what the fuck you want to do," says Josh, disgust in his voice.

"Yeah, but if I don't do it, I'll get beat up, right?"

"Fuck," he says. "No one's going to beat you up."

I don't believe him. The Surenos are like great-gulf-fixed demons and shit. They are the ultimate barbarians. Their only response to everything is raw, concentrated violence.

"Yeah, well. . . ."

"Look," he says, peeking at me with his peripheral vision, "I'll make sure no one touches you. Okay? I'll tell them you didn't even know about it till it was too late."

"No. I'll do it. I'll go along."

I pause, letting the thought percolate through me. The result is a slow-drip coffee composed of equal parts annoyance, fear, and hatred. Within the psychological and physical stress of adjusting to the pathology of jail, a hunger strike is just one more annoyance; I am fearful of physical retribution from either the guards or the inmates, stuck between a rock and a hard place, as it were, or more correctly between whackos in orange or reactionaries in black. And I hate everything about the posture in which I now find myself: bent over, ready to be butt-fucked.

"When does it start?"

"Tomorrow morning," Josh says.

I sigh to myself, a lame, ineffectual attempt to purge a rocket-tight stress situated around my chest, across my back, as if I am a fat chick in a corset.

"Okay, what do I do?"

"Nothing," says Josh. "Just don't go down for meals. Stay in the cell when they pop the doors."

"Well, aren't they going to get pretty pissed?"

"Fuck 'em," says Josh. And he means it.

The next morning, 5:15 a.m. to be precise, the doors pop. Not just once or twice but about fifteen or thirty times, like some death-wish dude unloading the banana clip of an AK-47. The explosions disintegrate my sleep, pop me into right now. I don't move.

Josh rolls himself out of the bottom bunk, walks to the steel door, looks out the window. He is naked from the waist up, his pale skin glows a yellow iridescence in the tier lights.

"What's going on?" I ask.

"Nothing," he says. "Nobody's going down for breakfast." A staccato laugh bursts out of his mouth, high-pitched and mocking.

"No one?" I say, hiding under my coarse sheet, my blue bedspread, thinking they will somehow, magically, wonderfully, protect me.

The death-wish dude carrying the AK-47 fires off another clip of thirty rounds, then another clip of maybe fifty rounds. Godawful racket. Fucking guards are playing with their control panel, wondering where the fuck the felonious fucking shits are.

"There's two guys going down," says Josh, still at his post.

"Who?" I say.

Goddamn traitors, I think. If I can do it, anybody can. That, in seven words, is my new philosophy and holy doctrine. Because if I can do it, fucking anybody can, even a nematode. Thus saith (pronounced "seth") Randy. At the same time, I'm jealous because the guards will like them, show them favoritism, smile at them, not yell at them. Simultaneous with the jealousy, I'm afraid, because these two, whoever they are,

are now noteworthy in the worst possible sense. Foredoomed.

"I don't know," says Josh. "Two of the fucking faggots."

He is referring to the single-occupancy cells, cells 40 through 50, although they aren't all used for homosexuals. Some of them are chomos of a redolent proclivity. Translation: child molesters so outrageous and vicious that even other child molesters think they're sick. Others are transvestites who are secluded for their own safety, although no one's sure why. For that matter, no one's even sure what their sexual preferences are or if they even have any.

"Are they stupid or what?" I say.

"What do you expect from fucking faggot-queers," says Josh. "Only thing worse than a faggot-fucking-fairy-queer is a fairy nigger," he adds for my benefit.

Josh maintains he was not a racist before jail. He is now.

"I'm a racist, and I love it," he says. It's his motto, his trademark, his brand, as it were. Proximity to niggers and Mexicans infects you, says Josh. He might be correct.

The first time he was in jail it was for arson. He told me the story. It was late at night. Josh was drunk and feeling mean and bored. To relieve his intolerable boredom, Josh needed excitement, so he torched a shopping cart filled with paper and cardboard. Then he pushed it down a hill. At the bottom of the hill sat an elementary school. Chaos theory imposed itself on Josh's world. A sudden, radical, irrational change took place in the very fabric of his existence.

The school burned down. It didn't catch on fire and sustain damage. It literally burned down.

Josh was arrested, booked, and, after the usual legal sequence of arraignment and hearings, received a sentence of six months in jail (local time, not prison). Once he was sentenced, Josh was placed on the Honor Farm, a sector of the county jail that ostensibly houses "honorable, nonviolent inmates" who are trustworthy. In reality, the Honor Farm gives rise to more fights, imports more drugs, and displays more raw violence than any other part of the jail.

The Honor Farm is controlled by the supreme white power boys, who are young skinheads who worship at the altar of Pandemonium. Their Holy Trinity is the father of hatred, the son of anger, and the indwelling spirit of violence. They hate everything, including themselves, are angry at everyone, and consider violence the only reasonable response to any event in their humdrum lives.

Josh calls them "the Pure Boys." Most of them are members of Norcal Woods, Aryan Nation, or Nazi Low Riders. Uneducated, unimaginative, mentally listless but simultaneously imbued with a dynamic fission-powered physical energy, and bored, they seek mental and emotional stimulation through sex, drugs, rock and roll, and sadistic brutality, devices for diversion and thrill and catharsis.

Because of his tattoos, the Pure Boys on the farm thought Josh was one of them — that is, "part of the woodpile." But he wasn't. And he told them so. Moreover, the Pure Boys discovered that Josh's mom was a deputy sheriff and, the ultimate transgression, worked at the jail. Josh became a walking, talking example of being in the wrong place at the wrong time: the Pure Boys would be "glad when he was dead."

Demonstrating copious amounts of élan, Josh decided on a lateral move: he requested protective custody. And he got it. They transferred him to Intake 2. Where, after forty-five days, he was "core-capped" out, released. Core-capping is when the jail gets too full, so they release the less violent offenders to make room for the latest scumbags.

Shortly thereafter, Josh was awash in an alcohol-induced rage (beer and tequila) and bored. Again. So he went home, which was a room in his married sister's house, and made a phone call to some guy he knew who had been bothering his girlfriend.

The conversation resembled a monologue rather than a dialogue because the guy wasn't home, but his answering machine was. So Josh spoke with the machine. Basically, he threatened, eight times, to kill the guy, his mother and his father, his brothers and his sisters, and anyone who knew the guy.

Josh's mom heard the recorded threats at a later time. She said, "It was the worst series of death threats I have ever heard . . . horrible things."

When they have a recording of it, it's hard to deny or amend or diminish the intent of terrorist remarks. So Josh was booked and charged eight times with "intent to murder." Facing twenty-five to life for, in essence, being drunk, disorderly, mean, and talkative.

So here he is. He's been here nine months, attending hearing after hearing, waiting like Jonah in the belly of the whale to see what happens. At all costs, he is trying to avoid prison, the fear of which surges like a current in every nerve of his body — a fear that has remapped his moral geography very quickly. He now constantly effervesces up Calvinistic-Latter Day Saint bubbles, things like "I'll never drink again" or "Alcohol is the demon of my life, but I am a changed man."

He can believe it if he wants, but I don't. He is a prime candidate for intensive anger management therapy, a course of antidepressants, and a session or two in the motivation room. Instead, he is a protagonist in a hunger strike.

Josh twists his neck, a kind of down and around motion that implies a double-jointed neck. "One of 'em's coming round opening each cell with his key," he says. Josh lies down on his bunk, pretending to be asleep.

I hear cell doors crashing shut, a booming reverberation that vibrates my bones, like too much bass in some badass lowrider as it drives slowly by your house, shaking the windows, oscillating your very skull. The CO is slamming the doors after he opens them.

Our door swings open. A large man, exuding primate dominance dynamics, stands in the door. I recognize him but do not know his name. He is harsh, inflexible, despises inmates, probably his job and himself too. That is my psychological profile of him. Balding, he is one of those peculiar blond-haired men who has masses of body hair. Flaxen, wiry body hair. It's like he is furred with blond shag carpet.

"Breakfast," he says.

I am looking at him, but I cannot move.

"We're not coming down," says Josh.

"Then fucking stay in your cell," he roars, smashing the door shut.

Five seconds later the cell door opens again. A furious, muscular guard with shag carpet sprouting from his forearms strides into the cell, walks to the back window, which over-looks the yard. He snatches Josh's tobacco can from the five-inch-wide sill.

"You fucks have been warned about stuff in your windows." He throws the can on the floor. "If I see anything there again, you'll be written up." The volume of his voice is at social engineering level: maximum so that we might be enlightened no matter what our IQs.

The door crashes shut again, an older, deeper invocation, a metallic fuck it!

I breathe.

Josh says in a loud voice, "Motherfucker! No right to throw my shit around like that. Fucking pussy!"

"Josh," I whisper, "not so loud, please." Visions of the hole do the fandango in my ophthalmic nerve.

"Fucker," yells Josh, even louder.

He rolls out of the cave of the lower bunk. Walking to the door's window, he growls, "Those motherfucking punks think they can do anything they want." Turning his head, he gives me his best Aryan Nation-social reality look, his eyes toxic black. "I'm gonna file a grievance against his ass. Get him fired. Fucker!" He punches the steel door — hard.

"What did you expect?" I say from my top bunk. I look at

the white ceiling, splotched with black marks. I wonder how the scuffs got there. "We are directly challenging their authority, not only on a personal level, but at an administrative level too. Their expected response will be astonishment, then anger, then retaliation, and finally harsher measures."

"Wha' the fuck you talking 'bout?" says Josh, doing his imitation of "jive nigger" talk, which is so lame. Because he's so proud of being a fucking "casper," you know, a white boy like Casper the friendly ghost, which he isn't; he is, in fact, half white and half Hispanic.

I decide to answer his question, although I know for a fact that he doesn't really want an answer. He's just playing a part, acting all bad and shit. "I'm talking about power within the social context," I say. "All of us are products of a vast socio-economic horizon called social reality — or perhaps "culture" would be a better term — the ballast of the time and place we live, which bisects vertically with the individual psychology, our urges. A person's psyche, and thus his behavior, is the result of this collision. And you, my friend, have just collided with the dominant psychology of the powers that be. You have directly challenged their authority."

Josh stares at me like a grasshopper on crystal meth. "The fuck?"

"Putting it in plain terms, they are going to kick our asses," I say.

"Shut the fuck up, Radic," he says. His voice is subdued now, which means he is thinking.

I eat one package of Planter's peanuts for breakfast, which, according to the nutritional chart on the back of the package, provides me with 105 calories, 90 of which are fat calories. I guess I won't starve. What I regret is missing my morning cup of coffee, served so elegantly in its white Styrofoam cup. We get only two cups of coffee per day: one cup of caffeinated coffee in the morning, and one cup of decaf at dinner.

Josh eats a bag of chips and two Lil' Debbie Nutty Bars.

Lunchtime. Once again no one comes out of his cell, except for the two gay guys, who for a fact look exactly like women, talk like women, move like women. Long, tinted hair, swishy-soft gesticulations, undulating hips — the whole package. One of them, Coco by name, recently exhibited "her" breasts for the guys in the yard. I didn't have the pleasure of viewing them, but I heard that they were nice tits. Small but definitely tits.

And Bob, my walking buddy, comes out too. We find out later on that he didn't know he wasn't supposed to, he had no idea what was going on. No one bothered to tell him about the hunger strike because he was white and an OG.

His full name is Robert Gay. Accused of murdering his wife, he's been in jail for almost a year. His trial will take place soon. Lucky for him, he has lots of money, because his attorney got $200,000 up front to take his case. He used to be a regional vice-president for Orkin, the big bug-killing company. Bob knows everything there is to know about killing bugs. And tennis. I guess he's hecka-good at tennis. Before he got to jail, he weighed 220 pounds. Now he weighs 150.

The COs determine when we get out for rec time. Usually, sometime in the afternoon and then again in the evening. Usually for sixty to ninety minutes each time; occasionally, depending which COs are on duty, for two hours. Rec time is split into two sessions. First, the Surenos get out for ninety minutes. After they are locked back down, we get out for ninety minutes. Or vice versa. There's no rhyme or reason to it. Rec time is at the COs' discretion.

Without a doubt, the COs favor the Surenos. Because their crimes are more "normal." Although brutally violent, the Surenos eschew certain crimes, such as rape, child molestation, and arson. They endorse more upscale, chic crimes: drugs, armed robbery, car jacking, drive-by shooting, attempted murder, murder, mayhem, assault and battery, domestic violence, racketeering in general. Surenos are the "swells" of the subcultural group most commonly known as "criminals."

It's after the aborted lunch, around 1:30 p.m. Josh is standing at the cell door, waiting for rec time. I'm in my penthouse bunk reading some forensic-mystery novel I borrowed from him.

"Soon?" I say.

"Any time now," Josh says. And he knows. He has some inner-cowboy-fuzz-grunge sense, he can predict almost to the second when the cell doors will pop. Eager for a cigarette, his impatience hangs in the air like a mist.

He starts punching the door but not too hard. Too hard and the COs will notice, use it as an opportunity to demonstrate their power and control by delaying rec time.

"Motherfucks," says Josh. "C'mon, c'mon, open the goddamn doors."

"Maybe something's going on," I say. It is my position that the COs actually "do" have duties to perform. My opinion is invariably discarded as the meandering thoughts of a "fucking asshole."

"Fuck!" says Josh. "The bastard punks are doing it on purpose. Their badges have gone to their heads."

The latter is a quote from Josh's mom, who sustains Josh's opinion that many of the COs are power-crazed punks. Only she packages it in more diplomatic terms.

A loud boom resounds nearby. One of the boys, angry because he wants out, is hammering on his cell door. Another boom, this one from someone else, sounds as if it's nearby, maybe around the corner, cell 56, wherein reside two Paisas (unaffiliated Hispanics: i.e., non-gang members who usually speak little English) who are in for God only knows. Probably drugs, domestic violence, or child molestation.

"Those morons better cool it," I say. "They're going to forfeit our rec time. I wish they'd just toss the idiots in the hole. All they do is mess it up for everybody."

Josh laughs. "It's jail. Whaddaya expect?"

"Not much," I say. "But those halfwits are creating their own environment."

"Wha' the fuck, Radic? I never know what the fuck you're talking 'bout."

I sigh audibly.

Due to the troglodytes, the tootsie wootsies with partial brains, the ones using themselves as crash-test dummies against steel cell doors, our rec time is delayed. Eventually, the doors pop.

"Name tags on! Fully dressed! Beds made! Cells clean!" shouts one of the COs.

Nelly, a petite, long-haired Asian gangbanger, blasts down the stairs. Physically perfect, covered with tattoos, he is like a twelve-inch Damascus steel blade with a file-worked ladder pattern. Beautiful, shiny, dangerous.

As he passes the podium, he snarls something at the COs. I hear him but cannot make out what he says. The ultrawide, ultrafat CO steps around the podium, staring at Nelly's back as he walks out to the yard.

"Watch your fucking mouth!" says ultrawide. "One more word out of anybody, and we'll lock it down."

Nelly looks back over his shoulder. "You're shorting us on our rec time," he snaps at the CO.

"Punk!" says the CO. He is now really pissed off. His voice volume is at shock wave level.

Like kids playing freeze tag, everyone in orange stops moving. Except Nelly. He keeps walking toward the yard.

"Three hours per week is all we have to give you. Fucking pukes! Three hours a week!" says the CO. His face looks like a red balloon.

"Three hours *minimum*," says Nelly, this time without looking back. He opens the yard door, passes through it into the yard.

Ultrawide stands debating with himself. Turning, he says, "All you fucks! Anything else and we lock it down! Don't approach the podium. Don't ask for anything. If it gets too loud, we lock it down!" He returns to his chair behind the podium, sits down, his fat ass rolling over the edges of the seat like saddle bags.

Staying far away from the podium, I walk over to pick up some inmate request forms. That's their official title. Everyone calls them "kites." You shoot a kite or fill out a kite. You even fill out a kite to request a grievance form. I just want to request some books from the jail library, which books, of course, will not be available.

As I take three, Anthony, one of the gays, approaches me. I know what he wants. He's carrying a white Styrofoam cup.

"Hey, OG," he says in a patronizing voice. "Got a shot of coffee?"

I sigh out loud to manifest my annoyance.

"C'mon, man," he says. "I need a shot. I'll pay you back."

And he will but only half of what he owes me. One for two is his idea of reimbursement.

I sigh once more, this time at myself — sucker. "Okay," I say. "I'm going back up anyway. Meet me at my cell."

I give the podium a wide berth, climb the stairs. Anthony tags along like a puppy.

Entering the cell, I open my steel drawer, find my packet of instant coffee. I never drink the stuff because it gives me explosive, stinking gas. I use it to trade. Cigarettes, coffee, soups, and sweets are best for trading, in that order.

Anthony stands at the brink of the cell. Entering a cell other than your own is not only against the formal administrative rules but also violates informal jail etiquette, which carries even harsher penalties, such as getting your ass kicked.

I pour a large portion into his cup. "That enough?"

"Thanks, man. That's good for two cups."

He leaves happy. Not only is he gay, which means most of

the guys in PC won't have much to do with him, but he is also a swishy gay, and black, which ushers in racism. Worst of all, he has no money on his books. I trade without regard to race, creed, or color. My only rule is this: they owe me, I never owe anyone.

Josh comes bustling in to roll more cigarettes as I am shutting my steel drawer.

"You giving that black faggot more coffee?"

"Yeah."

"Why? That nigger jive ass faggot is nothing but a mooch." He sits in our only chair, begins lining tobacco on the desktop, as if he's preparing lines of cocaine to snort. Then he brushes each line onto rolling paper with a straight edge made of folded yellow legal pad paper.

"That's probably why," I say.

"Why what?"

"Why I give it to him. He doesn't have any money on his books, so he mooches. I guess I feel sorry for him."

Josh snorts his derision. "I don't give a fuck about anyone in here," he says.

I make a mental note to remember those words. "Then how come you're all chummy with the Asian gangbangers?" I would like to understand.

"'Cuz I got to hang with someone," he says. "It's just someone to talk to. But I don't give a fuck about them."

Rising from the chair, he huffs and puffs like the Big Bad Wolf in *Little Red Riding Hood*, blowing the remaining tobacco all over the floor. I cringe. No wonder I have to clean the cell every day. I live with a big, bad, protopunk pig.

Josh leaves the cell with a whoosh of speed, in a hurry to smoke with his gangbanger buddies. They stand in the yard passing around cigarettes, hands in the fronts of their pants, looking as if they're playing with themselves. Their pants are tucked into their white sock tops, giving them the appearance of dancing harem girls in those B movies on television. On their feet they wear shower thongs. And when they walk, they leave their hands in their pants, swaying, rolling, gliding — all at the same time. It's called the "pimp roll." It is gang shit. All of it.

They think they look supermotherfucking cool and bad. And cool and bad are status. And status, in jail, is everything. In reality, they look like certified nitwits in chirpy gaucho outfits.

I decide to clean the cell. Maybe I'll stop thinking about food.

Day two of the hunger strike. The rapid-fire popping of the cell doors for breakfast. Then a thirty-second pivotal pause while the COs wait to see if anyone's coming out.

"You got fifteen seconds to come out!" bellows a voice. "If you don't, you fucking retards can stay in your cells all day. I don't give a fuck!"

The two gay guys and Bob Gay come out to eat. The snapping of the doorlocks comes in waves as the COs palm the switches in groups of ten. Locked down.

Climbing out of my bunk, I retrieve my last package of peanuts. I toss a handful in my mouth, hold them there, letting my saliva rinse the salt and oil from them. Then I slowly chew them, like a cow chews its cud, in a vain attempt to make them last longer, be more than they are.

Josh is awake, lying under his blue bedspread like a great pale beast of the sea. He just looks at me, his rare Noriego blue eyes peering out from beneath the black-watch stocking cap on his head. He pulls it down over his eyes and nose when he wants to sleep, his version of a sensory deprivation device. He ordered the stocking cap from commissary. Most of the badass gangbangers, all attired in identical raffish fashion, swagger out to the yard in them.

"You got anything left to eat?" I say.

"No."

"You can have half of these if you like."

"No. You eat 'em. I'll be okay." He rolls over to sleep.

At lunchtime, Josh stands at the cell door studying the bleak landscape of our cement and steel Club Med. He is bare from the waist up, glistening and sweaty from his calisthenics, which he keeps track of by making hieroglyphic marks on the wall above the sink. His tool of defacement is a four-inch number two pencil, which, when not in use, resides at the crest of his right ear. That is where the cool-bad dogs store their extra cigarettes and pencils. I call it the Position of Efficacious Immediacy: it provides that which they will soon need.

Twice a day Josh performs his exercise routine: push-ups in groups of twenty-five; jogging in place (in front of the six-inch-by-nine-inch mirror above the sink) with his hearing-secret-harmonies expression; twenty rows, which stimulate the lat muscles, the theory being that he will thus attain the ultimate V shape. He hangs a towel from the top of the bunk frame, leans back, and rows his face up to kiss the metal. Then fifty sit-ups, then twenty-five dips on the desk (for his triceps). Repeat endlessly or thirty times minimum or until boredom collects him.

"The trays are here," he says. "Only they're not trays, they're the Styrofoam boxes."

"Well, what does that mean?" I say from my top bunk, where I am doing sit-ups in groups of two hundred, followed by twenty push-ups, repeat.

"It means that anyone who decides to eat will eat in their cells. The fucking punk guards are getting pissed off at us." He sniggers.

"You mean we're being locked down indefinitely?"

"Fuckin' A! What else can they do?" He looks toward the podium, which is invisible from our cell. "Pussies!" he yells. He puts on his T-shirt and his orange top.

The machine gun rattle of the door locks sounds. Josh

pushes open the cell door but does not exit. I stand behind him.

"Stand by your doors!" booms a voice. "Fully dressed and standing by your doors!"

Josh passes me my name tag. We clip them to our respective tunics. I check to make sure my T-shirt is tucked in. We exit the cell. Josh stands to the left of the door, I stand to the right, in front of the fully opened door itself.

Mikey and Porky from next door, cell 51, each touch fisted knuckles to Josh, saying, "Dog." They nod to me.

Porky is here for a probation violation — one year, local time — and is on probation for armed robbery, drugs, racketeering. He is in PC because he used to be active, a member of the Nazi Low Riders, who are king crimson mo'fuckin' badass supreme white power dudes. Major into racism, white power, guns, and crystal meth. And by "guns" I mean fully automatic military-grade weapons, not piddly handguns. NLR dudes think Hitler was all right, a righteous dude. Anyway, Porky quit the NLR. You die, but you don't quit the NLR. So Porky's in Protective Custody.

Mikey — he of the narcotic eyes — is twenty-three years old. While his wife slept, he pressed a shotgun to the side of her head — which, when he pulled the trigger, popped like a honeydew melon, spraying a corona of blood, bone, and brain all over the bedroom. Fifty thousand dollars. That's why Mikey did it, to collect the insurance policy.

He just got sentenced: fifty-five years to life. Like he told me once, "I ain't in no hurry. I got plenty of time." Then he brayed like a jenny in heat. "Shit, man, I'll be seventy-eight when I get out."

Upstairs and downstairs, cell doors are outlined by their orange-clad occupants. They talk, talk, talk to each other, to their neighbors. Shrill laughs spike the machine-regulated air.

"Quiet!" says one of the COs. Along with his partner, they stand in the quad below.

"Shut the fuck up!" yells the other one.

Reluctant silence ensues.

"Okay. Now the sergeant has something to say. Stand still and listen up. Anyone moving or talking will lose privileges!"

A dark-haired man with three chevron stripes on the sleeve of his black uniform steps into view, a clipboard in his hands. He is a smooth, ovoid man of middle years and assured style.

"Gentlemen," he begins. "We're all men here, so let's keep it down and listen, please." He checks his clipboard and continues. "You have determined to pursue your hunger strike with regard to your grievance about rec time and scheduling. This is against the rules. The captain and the director are aware of your grievance and are addressing the problem." Pausing, he again checks his clipboard. "Rather than using up all your commissary, we propose that you stand down from your hunger strike and allow the administration to discuss various alternatives. And just for your information, they have been formulating a schedule for the last two weeks. It should be ready in a couple of days."

An angry murmur drifts up like a fog from a swamp. The murmur swells, becoming a strident boo. Orange-clad elbows begin thumping against concrete walls, steel doors. The noise becomes deafening.

The two COs and the sergeant stand still. After thirty seconds, the sergeant raises his hand. The noise diminishes.

Down below, Chuckie steps forward. This means he wants permission to speak.

The sergeant points to him.

"That's bullshit," says Chuckie. "If we give up our strike, things will just stay the same." Looking around at his peers, he says, "I say we keep striking until they give us what we want!"

Wild clapping and hooting ensue. Middle fingers appear and power signs and barking animal noises. Mikey releases an eloquent fart, then laughs like a hyena.

Again the sergeant's hand goes up. The two COs look sourly amused, as if they'd like to pepper spray the whole lot of us.

I stand frozen, my stomach a hurricane of fear-induced nausea.

In a measured voice, the sergeant says, "Okay. If that's the way you want it, that's how we'll play it. But again, I'm telling you that your grievance is being addressed."

Silence greets his words. The air is thick with malevolent energy, anger, sheer hate.

The sergeant nods to the two COs, lowers his clipboard.

"Lock it down!" shouts one of the COs. "Lock it down!"

I enter the cell as fast as I can. Josh remains at his post, rocking from foot to foot, a menacing movement.

For a moment, by some kind of mutual impulse, the insane exhilaration of riot punctures the atmosphere. The COs glare, hands moving to their Sam Browne belts.

I can feel the inmates' emotion; it is almost palpable, a crazy, irresponsible ferocity.

"I said, LOCK. IT. DOWN!" A warning resonance shimmers in his tone, as if he is under violent self-restraint.

His partner is speaking into his shoulder-mounted radio. I realize with dilated certainty that he is calling for reinforcements.

Fifty-two orange-clad shoulders rise and fall in faint shrugs, as if of no importance. The moment of convergence passes.

"Fucking punks," says Josh as he turns to enter the cell. Before he does, he once more touches knuckles with Porky and Mikey.

"Fucking bullshit is what it is," says Porky. "They can throw me in the Hole, I don't fucking care."

Mikey laughs like a hyena in heat.

Cell doors slam shut. The door locks snap into place with an inexorable finality.

I look out the cell door window to the quad below. The two

COs float back in triumph. One of them gestures largely to someone I can't see, probably the sergeant. I climb back onto my bunk, sit down Indian style.

Josh moves to the window, begins signing to the gang-bangers across the way. He is still vibrating with energy.

Porky, from next door, thumps on our adjoining cement wall. His muffled voice yells something I cannot make out. But Josh can.

Josh laughs. "It's fucking jail! Whaddaya expect?"

More muffled pronouncements from Porky. Then Mikey says something unintelligible. Even though locked down and presently bankrupt, their slo-mo atomic anger hisses within the reactor of their emotions. Like a perpetual motion machine, it fuels itself. It has to come out. Or explode. One or the other. Thus, their mouths, their words, become fail-safe mechanisms, gradually siphoning off the mounting pressure.

Porky says something else. Josh's laughter sounds like a lone rooster crowing.

I give Josh my "what did he say?" expression, lifting my shoulders and holding them up, a kind of interrogatory pause.

Josh raises his hand, his signal for "I'll tell you later, be quiet so I can hear."

I hear Porky and Mikey: Porky's subterranean rumblings, Mikey's little-girl shrieks.

"Josh! Josh!" says a voice from below, as if God is speaking to us. Only he has a Hispanic accent and a shrill voice. It's the trustee, Sleepy, shouting into the ventilation shaft. His cell is on the first tier, below ours.

Josh kneels down by the sink, puts his mouth close to the intake vent, shouts into it. "Sleepy! Sleepy! What?"

"No lunch today, dog!" says Sleepy, his voice thinning as it travels up the shaft. "They're sending the trays back. Lock-down, dog. Everybody's fucking locked down!"

"Wait," Josh shouts into the vent. Scrambling to his feet, he jumps to the cell door window, looks out.

"You mean they're not even going to give lunch to the guys who want it?" I say. I don't believe it. Legally, they have to feed us — at least offer it to us.

"Fuck!" Josh yelps. He kneels in front of the vent. "Sleepy! Sleepy!"

"Yeah."

"What the fuck, dog? They're really sending it back?"

"Yeah, dog," says Sleepy. "We're locked down too. The cos are pissed, man. Won't even let us out to fold laundry."

"Fuckin' A, dog," says Josh. "We're getting their attention now!"

Three heavy thumps sound on the other cement wall of our cell. It's Aaron Woods, next door in cell 53. Without waiting for Sleepy's reply, Josh jumps up on the sink. Balancing precariously, he shouts into the exhaust vent.

"Woods! Can you hear me?"

Woods' jive tones emanate from the vent. I can't understand him. For that matter, I can't understand him when he's standing in front of me. He's got this chocolate-dandy lingo he uses. Maybe it's ebonics, I don't know.

Josh listens, laughs, derision in his tone. "Stupid ass nigger," he says to himself, to me.

"Woods!" he shouts. "Sleepy says there's no food today, dog. They already sent it back. We are locked down, dog!"

Muffled words float out of the vent next to Josh's ear.

"No," says Josh. "I don't know for how long."

Vague sounds issue forth, as if filtered through cotton bales. Woods discourses at length about something. Josh listens. Finally, Woods stops.

Josh shakes his head, looking at me. "I can't understand what the fuck he's saying."

"Woods!" Josh says. "I'll get back to you, man."

Jumping down from his perch on the sink, Josh thumps the wall adjacent to Porky and Mikey. A rapid tapping answers — Porky's signal to go ahead.

"Porky," says Josh. "Woods is hungry. Says he's got no food. You guys got any sweets he can have?"

"No," says Porky. Even I can make it out.

Josh thumps once, indicating end of palaver. He moves to the cell window, begins signing the gangbangers across the way.

I lose interest, decide to settle in for a protracted wait. Fluffing my pathetic, generic jail pillow, which is more of a foam-filled plastic bag than a pillow, I lean back to read.

My pillow is compliments of Josh. He nabbed it from an empty cell two days ago. Somebody got core-capped out, and he just grabbed it. Handed it to me matter of factly. I thanked him profusely. He responded in classic Josh fashion: "It's no big deal. Just a fucking pillow, man. I'm tired of seeing you sleep on your fucking sweatshirt."

Fifteen minutes later, Josh turns from the window. "Fucking Tommy is standing in his cell. Just fucking standing there, like someone's going to deliver him a package or something." Josh lies down on his bunk. "I hate that fucker," he says to the steel plate that functions as my luxurious box spring.

"Who?" I say.

"That fucking Tommy," he says, punching the steel plate. "He's doing local time for molesting some five-year-old boy, and I'm in here for fucking eight months now, and that cocksucking shithead will get out before me." He pauses, allowing his hate to saturate the cell. "Anybody touched one of my family members I'd fucking kill 'em. I don't care how long they lock me up for. Motherfucking chomos!"

I just grunt, realizing he's not really talking to me. He's just discharging his anger, his hate, his frustration.

After a few moments, I say, "How long do you think we'll be locked down?"

"Till the punks *have* to let us out," he says.

"Well," I say, "how long will that be?"

"Till some captain tells them to," he says, tap, tap, tapping on the cement wall.

"So I shouldn't count on any rec time any time soon, is that what you're saying?"

"Fuck, Radic. It's jail. Whaddaya expect?" He snorts at my stupidity.

"Okay. Just asking," I say, trying to soothe him.

I hear him roll over to sleep.

Dinner time. Josh is at the cell door window; he stands motionless, like a skinhead Cassandra. And like Cassandra he has already read the auguries and pronounced his prophecy: "We'll be locked down the rest of the night. Probably tomorrow too," he said earlier.

I didn't ask because I didn't want to know. But Josh told me anyway. It's like he couldn't resist telling me because his only pleasure right now is suffering and being miserable and spreading his suffering and misery to others.

"You see anything?" I say. I am flat on my back on my penthouse bunk, with my orange sweatshirt draped over my upper body like a bodice. It's fucking freezing in here.

The machine-washed, machine-cooled air in PC is kept at a constant sixty-eight degrees Fahrenheit, with sporadic drops to sixty-five degrees Fahrenheit. Ostensibly, this is to mitigate the spread of infections and diseases. Which may be true, but I believe it is a postmodern form of passive torture too — a subtle sort of physical control. If you're cold you're too busy thinking about getting warm to think about making trouble.

"Fucking nothin'," says Josh.

I grunt, a monosyllabic manner of speaking volumes. My grunt says, "Well, what the fuck? What's taking them so long? I hope they at least let us out to eat. Just fifteen minutes out of this eighty-four-square-foot oblong cement box would be nice."

Josh understands me perfectly. "Forget about it," he says. "They're not letting us out 'cuz they fucking don't have to."

I grunt again.

"I told you," snarls Josh. "Don't sit there thinking about it. It just makes it worse when it doesn't happen. Like thinking about banging your girlfriend — it just makes it worse."

He pauses. Then speaks one of those intimate confessions that make me like him. "I don't let myself think about anything. Nothing. I don't ever think about what I could be doin' or what I'll do when I get out. It just makes the time go even slower."

He turns to look at me. "That's why I sleep so much. It makes the time go faster, and I don't have to worry about not thinking."

I grunt.

"The trays are here," he says in a quiet voice.

I struggle up to one elbow, crane my head around to gaze out the window. I can see the trays in the dock, on the stainless steel cart, where the Honor Farm guys park it three times a day.

Then the trustees wheel it in, set up the tables and chairs, brew the coffee, put on their little plastic aprons and gloves, their little old lady caps to keep their hair out of our food, which is a joke. Because all four of them have peach fuzz-length hair or less. Todd, the "head" trustee, is totally bald. But he has this Asian-Egyptian imperial, like a dragon's curl, on his chin.

"Are the trustees out?" I say.

"No," says Josh, a prophetic "I told you so" smugness in his voice. "One of the COs is by the dock door," he reports, as if he's a fucking play-by-play commentator on ESPN. "Talking into his radio now. Standing there, listening to the reply. Laughing — the cunt punk. Walking back to the podium."

We wait. Josh at his post by the cell door window. Me in my bunk.

I hear a muffled thud — the sound of the outer dock door closing.

"Fuck!" says Josh. There is shrill anger in his voice.

"What?" I say, lurching up on my elbows.

"Fucking kitchen workers are taking them back," he says.

"What? You mean the trays?" I roll over, climb off my bunk. I want to confirm this for myself.

"Fucking guards are sending them back!" says Josh.

I am behind him now, peering over his shoulder, trying to get a glimpse. But his big, bald head with its quasi-white-power star tattoo keeps getting in my way.

"Here, see for yourself," he says. He moves out of the way, throws himself on his bunk.

I can see the Honor Farm guys, dressed in white, which designates kitchen workers, tugging the tray-laden cart out.

"What the hell?" I say, as much to myself as to Josh.

"I told ya," says Josh. "We are locked down, baby."

I turn and look at him.

"Motherfucking locked down!" he yips.

"You're right," I admit. "How come you're always right? It's not a very endearing quality, I must say."

He's not listening to me. He's out of his bunk, thumping on Porky's wall.

I decide to take a piss. I sit on the toilet like a female, watching Josh, who, because he's very private about bodily excretions, politely turns his back, still thumping on the wall.

"Porky! You guys up?" he shouts at the wall.

Thump, thump is the reply.

"Did you see? No food tonight! Locked down, dog!" There is excitement in his tone.

I shake my head to myself. He actually likes this shit, I think.

Porky's muffled voice says something.

"Yeah!" booms Josh. "Fucking punks!"

I shake my penis, stand up, pulling up my boxers and pants.

"I'm gonna flush," I say. It's more a question than a statement. I'm asking permission because I don't want to interrupt his dialogue with Porky. The toilets are pressurized to avoid clogging, thus really loud.

"Go ahead," says Josh, throwing himself on his bunk.

Whoom! I wash my hands using my bottle of liquid shaving soap, which stands on the edge of the sink.

As I climb up into my bunk, Josh already has his black-watch cap pulled down over his face.

"You going to sleep?" I say.

"Fuck, yeah," he says. "Nothing else to do. I'm tired of reading. Might as well settle in for the long haul."

"I'm gonna read for a while," I say. "I'll put out the sign when I'm done."

He doesn't answer. He doesn't care. But he does, really. That's why he goes to such pains to demonstrate his nonchalance.

The sign, our sign, is a piece of yellow paper from my legal tablet. Folded lengthwise, one end says "Lights out, Please." The other end says, "Lights on, Please." We slide it out the crack between the steel door and the steel jamb. When the COs make their rounds, they either turn the lights on or off. Usually. The light switches are on the outside wall of each cell.

Next morning, 5:00 a.m. I wake up and roll over because my shoulder is aching. Josh is at the cell door window.

"Trays?" I say.

"Yeah, inside the dock. But I don't think they're letting the trustees out," says Josh. His black-watch cap sits jauntily atop his head, his torso is naked above his orange pants.

"Who are the COs?" I say. In my opinion, you can forecast what's going to happen based on the personalities on duty. It makes a difference.

"Jackson and Little Hitler."

"Great," I say with sarcasm.

Jackson, a tall, lanky black CO, is strict yet fair. Just remain inconspicuous and don't make any noise, and everything is cool. Little Hitler, though, is another story. He sports a Hitleresque mustache and is short, with the attendant little-big-man complex. He hates everyone, including himself and his fellow COs.

"No way," I conclude.

Josh moves to his bunk, lies down. His silence tells me he agrees.

I stare at the cement ceiling. "I'm starting to get a little hungry."

"I'm fucking starving," says Josh.

"You want some of my rice?"

"Fuck rice, man. That shit just makes you hungrier."

"I know," I say. It's packaged, precooked rice. Comes in these eight-ounce red packets with tear tops and an inner reseal top. Just add hot water, and it softens and swells up. But it tastes like old cardboard and smells like baby vomit.

"I'm going back to sleep," says Josh.

I lie on my ruthless bunk, breathing machine-cooled, merciless air, wishing I were anywhere but here. I cannot believe this is happening. Not only am I in jail, feeling like Prometheus bound, but I am also participating, because I have to, with a bunch of supermorons from the first ice age in a hunger strike.

Lunchtime comes and goes. We remain locked down. Josh is still asleep or pretending to be anyway. At 1:30 p.m., the hydraulic door locks pop three times.

"Fully dressed and standing by your doors!" yells a CO.

Josh leaps out of his bunk, slips on his T-shirt and orange top, plunges his feet into his rubber slippers, pushes open the door. I'm still climbing out of my bunk when the voice booms again.

"Fully dressed, name tags on. Standing by your doors!"

I snap my ID and Josh's out the door, step outside. Handing Josh his name tag, I stand at attention on the other side of the door.

"Thanks," says Josh. He clips his ID to his orange blouse.

I give him a tight you're-welcome nod, then I give a chubby nod to Porky and Mikey. Porky's pot belly billows out front, like an orange spinnaker; his tattooed hands are pulling at his pants. He is groggy with sleep. Porky has spent most of his life in one prison or another. He's a former supreme white power dude. He withdrew from the woodpile, which explains why he's in PC.

Mikey's cocaine eyes spin with alertness. He has his hands inside his pants, pressing out from his crotch, as if he has a large Idaho potato in there. This is Mikey's way of mocking the gangbangers, whom he calls pussies to their faces.

His head is shaved bald, and his face is clean shaven except for giant mutton-chops on each side of his jaw. Mikey's presence is wickedly noxious and bizarre, with an extraterrestrial urethane tang.

"Good morning, gentlemen," says Mikey. His voice tinkles with burlesque.

I want to correct Mikey, tell him it's afternoon, not morning. But I mind my tongue. I don't want him staring at me with those eyes of his. They have this alien glow to them, as if he's the male version of the Witch of Endor.

"Dog," says Josh, extending his knurled fist to Mikey, then to Porky.

Mikey laughs like a little girl. He is having fun.

Porky mutters something about "too fucking petty." I assume he is referring to the COs, whom he openly despises and frequently describes with the adjective *petty*.

"Okay," says one of the COs. "Shut the fuck up and listen."

The same sergeant as before steps forward with the same clipboard. He glances down at it, clears his throat. Not because there's any phlegm in it but as a prologue, a kind of official introduction.

"Okay, gentlemen," he says. "The director of the facility and the captain have issued an official schedule. I will post a copy of it over on the bulletin board." He waves his clipboard back toward the bulletin board. "The new schedule will not go into effect until next Monday. The duty officers will try to follow it between now and then. But because these things take time to implement, I'm warning you it might not go smoothly in the beginning."

He looks up at all the orange-clad bodies beside their doors, gives a perfunctory smile. "So," he says, "you can stop wasting all your commissary and start coming down for meals."

He looks at the COs, as if to say, "Anything I've forgotten?" They stare back at him. Consulting his clipboard, just to be sure, he concludes his oratory, "Okay. . . ."

A wave of sound, shot through with sudden eddies of need and gratification, erupts. Cheering, applauding, laughing inmates. They think they won. They really believe they are in control and have asserted their "rights." They think they have received respect.

I shake my head to myself. They are so stupid. I stand mute.

Josh is flashing power signs to Sleepy and the other gang-bangers. He is smiling and laughing. Porky is hitching at his pants again. Mikey is "dogging" knuckles with Allen out of cell 54.

The cheering subsides. Everyone is staring at the two COs, the sergeant. The sergeant leaves, reading his clipboard.

One of the COs checks his wristwatch, shouts, "Rec time begins now! Be sure your beds are made, your cells are clean, T-shirts tucked in, license plates on, fully dressed!" He turns away, then adds, "And keep the fucking noise down!"

I go back into our cell to make my bed. Josh is already opening his drawer, reaching for his tobacco and rolling papers. "We showed them, huh?" he yelps at me. "We fucking showed them!"

"Yeah, boy."

"C'mon, Radic!" He slaps me affectionately on the arm. "You were part of it. You did it. One of the white brothers."

He presents his "dog fist" to me. I hesitate. Then, because it is expected, I touch his knuckles with my knuckles. "Dog!" says Josh, as if I'm an initiate in some exclusive club.

Porky's close-cropped head floats in our doorway. "Josh," says Porky, "you got a smoke for a dog?"

"Sure," says Josh. "Let me roll five or six. I'll meet you down in the yard."

Mikey moves into the doorway, his shoulder rubbing Porky's. "You guys hungry?" says Mikey.

"Fuck, yeah," Josh says.

"What about you?" says Mikey, nodding at me.

"Yeah, a little bit," I laugh.

"Come out in the yard when you go down," he says in a hoarse whisper. "Got something for you."

"That's okay," I say. "I can wait till dinner." A patent lie. I just don't want to go into the yard with all the full-spectrum freakoids.

Mikey won't take no for an answer. "No, no. Come out and get something to eat, man. You earned it. You're one of us."

"Okay," I say. "After I clean, I'll be down."

A squeal mushrooms from Mikey's mouth, like a pig oinking.

"Got a smoke, dog?" he asks Josh.

"Sure, dog." Josh blows the excess tobacco all over the cell floor, gathers his smokes, and they all depart.

I gather my cleaning supplies: agent orange, paper towels, broom, mop. After I finish, I wash my hands repeatedly.

As I descend the stairs, I see the cos sitting behind the podium. One is reading the newspaper, the other is tilted back in his chair reading a hardback novel.

The yard has four walls that rise about thirty feet up. One wall is nothing but glass windows. In it resides the door into the yard from the unit. This wall of glass sits about twenty feet in front of the podium, so the guards have a full view of the yard and its occupants. The yard is full of smoking inmates, all talking animatedly.

Porky, Mikey, Josh, Slim, and Nelly stand against one wall, smoking. One hand in their pants (the other hand holds their smokes), Josh, Slim, and Nelly pose as they smoke. Badass-cool poses, like models in a magazine. Mikey is talking to anyone and everyone, nodding to inmates across the yard, while he half-listens to Porky.

Porky sees me coming, heads toward the door to meet me. He's hitching at his pants.

I open the door, step out into the yard. The heat from the sun falls on me, like warm rain.

Porky puts his arm around my shoulder.

"Come over here," he says, glancing over his shoulder to the podium. As we move toward his place on the wall, he motions to Sonny, one of the trustees. We all converge at the wall.

"My dog needs something to eat," Porky says to Sonny.

Sonny regards me suspiciously. I'm white, I'm an OG, I'm new. Sonny is Mexican, a tall, powerful man swimming in swarthy handsomeness.

"He's cool," announces Porky. "One of the white brothers who stood with us."

Reassured, Sonny moves in front of me, his back to the podium. He lifts his orange tunic. There is a plastic bag stuck in the waistband of his pants. He removes the bag, opens the top. Inside the bag is five pounds of yellow crumbs from corn muffins. "Go ahead," he says. "Take a handful."

Porky dips his hand in, takes a fistful. Porky eats the cornmeal out of his hand, like a dog, getting it all over his lips and cheeks. Half of it falls to the yard floor. "Go on, dog," Porky encourages me, "take some."

I stare aghast at the bag, wondering how many crotch-riding hands have been in it. "That's okay," I say. "I'm not fond of corn muffins. But I appreciate the offer."

"You sure, dog?" Porky says. He sounds concerned, like a

father for his child.

"I'm sure. But really, I do appreciate it."

"Okay, dog," says Porky. He shoves his hand into the bag once more, gobbles it up.

Sonny shrugs. Puts the bag back in its hiding place, moves off.

"I think I'll go watch some TV," I say to Porky.

"Dog," he says, giving me his knuckles.

This is my first and only foray into the yard of Intake 2.

CELL 52

———————————

———————————

———————————

———————————

My cell. Coincidence or fate? I mean, my birthdate is 1952, and I was arrested when I was 52 years old. And I was born in Roswell, New Mexico, which is infamous for Area 51, which is only one less than 52; and Area 52 is Haute-Marne, France, whose total area is 2,398 square miles.

I pull the cell door open. It's heavy, once moving it's hard to stop it. Always reminds me of that song from the animated movie of the same name: heavy metal. The Deluxe Suite, I call it. Seven feet by twelve feet. White cement walls, gray cement floor. Only the finest furnishings, including a three-inch-thick plastic mattress filled with, at a guess, steel shavings or Brillo pads. It smells like agent orange, that's what I call the disinfectant they provide us with.

Every day, at the beginning of rec time, I go down the stairs and ask Chevy for some agent orange. Then I retrace my steps back up to the Deluxe Suite, where I spray the toilet, the sink, and the cement floor with the disinfectant. Taking paper towels, I wipe everything down, then wipe it dry. And I'm not talking about Bounty paper towels — the picker-uppers. I'm talking about the coarse, beige paper towels you find in bathrooms of automotive shops. The ones that just get wet but don't seem to absorb anything. When I finish, the place smells like Pine-Sol, sharp and tangy. You can taste it in your mouth as the molecules coat your tongue.

Five minutes until lockdown. Josh is already in the cell. Which is really weird. He is never ready for lockdown; in fact, he's usually the last one up the stairs. Rec time is all but over — thank God, because I'm so bored I'm hypnotized. I'm ready to do some reading. Lock me down! Let me read! Engage my brain.

Josh is my cell mate, or cellie, or bunkie, whichever term strikes your fancy's fancy. He's twenty-three years old. Caucasian features and complexion, but he is a halfer — half Hispanic and half white. He thinks of himself as white. Josh is mui macho, which means he's into macho symbols. Which means he has three or four tattoos scattered about his body.

The noteworthy tattoo is on the back of his neck: a five-pointed star in black with red hatching. Supreme white power shit is what it is. Nazi Low Rider, Norcal Woods, Pure Boys kind of shit. Those guys are just dumb enough to tattoo their faces and necks. Not even the Surenos do that, and they are major into tattoos, real fetishists. Five-pointed stars, like Josh's, or their girlfriend's name on their neck, near the jugular vein, or the granddaddy of supercoolbadness, according to these supreme white power klan-assed Nazi robots, they shave their heads and get the word *notorious* tattooed on their scalps.

Except Josh isn't "active," which is gangslang for gang-affiliated. He's friendly with the Asian gangbangers, slender, reed-like figures with rapid gestures, balletically defiant stances. A stance I can't emulate, although I try, when no one is looking. I don't have the attitude, the linear, superbuckled arrogance necessary to achieve it. I can't do it by merely practicing it; it's more an arcane energy or some type of innate disdain. Whatever it is, I don't have it and don't know how to get it. But I will admit this: I'd like to have it. I like the way it looks: stylized, self-empowering, totally cool, what I now call "primate dominance dynamics."

Josh hangs with them, smokes with them, plays handball in the yard with them, but only because he's trying to be supercool. But he's not part of the woodpile (gangslang for white power or skinhead affiliation), despite the fact that his head is shorn peach fuzz short, so he looks like a cancer patient undergoing chemotherapy. So why does he have the tattoo?

I asked him once. His reply was, "'Cuz I thought it looked cool, man." What else matters, right? Packaging is everything, especially in the rarefied realm of "cool."

Standing just over six feet tall, Josh is rolly-polly fat with puffy features, as if somebody took him to the Shell station on the corner and inflated him thirty or forty pounds over the recommended pressure. Our relationship is ambivalent, depending on location: in the cell, we're easy companions, discussing sex, love, hate, anger, jail, girlfriends, literature, the guards, other inmates, but once the door pops and we're outside the cell, Josh refuses to acknowledge my existence. He's young and I'm an OG, and he's supercool and I don't even register on the cool-o-meter.

As I enter the cell, Josh peeks back at me over his left shoulder. His posture, his entire body language, indicates he is hiding something. "Good rec?" he asks me. He always asks that, as if it matters.

"Okay," I say.

"What'd ya do?"

"Same as always. Walked. Talked with Bob." That's all I ever do on rec time.

"The fuck ya doin'?" I ask him. My utilization of the graphic *fuck* demonstrates my ennui, as I assiduously avoid its usage in here, 'cuz everybody else, all the full-spectrum Neanderthals who populate this place, use it like breathing — once every three or four seconds, without fail.

He's seated on our plastic maroon chair, our only chair, which is less a chair than a glorified stool, at the desk. *Desk* is kind of a pretentious word for a five-inch-thick block of wood, eighteen by twenty-four inches, bolted to the wall. *Shelf* would be more accurate or perhaps *thick wooden projection* upon which one may write if so disposed.

"Sewing," he replies. Terse, that's Josh. Although I doubt he knows the definition of the word.

"Sewing?" My voice rises halfway through enunciating the word, as if somebody grabbed me by my balls, partly in disbelief, partly because voice modulation is the way we frame questions in Western culture.

"Yeah. I'm taking a thread from one of my socks."

I lean forward, peer over his sumptuously orange-clad shoulder. He smells like Pine-Sol and sweat, and, even though I can't see it, I know his mouth is making those funny fish-lip motions that he makes when he's concentrating. He's right. He's dismantling one of his socks with a white plastic spork, the only utensil we're allowed to have, other than four-inch number two lead pencils.

"Excuse me for asking," I say, "but why?" I already kinda know the answer: an agenda, as in a scheme, a ploy, a ruse. No one in here, including Josh, does anything without an agenda, an ulterior motive. They're always looking for an advantage, a way to scam somebody.

"I have court tomorrow," Josh reminds me, working industriously to produce a single white cotton thread.

"I know," I say. My voice has that "Tell me something I don't know" rasp in it.

"I'm gonna sew some cigarettes into my underwear," he says in a flat voice.

I knew there was an agenda. And I should have figured it would involve tobacco; most things revolve around tobacco in jail. Tobacco, soups, candy bars — the currency of jail, tobacco being the gold standard. Tobacco products are verboten in the holding tanks at both Stockton and Manteca courts. But that's just a technical detail to these guys. Like throwing down the gauntlet, it's a challenge. Where there's a will, there's a way.

Sure enough. Next morning Josh is dressed in pristine, cunt-blazing-orange clothing — clothing that he rates because he is "tight" with the trustees, who are young and Mexican and supercool too; most actually worry about making a good appearance in court, so they want the newest, orangest, loosest-fitting clothing (loose is gang, loose is cool). The door to cell 52 is popped, a voice bellows, "Ordonez! Come down for court!" And Josh walks out the door with one hundred hand-rolled cigarettes strapped to the length of his flaccid penis. They are held there by a slender white cotton thread, wrapped many times around his tobacco-ensconced dick, like having his cock in a Marlboro pussy.

DENTISTS

_____

_____

_____

_____

Morning rec, circa 8:30 a.m. Bob and I have just begun walking.

One of the COs steps from behind the podium holding a computer printout. Reading from it, he shouts, "Listen up 23, 17, 26, 27, 52. Dental clinic in five minutes! Line up!"

Cell numbers whose occupants have requested dental care. My cell is 52, but I doubt it is me as I turned in my request just two weeks ago. It must be Josh. He has been waiting two months to have an abscessed tooth pulled. I look around the unit for him.

The CO begins reading off names in a bugling voice. "Brown, Hayford, Herbert, Killian, Radic, Ordonez! Dental clinic! Now!"

I look at Bob, checking to see if I am hearing correctly.

"You better get over there," he says, looking back at me over his shoulder.

"I guess so," I say. "Well, have a nice walk."

"Too bad they didn't wait till this afternoon when we're locked down to call you," Bob says.

"Yeah. See ya at lunch," I say. I begrudge my time with Bob walking, talking, being confiscated.

I know the routine, so I walk to the railing in front of the podium, stand waiting.

Todd and Chuckie are already here. I see Mike Brown out in the yard puffing frantically on a cigarette. Thomas Herbert joins us at the railing. He farts wetly, a lengthy, moist, ripping sound. He giggles.

"Goddamnit, Thomas," says Chuckie, his ears sticking out from his head like those of Dumbo the elephant. "Do you have to fart all the time?"

Todd shakes his head in disapproval. "You know, Thomas," he says tightly, "that isn't going to cut it in prison. Somebody's going to kick the shit out of you for that."

Thomas giggles, farts again, with a sound like knotted rope being pulled from a tank of oil.

As he farts, Josh joins us at the railing, orange pants tucked into his socks, shower thongs on his feet, hands in his pants. Gangbanger haute couture. Josh shoves Thomas with both hands. "Motherfucker!" Josh says, his face twisted in loathing. "Do it again, motherfuck, and I kick your ass."

I look at Todd. "Jesus," I complain. Todd is white, bald, and educated. He's in jail for drugs and has a knack for getting along with people, which probably explains why he's head trustee.

"Look, Thomas," says Todd, "just hold it for a while, okay? Give us all a break. You're an embarrassment. Even for jail, man."

Thomas titters insanely. I feel like slapping the goofy, arrogant grin off his face. Then I remind myself: never get angry, never threaten.

Thomas is here for arson and, I suspect, other stuff that he's not revealing. He torched some trees in a park. Soaked brown paper bags in gasoline, wrapped them around the trunks of trees, and lit them up with a flick of his Bic. *Why* anyone would want to torch a bunch of trees is the question. I don't know the specific answer. But insanity might have something to do with it.

Short and plump, he has reddish brown hair, a scraggly mustache of the same color, and blemished skin. He looks like a toadstool, pale white with blotchy discoloring. One of those people everyone instantly hates, curses, and avoids; he hangs with the chomos because no one else will have anything to do with him.

A middle-aged CO comes into the unit to escort us to the Medical Clinic. He is ramrod straight and walks with power and purpose, as if he's in the military. I have seen him before in Transportation. He's cool.

He reads our names off his list, stepping forward to check each ID. "Brown, Michael," he reads from his list. He looks around. "Brown?"

He's about to draw a line through Brown's name when Brown comes hustling through the yard door, his long hair bouncing as he trots up to the railing.

"Brown?" asks the CO.

"Yeah," replies Brown. A crooked smile angles across his lips. It is a scamp's smile, almost cute, except that Mike Brown is an ugly young man so he can't pull it off. Brown is gregarious, likable, and easy to get along with as long as you give him food, but he's as stupid as a rock.

Doing a year of local time for robbery and drug possession. However, when he was first sentenced, he got five months, and his attorney got him released on a thirty-day OR so he could "take care of some personal business" before he began doing his time. Well, when it came time to surrender to the authorities, Brown blew it off. He didn't show up. So they issued a warrant for his arrest. When they finally located and arrested him weeks later, he had a gun on him. In a New York minute, his sentence escalated from five months to twelve months.

"Okay," says the CO, "let's go."

He leads us out the massive doors into the wide hallway. We walk single file, each inmate three feet behind the one in front. The CO is to our left; he is relaxed and whistles a tune as he steps out.

Brown has a finger in his mouth, poking at a tooth. "Fuck, man," he says to no one in particular, talking around his finger so his voice sounds hollow, "this fucking tooth is killing me. I hope they fucking pull it."

Josh, who is walking behind Brown, is in front of me. "Fuck, dog," he says, "I don't want 'em pulling mine. I just want 'em to fill it. I ain't into having no tooth pulled."

Brown looks over his shoulder at Josh. "What? You never had no tooth pulled?"

"No," replies Josh. "And I don't want to. Must be fucking painful ripping a tooth out and shit."

"Fuck," exclaims Brown. "It don't hurt, you pussy. They give you a shot so you don't feel it."

"Yeah, I heard that," says Josh. "But I still don't want no tooth pulled."

Brown shakes his head, laughs.

"Okay, guys," says the CO. "Hold up."

We stop outside a door that reads "Medical Clinic." The door opens, and another CO walks out into the hallway. Behind him, following along like chicks after a hen, trail four orange-clad inmates. All four are white dudes, superscuzzbags, scruffy beards, dirty hair, filthy oranges.

Our CO holds out his hand, a warning to us not to move. As the other CO and his scummy orange chicks walk away, our CO turns to us, gestures toward the door.

We file into the clinic. It is just like any doctor's office. The walls are hospital white and devoid of graffiti, the carpet is dark blue. A TV, with cushioned chairs to sit in, plants, a real bathroom that is as big as my cell, and a reception desk. Only there is no cute receptionist. A burly, black-clad CO sits behind the desk. His arms are as big around as my thighs, and he is hairy. The butt of a big semiautomatic sticks out of the holster on his hip.

"Line up. Give me your name, then go sit down," he commands.

One at a time we step forward and give him our names. He checks each name off his list. I am last. After reciting my name, I walk over to the lounge area, where the other five are seated around the TV.

As I sit down, the clinic door opens, and in walks Bakr, who is also from our unit. He is a late addition to our group. His escort checks him in. Bakr comes over to join the rest of us.

Bakr is Egyptian; tall and slender, he wears glasses, a Cheshire cat grin, and heavy silver braces on his teeth. Outside in the real world, he is a dentist. He was busted for fondling his female patients while they were sedated. In addition to his sexual molestation charges, he is being sued by every female patient who ever entered his offices at Western Dental.

I nod to him as he sits down.

"Hey, Bakr," says Todd, "you going to let the dentist work on you, man?"

"I will talk to him," says Bakr in his syrupy accent. He smiles. "But probably not."

"Well, fuck me," says Chuckie. "If a dentist won't let this guy work on him, I don't know if I'm going to either."

A nurse comes out of a door with two other inmates: one male, one female. The female is twenty-something, with long dark hair and large, liquid breasts evident under her orange blouse. The male is nineteen or twenty, and his head is shaved clean. He wears black Nike cross-trainers on his feet.

"Have a seat," the nurse tells them. Then she hands out clipboards to the rest of us. A blue Bic pen resides on each clipboard. "Please fill out the form, gentlemen," she says to us. "Then return it to the guard at the desk." She turns and leaves.

The form concerns health and dental history. As I fill mine out, I hear Chuckie ask the female inmate, "You here for the dentist?"

"No," she replies. "I'm here for the doctor. Some blood test for my foot." She points to her ankle, pulls up her orange pants, revealing a bandage on her ankle.

The young guy, who sits two seats to her right, says, "I ha' a 'ooth pulled." He points to his mouth, which is full of little cotton logs. Saliva dribbles from his mouth as he speaks. His complexion is the color of oatmeal, his eyes a bleached blue, an icy baby blue.

Chuckie scowls at him.

"What unit?" Chuckie asks the woman.

"The Hole," she says, smiles. It is a pretty smile in a semi-good-looking face. Hardness lurks just beneath her skin.

Chuckie guffaws, his mouth wide open. "The Hole? Fuck! What'd you do to get the Hole?"

"Hit some bitch in GP," replies the woman, grinning.

"Get back," exclaims Chuckie, swinging his arms wide, scooting back in his chair. "So you're all bad and shit, huh?"

She smiles, gives a little shrug.

Chuckie smiles. He is impressed.

Todd looks at me, raises his eyebrows. His face wears a leer.

"What the fuck you hit her for?" asks Josh, who sits next to me.

"She stole some personal property of mine," the woman replies. She curls her legs up into the chair, like a cat.

"So you just smacked her, huh?" asks Josh.

She shrugs. "Had to, you know? I mean, I can't let something like that slide, can I?"

"No, ma'am," says Chuckie. "Got to have respect."

"How long you been in the Hole?" asks Josh.

"Two months," she replies, pushing her hair back from her face with a hand.

"Two months!" ejaculates Josh. "Fuck! You must a done more than hit the bitch." He gazes at her expectantly.

She shrugs.

The young guy with the mouth full of cotton gets up, goes into the bathroom. He's in there for about ten seconds, then comes back out.

"What you in here for?" asks Chuckie, leaning forward.

"I don't want to talk about it," she says.

"That's cool," says Josh.

Thomas Herbert is one chair over from me. He releases a squelching fart, like car tires splatting through puddles on a rain-drenched road. He titters.

"Fucking Thomas!" shouts Josh. "You fuck. I told you to cut that shit out or I'd kick your ass."

"Goddamnit!" says Chuckie. "You piece of shit."

Thomas sniggers.

The young guy gets up and enters the bathroom. Fifteen seconds later he's back out.

Chuckie looks at him as he sits back down. "The fuck?" asks Chuckie.

"I 'ot a 'ooth pulled?" says the dude.

"What's your name?" asks Chuckie. There is a vicious glint in his eyes.

"'avid 'ohnson," slurps the dude.

"David, huh? Well, look, David," says Chuckie, "I don't know what your problem is, but if you're sick you wash your fucking hands after you use the toilet." Chuckie leans back in his seat. "More'n fifty percent of all inmates have hepatitis. I got hep-C myself, so I'm real careful not to expose anybody to my saliva or my blood."

David nods, but his face manifests no understanding.

Todd gives me a funny grimace.

"What I'm saying, David," Chuckie continues with dark menace in his voice, "is you better be washing your fucking hands in there and using a towel to open the door. 'Cuz I don't wanna get whatever shit you got. Ya understand?"

As David nods, drool drips from a corner of his mouth.

Todd puts his hand on Chuckie's leg. "Relax, man," he says in a low voice. "The guard is looking."

I glance over at the guard who sits at his desk. He is staring at us.

Chuckie brushes Todd's hand off his leg and shifts forward in his chair. "What the fuck you in here for?" he asks David.

"'omping 'iggers," replies David.

Chuckie thinks about this for a second. "So you're a SWP?" he asks David.

David smiles, nods, snaps his fist to his chest. "'orcal 'oods. O'er Oak'ille way."

"Fucking skinhead," announces Chuckie, glancing around at us.

David looks pissed. "'at 'ou say?" he demands.

"I said you're a fucking skinhead," replies Chuckie, staring straight at David. "You guys think you're so bad. You ain't shit." He waves at all of us. "We're from PC. You know what that is? Protective Custody. They put us in there to protect the other inmates from us. That's how bad we are. They got to protect everybody from us."

I look at Todd, who is smiling at Chuckie's interpretation of PC.

"Yeah," chimes in Josh. "We're badass dudes, so cut the shit, huh?"

Todd laughs out loud, shaking his bald head.

"'at you 'aughing at?" demands David.

Todd looks at him, keeps laughing. "You," he says.

"He can't believe how stupid you are," says Chuckie. "I didn't know people could get so stupid as you, you dumb cocksuck."

David looks like he's about to say something because his mouth pistons like a fish. Then he gets up and goes into the bathroom. Fifteen seconds later he's back out.

"Hey, shithead," says Chuckie, shaking his head. "What you got? VD, some other disease? I told you, asshole, wash your fucking hands!"

The guard looks over. One page of the magazine he is reading stalls in the air, half turned. "Keep it down!" he growls. The page flips over.

"Yes, sir," says Todd. He nudges Chuckie with his elbow.

Thomas Herbert farts, long and loud.

"Jesus!" I exclaim. I get up and move over four chairs.

"Thomas, you fuck!" yells Josh. "Go in the bathroom if you have to fart!"

"Yeah, Thomas," shouts Chuckie, "you piece of shit. Go in there," he points at the bathroom door, "if you have to do that."

David is laughing.

Todd says, "Hey! Look! It's Bakr." He is gesturing to the TV.

Everybody looks at the TV. Sure enough, there he is. Bakr's photo is on the screen behind the newscasters. We listen. The newscasters report that Bakr will soon be released. He may or may not be deported.

After the segment is over, Chuckie turns to Bakr. "You're famous, man," he says. He looks at David. "There's three famous people in this room. Me," he thumps his chest, "Radic, and Bakr. We've all been on TV because we're such bad dudes. You ever been on TV?"

David stares dumbly at Chuckie. Chuckie looks like that evil doll in the horror flick *Chuckie*. Thinks he's bad and all that shit. In for grand theft — auto, armed robbery. His real name is Charles Killian; he's addicted to the media. Wants his name, his story, his mug shot in the newspapers all the time and, hopefully, on the ten o'clock news — the local news, where polymer dolls, Barbie and Ken resurrections called newscasters, engage in snappy witticisms: a culture medium for a medium culture.

"I didn't think so," says Chuckie. "Fucking skinhead pussy."

David sits mute, looking half pissed off and half depressed. He leans forward, elbows resting on his knees, staring down at his black cross-trainers.

Josh rises from his seat and walks over to sit next to the female inmate. He strikes up a conversation with her. I watch as she uses her hand to adjust her hair around her ears, her forehead. Josh smiles like a little boy, sweet and charming;

there is a tenderness in his eyes, a kindness about his face as if, for just a moment, he isn't in jail.

"Nice shoes," Chuckie says to David in a snotty voice. He is looking right at David. "Where you at? The Honor Farm?"

"Yuh," replies David, his tongue surging around the small cotton logs in his mouth.

Chuckie nods to himself. "I thought so. That's where they put all the supreme white pussies — on the fucking farm."

Chuckie, sitting on the edge of his seat, leans back, crosses his arms over his chest, stretches his legs out straight, so he looks almost like he's standing but in defiance of gravity. "You guys got it pretty sweet over there, huh?" says Chuckie. "Hamburgers, sodas, even milk shakes. Fuck!" He shakes his head in disgust. "Goddamn pussies!" He glances around. "We eat slop I wouldn't feed a pig. But you fucking supreme white pussies live like fucking kings."

"I thidn't ask 'o be put there," states David, defiantly, looking down at the floor.

Chuckie laughs, a chuffing sound, like a car engine that will turn over but won't start.

Todd places his hand on Chuckie's leg. "Ease up, man," says Todd. "You don't want any shit in the clinic, and you certainly don't need any more charges against you."

Chuckie thinks about this, decides Todd is right. "Shit," he ejaculates, then turns to look at the nurse, who is picking up the clipboards.

After she gathers all of them, she says, "It won't be much longer." She leaves.

Chuckie eyes her ass as she walks away. Smiling, he nudges Todd with his elbow. Todd is fiddling with the elasticized waistband of his orange pants.

"The fuck?" whispers Chuckie.

Todd holds up a blue Bic pen, which used to reside on a clipboard.

Chuckie smiles. "Cool, dog. That'll come in handy."

"Yeah," says Todd, "but I got to find some place to hide it." Glancing over at the guard, he adds, "Keep an eye on him, will ya?"

"Gotcha', dog," says Chuckie, turning his head slightly so he can watch the guard.

Todd slips the Bic pen into a hole in the waistband of his pants. Then takes it out. He ponders for a moment, then slips the Bic pen into his sock.

The nurse comes out of the back room and walks over to the guard. She looks intently at us as she says something to him.

Turning his head, the guard eyes us like a bullfrog watching a buzzing fly. Shifting in his seat, he turns toward us. "All right, punks," he booms. "A pen is missing. Who took it?"

I sit motionless.

Chuckie turns and shrugs his shoulders.

Todd's face is blank, like a canvas without paint.

"Don't fuck with me," commands the guard in a woolly voice. He asks the nurse something. She replies.

The guard looks at his clipboard. "Hayford!" he yells.

Todd turns his eagle's head to look at the guard. "Sir?" he says.

"Get your ass over here!" snarls the guard.

Todd walks over, stands in front of the guard, who reaches over the counter and runs his hands around Todd's waist. Then he orders Todd to pull up his pant legs. The guard scrutinizes Todd's socks.

I note that Todd has no hair on his calves.

The guard is not satisfied, but Todd doesn't have the Bic pen.

"Go sit down," orders the guard.

Todd walks back and takes his seat. There is a little smile on his face.

"Okay, punks!" shouts the guard. "I want the pen. If it doesn't turn up in the next sixty seconds, we'll have strip search right here."

Everybody sits still, silent, staring at the guard. Except for David. He makes little slurping noises with his mouth.

Chuckie shoots Todd a questioning look.

Todd gives a little nod.

Chuckie magically palms the Bic pen from his person. He drops it on the floor. Sitting up straight, he peers around the waiting room, as if he's searching for the lost pen. Bending over, he says, "Here it is!" He carries it over to the guard, holding it up like the torch on the Statue of Liberty. He slaps it down on the counter in front of the guard. "Must've dropped off the clipboard," he says.

"Right!" snarls the guard. He picks up the Bic pen and hands it to the nurse.

She leaves. The guard goes back to his magazine.

Chuckie sits down with a huge grin on his face. Todd laughs silently, shakes his head in regret.

A black-clad CO enters the clinic from the hallway. He looks at the guard, nods. Then he points at David. "Okay, let's go," he says.

David stands, flicks his eyes over us. "Yuh," he grunts, dribbling saliva.

"See ya, asshole," says Chuckie, giving David his best happy face.

With his ice blue eyes, David glares at Chuckie, turns to follow the CO.

The CO stares hard at Chuckie. The CO's body is stiff with latent menace. Tension crackles in the air.

The guard behind the reception desk is staring too. He shifts in his chair, and his hand moves to his Sam Browne belt.

Chuckie keeps smiling.

With one last glower at Chuckie, the CO barks at David, "Move, punk!"

They leave.

FEROCIOUS ANIMALS

One evening, some of the boys from the other side of Intake 2 decide to have a soiree.

It is almost 9:30 p.m. Presently, the other side, the Surenos, are out on rec. In about ten minutes, they will be locked down, and our side will get out until 11:00 p.m.

Josh stands at the cell door window, looking out. "Yeah!" he screams.

"What?" I say from my top bunk.

"Two of the Surenos are killing each other," he shouts, raw pleasure in his voice.

"What?" I repeat.

"Lock it down!" roars a voice from the floor. "Lock it down!"

A grim, urgent color infuses the voice, like a ferociously goosed-up compact shock wave ramped with a metallic filament.

Steel cell doors crash shut. I hear the distinctive deep thunk of the intake doors. Rushing sounds, as if a pack of wild dogs is running loose in the unit.

Josh remains at his post, a front-row seat to the carnage. He yells his commentary to me. "Two of 'em! Jesus fucking Christ! They got shivs. Slicing at each other. Rolling on the ground. Oh, fuck! Blood is flying. One of 'em caught it in the arm! Bam! Bam! Fuck me, dog! These homeboys are fucking getting after it! Oh, Jesus! Right in the head!"

A chill deepens and spreads through my vitals. I am sitting on my top bunk, legs hanging over the side. I watch my legs twitch and kick as if they have a life of their own.

"The guards are in it now!" screams Josh. "There must be ten of 'em." He watches, gasping, bouncing up on his toes.

Steel doors keep slamming, pounding, like a battle of armor-clad Titans.

"Fuck, yeah!" shouts Josh. "Spray 'em! Spray 'em!"

"What? What?" I say.

"Pepper spray," yells Josh. "They're spraying the shit out of 'em! Everywhere!" He pauses. "Goddamn, that's gotta hurt! Fuck me. Fuck me."

Silence.

"What?" I whisper.

"They got 'em on the floor," Josh says. "Four guards on each of 'em. Fuck!" he screams. "They're spraying 'em right in the face while they got 'em down! Those guys are pissed!"

"Who? The guards?" I rasp.

"Yeah, dog. Really roughing them up. Now they're up. Got 'em on their feet." Josh pauses. "Fuck! Fuck! Fuck! They're going after each other again! Broke from the guards!"

Enthusiasm drips from Josh; it's as if violence is his art form, and the beauty of the spectacle has ripped him out of himself, has made him forget the emptiness of his own life.

I hold my breath, watch my legs twitch. I am literally wringing my hands.

"Oh fuck, man!" shouts Josh. "They're spraying 'em again! Now they're cuffing them. They got 'em. They got 'em. It's the Hole now, baby!"

Josh turns to look at me. His face is flushed, his eyes coruscating tiny speckles of energy, glee. "Fuck me," he says, turns back to the window. "They're marching them out. Four guards on each of 'em. To the Hole, baby! To the mo'fuckin' Hole." He splutters a giddy laugh.

I lie back on my bunk.

"Well," I say, "there goes our rec time."

"No shit," agrees Josh. "Locked down now, baby. Probably lock the whole fucking place down."

"Whaddaya mean?" I ask.

He spins around to gaze at me. "Fuck, dog," he says. "They pulled guards from everywhere. They'll have the whole fucking jail locked down. That's big-time shit, man."

Josh returns to the window. Two minutes of serene quiet pass. Then a staccato banging begins. Muffled yet forceful.

"What's that?" I ask.

"The Surenos, dog," says Josh. "Pounding on their cell doors." He shakes his head, a gesture full of respect.

"What? Why?" I ask.

"They're rioting, dog," Josh explains. "The shit is about to jump off."

"From inside their cells?"

"Fuck, yeah, dog. Those homeboys are fucking angry," Josh says.

This place has the potential to wound you, to make you something less than you are. As if merely by seeing a thing some part of yourself is taken away from you.

A CO walks by our cell door. They're still making rounds. I hear him say to someone, "Probably not. The jail is locked down. I don't know when you'll get out. That's up to administration."

"Ya hear that?" asks Josh. "The fuckin' whole fuckin' place is locked down."

Thumping noises reverberate through the unit. Heavy whumps, flesh pounding on steel.

"Josh! Josh!" Sleepy's voice distends out of the exhaust vent from down below.

Josh kneels in front of the vent. "Sleepy!" he shouts.

"Josh! You see those homeboys? Dog, it's the Hole now. We are in the Hole now, dog."

"Sleepy!" Josh yells. "What? What about the Hole?"

"We're in the Hole now, dog," Sleepy says. "Those home-boys are flooding their cells."

"Fuck me, dog!" shouts Josh.

"Yeah, dog. They plugged their sinks and toilets, flooded their cells. I can see it from here. They got crews with mops cleaning it all up. Fucking flooded the whole end of the unit."

"Yeah, dog!" Josh sparks. "Later, dog!"

He jumps up to the cell window. "Fuck," he tells me. "They got guards all over the place down there."

"They flooded their own cells?" I say, more to myself than to Josh.

"Yeah, dog," Josh says. "Fuck, fuck, fuck." He glances over his shoulder at me. "You gotta love this place, dog. You gotta." Laughing, he adds, "It's fucking jail, Radic. Whaddaya expect?"

I lie motionless on my bed, waiting.

"Oh, fuck," Josh whispers to the door.

"What now?" I ask.

"They're lining 'em all up," Josh tells me.

"Lining up who?"

"The Surenos."

"All of 'em?"

"Yeah, dog. They all going to the Hole," Josh squeals.

"All of 'em?" I can't believe it.

"Yeah, yeah, yeah," sings Josh. "They got 'em all lined up with their stuff. In plastic bags. They're all going to the Hole. They got 'em all cuffed. Fuck! They even got shackles on 'em."

"Jesus," I mutter.

"Fuckin' yeah!" shouts Josh. "Take 'em all to the Hole. Every last mo'fuckin' one of 'em." He counts out loud. "One, two, three, four . . ." then under his breath. "Fifteen! They got fifteen of 'em going to the Hole!"

"Where will they put 'em all?" I ask.

"Fuck, Radic!" Josh snorts in derision. "They got a shit load of cells in the Hole."

I shiver as a chill runs up my spine.

"All of 'em," Josh intones to himself. "Fuckin' all of 'em." He turns to look at me. "Sleepy's right, dog. We are in the Hole now, baby."

"I just want to do my time, not bother anybody, and go home," I say.

"Fuckin' right," Josh says. "But this *is* fuckin' jail, man. Whaddaya expect?"

"Well, not this," I snap. "Not this."

"Josh! Josh!" Sleepy's diluted voice circulates out of the vent.

Josh drops to his knees, like a pilgrim worshiping. "Go, dog!" he shouts into the vent.

"Didja see, dog? Didja see? Takin' 'em all to the Hole!" says Sleepy.

"I know, dog! I seen it! Fifteen of 'em!" shouts Josh.

"The fuckin' Hole, dog! The fuckin' Hole! All of 'em!" Sleepy says.

"Later, dog!" Josh shouts.

He jumps to the window. "There they go," he tells me. "There they go. Homeboys to the Hole. Homeboys in the Hole now."

"They're taking 'em out?" I ask.

"Every last one of 'em," Josh says. "Marching them and their shit right out the dock door. Fuckin' guards everywhere. Keepin' 'em 'bout ten paces apart."

Josh throws himself on his bunk, begins hitting the steel frame with his fist, as if he's drowning in energy, an energy shot through with points of luminescent violence.

I lie on my hard bunk, thinking hard thoughts about hard people. I abide among savage beasts residing in a concrete landscape, wherein, like shapeless wraiths submerged and drowning in icy waters, exists more punishment than crime.

These Surenos make themselves so hard that nothing can affect them anymore. But when they do that, they're alone, so completely cut off from everyone else that life doesn't work.

And there are others here, like Roy Smith, who manage to make themselves more than just hard. They find the strength to turn themselves into monsters. And monsters thrive in being alone. Alone as a way of life works for monsters. But there aren't many. Not many can so desecrate themselves and become monstrosities. Or try it this way: most of the individuals in here are animals, but there are only a few monsters.

FEEDING THE LION

I first hear of Roy Smith from Sharla. It is December 2005, and I am in cell 52, Intake 2. I am on the phone with her, circa 9:00 p.m.

"Randy," she says, "the newspapers say Roy Smith, you know, the man who killed Mary Starkey, is in jail with you."

"What?"

"Remember? Last summer. The woman who was killed. It was on the television news, in the *Ripon Record* and the *Modesto Bee*. I'm sure you read it."

"Oh, yeah. I remember. What do you mean he's in here? I haven't seen him. And I never heard of anyone named Roy in here," I say.

"Well, he's there." She pauses. "I never thought about it, but that's where he would be." Her voice is thin, like a wire supporting too much weight.

"Well," I say, "he must be in some other part of the jail. Because he's not in here. I'd hear about it. Josh for sure would know. He knows everything about everybody."

"Well . . . okay. But be careful."

"Okay. Don't worry. I'm getting better at this. I just mind my own business." Then with a rush, I add, "I love you. More than you'll ever know. And I miss you." Tears leak from my eyes.

"I love you too. Don't ever doubt that. Not for a minute," she says.

"Okay. Bye, sweet girl. I love you."

"Bye, Randy. I love you."

I hang up. I am lonely. I feel cold.

It's 9:30 p.m. "Lock it down!" shout the COS. "Lock it down!"

Josh enters our cell, shuts the cell door. The hydraulic locks slam into place. Already in my bunk, I am flat on my back, staring at the ceiling.

"Did you hear?" says Josh. His voice is a plump partridge of gossip, strutting and bobbing and twitching.

"What?"

"Roy Smith is here."

A chilly déjà vu cuddles me. "What? Where?"

"Over in one of the lockdowns," Josh says. "Everybody knows. I heard it from Slim and Nelly. They saw his ID in the door on the way back from their visits."

"Jesus," I say.

"Yeah," says Josh. "That dude is one bad motherfucker. He's facing a death penalty. Kidnapping, murder, and" — Josh emphasizes grandly — "lying in wait."

"How do you know all this?"

"It's in the fucking paper, man," Josh says.

Josh has a subscription to the *Stockton Record*. It arrives daily with the mail. Josh pores over it, grants special, almost voyeuristic attention to the local section, which is where all the crime shit is reported.

"So he's here," I say.

"Yeah. They'll assign him a cell sometime tomorrow," states Josh.

The next day, at dinner, I get my tray, my orange, my milk, my decaf coffee and walk to my table, which is on the other side of the unit. Josh and his cronies, and the other supercool dudes, sit on the supermotherfuckingcool side of the unit.

On my first day, I wanted to sit with Josh because he was

the only guy I knew. Of course, I'd only known him for about four hours. So at my first meal in Intake 2, I followed him to his table.

Halfway there he turned to me, said, "New guys sit on the other side."

So here I am. At my table I eat with Pope, Tommy Covey, Harry Potter, and Thomas White. But this evening there's a sixth person at the table. About my age, dark hair, a goatee, and sloping shoulders. He eats in silence, never looking up from his tray.

As I take the chair next to him, I glance at his ID. Smith, Roy. Jesus, I think to myself.

Pope is to my left. Harry Potter is across from me. To his left sits Tommy Covey, and to Tommy's left perches Thomas White. I think about my dining partners, and it hits me: everyone at the table, including the new guy, is a chomo. Jesus.

Picking up my spork, I prepare to dig in. But beans, rice, and dry cabbage that's been run through a Ronco Chop-O-Matic fail to seduce me. So I peel my orange, halve it, and slip both halves in my mouth. Then I drink my coffee, which, lo and behold, for once, is hot.

Glancing around the table, I hold up my milk carton, the beacon for "Who wants this?" Everyone does, except for Roy, who continues to be mesmerized by his tray, which is almost clean.

"What'll ya trade for it?" I say.

Nothing is free in the marketplace of jail. If you want to play, you pay, is the unspoken rule.

Tommy Covey glances at his tray, assessing value. He shakes his head.

"Unh," grunts Thomas White.

I assume this indicates a negative desire.

Harry Potter, though, holds out his dessert, two sugar cookies of tectonic hardness. "I'll trade my cookies for it," he says.

I look at Pope.

"Tomorrow's coffee," says Pope.

"And we have a winner," I say, dropping the milk carton next to Pope's tray.

Harry Potter pouts, which pleases me because he's such an asshole. Of course, Harry Potter is not his name. Adam some-thing is his real name, but everyone calls him Harry Potter because he looks just like the actor who plays Harry in the movies.

Milk is like crystal meth to chomos. In the best Faustian tradition, they will trade their souls for it. It is not unusual to watch Harry Potter consume four or five milks at a meal. I don't know why they crave it the way vampires crave blood, but they do. Must be some chemical in milk their bodies need.

I sit back and watch the chomos watch me. They stare at my face, then at my tray. They know I will not eat the food. Rather, I will give it away. Lust leers on their faces.

I look at Roy Smith. "You want any of this?" I say, pointing at my tray.

He glances at me. "You don't want it?" His voice rumbles like a kettle drum.

"No," I say.

"I'll take it," he says.

I push my tray next to his tray. He unloads all of it, using his spork and his left hand.

"Thanks," he says.

I nod as I look around the table. Pope doesn't really care. But Harry Potter and Tommy Covey fail to conceal their disappointment.

"Coo, coo, coo, coo," streams out of Thomas White's mouth. Pigeon noises. One of White's many talents, along with projectile vomiting — usually all over the dinner table — child molestation, and general insanity in all its colorful variations.

White presses his index finger against his right nostril, closing it off. Inhaling sharply through his left nostril, he slurps up a giant wad of mucus, swallows it.

I feel nauseous.

"Gross," mutters Raymond Pope.

Pope is twenty-seven years old, short, plump, and has burnished red hair, which he rarely combs. He rarely bathes, rarely shaves, and speaks through thick lips in an outlandish version of the English language.

"Uh huh," Thomas White says.

Tommy Covey laughs. Harry Potter looks annoyed. Of course, Harry's always annoyed.

"You know," says Harry Potter, "I heard we're not getting out tonight for rec. The Surenos are going to get our rec time plus theirs."

"That's bullshit," says Pope, making circles in his beans with his spork. Looking up from his culinary excavations, he asks, "Where do you get this shit?"

"It's not shit," Harry Potter says. "Chevy told me. And he knows!"

Pope shakes his head, returns to his excavations.

"I heard it too," chimes Tommy Covey. "The cos are always trying to fuck us over."

"Uh huh. Uh huh," says Thomas White, stuffing food into his mouth with his fingers. Then he examines his fingers, all covered with rice and beans, as if they're some undiscovered species. After a few seconds, he licks them clean.

"I doubt it," I say, looking at Tommy Covey.

"No, no, it's true," Tommy says.

"Bullshit," says Pope as he rises, picks up his tray, and shuffles off, his chubby thighs rubbing each other.

I gather my trash, place it on my tray. "See you gentlemen later — at rec," I say, giving them my best disparaging stare. I get up, push my chair in, pick up my tray, and head for the garbage barrel where I will dump my tray.

Roy Smith gets up too.

I turn to the table next to ours as if I'm going to say something to Lane so Roy Smith can go first. As he walks away, I fall in behind him. He is my height, around two hundred pounds, I guess. His movements are compact, powerful, as if packed with secrets.

I return to my cell, looking out the door as a mass of orange-clad inmates dump their trays. Thump, thump, thump. They bang the trays against the inside wall of the garbage barrel.

"Hurry it, gentlemen," shouts one of the COs. "We've got the other side to feed."

I watch Josh climb the stairs, taking them two at a time. He's in a hurry, which means he's going to smoke in the cell.

Lickety-split, Josh enters the cell. He carries a burning cigarette in his hand. Kneeling next to the intake vent, he puffs rapidly then hangs the cigarette in the vent, which keeps it lit and siphons off the smoke.

Moving to the doorway, he stands in it, hands in his pants, checking on the location of the COs.

Slim passes the cell door, walking slowly and arrogantly — the Asian gangbanger version of the pimp roll. Hands in his pants, he appears to have a giant tumor in his crotch rather than a dick.

"Where are they?" Josh asks.

"I don't know," Slim says.

"Are they making rounds?" says Josh.

"I don't know. I can't see 'em."

Slim pimp-rolls to his cell.

Josh kneels again, taking quick puffs, blowing the smoke out into the vent.

Like a fat orange snake, Porky appears in the doorway. He is lying on the floor.

"Hey, dog," he whispers. "Got a light?"

"Yeah," says Josh, spinning on his knees.

Porky tosses him two rolled cigarettes. Josh nudges them both, one at a time, one after the other, to the red tip of his cigarette, a tindery kiss. He flips them back to Porky.

"Thanks, dog," says Porky.

"Sure thing, dog," Josh says.

Porky rolls and slithers out of sight, as much as a guy with a belly like that can.

Josh is still on his knees. He takes a flurry of final puffs, tosses the butt in the toilet, flushes it.

From my top bunk, I say, "It stinks in here, man."

Standing, he reaches for his towel, begins flapping it at the doorway, like an old lady shaking out a rug. He's trying to get the smell out of the cell.

"Shut your fucking doors!" yells one of the COs. Doors begin slamming shut, a cold steel wave of sound. The hydraulic locks crack into place.

Josh looks out the cell door window.

"Guess who's sitting at my table?" I say.

"Who?"

"Roy Smith."

Josh turns to look at me. "Fuck me, dog."

"Sat right next to me," I say. "In fact, I gave him most of my dinner."

"He say anything?"

"About four words. Otherwise, just looked at his tray the whole time."

"Why the fuck he sittin' over there with all the losers?" Josh asks.

"I don't know."

"Tommy Covey and Roy Smith," Josh says, chuckling. "Does Tommy know who he's sittin' with?"

"I don't know," I say. "I doubt Tommy knows much of anything."

Josh sniggers then flushes with anger. "Fuckin' chomo faggots. Goddamn, I hate 'em."

"Yeah, they're kinda creepy," I say.

"Creepy? Fuck creepy," Josh snarls. "They're fuckin' way beyond fuckin' creepy."

He walks three paces to his bunk, throws himself on it.

I pick up my book, begin reading. But I can't stop thinking about Roy G. Smith. Lying in wait. Kidnapping. Murder. Sounds like a lion stalking Bambi, then pouncing on him, tearing his throat out. Of course, a lion kills to eat. Roy kills because he's a cannibal. Only he doesn't eat flesh, he eats souls.

JIMBO

_____

_____

_____

_____

His full name is James Allen Holden. But he goes by Jimbo. Kind of like Jumbo. And he is imposing, both in a physical sense and in personality, kind of like Jumbo. A six-foot-one-inch Pillsbury dough-boy with strawberry blond hair greased straight back.

Jimbo is more than anyone bargains for.

I am coming back to my cell, rounding the corner on tier two, when I encounter Porky and Mikey, who are inseparable. But now there's a third member of their two-member gang. Someone I've never seen before. As I approach, I stare without staring at the guy. A visible disturbance surrounds him, as if a hurricane just passed over him. He's a mess. Like his clothes don't fit right.

I stop in front of Porky because I have a vital question to ask him. My sentencing hearing is soon, and subsequent to that I will be transferred to DVI for processing. From there, I will most likely transfer to a minimum-security facility, maybe a fire camp, if I'm lucky.

Quite frankly, the looming and ominous specter of DVI horrifies me. I need reassurance. And I need survival techniques, a kind of personal defense policy — my own little private Monroe Doctrine, as it were.

My presence brings their conversation to a screeching halt, as if I'm an OG with warning lights.

"Porky," I say, "when you have time, I'd like to talk to you for a few minutes."

Porky hitches at his pants, pulling them up snug below his convex belly. "What's up, dog?"

"I have some questions about DVI," I say, wishing we could speak confidentially.

Mikey laughs like a girl. His hands fisted in his pants.

"Ask," says Porky.

"Well," I hesitate. What the hell, I decide. "I'm scared," I say. "I don't know what to expect."

The blond dumpster regards me with big brown eyes, with a sensual, more alive than alive look. "It's nothing," he says as if we're best buddies. There's a sheen of perspiration on the dumpster's face and arms.

"Well, what's gonna happen? I mean, tell me what to expect."

Porky pulls at his pants again then holds his hand out front of his belly, as if he's trying to catch a ball. "First off, when you arrive they'll give you new clothes. CDC shit. The same as you wear now, but they'll say Prisoner 'stead of Jail. And CDC on 'em," Porky says. His voice is a rumbling rasp, as if someone's tearing paper in the bowels of hell. "The guys who give you your stuff are inmates," Porky continues.

I look at the gang tattoos on his knuckles. Black dots and squares, one on each finger.

"Don't say nothing to 'em. Don't give them any personal information 'bout yourself. 'Cuz they'll be pumping you ta see if you're lying. 'Cuz they already know all about you."

"How?" I say.

"From the paperwork that arrives with you," he says. "It says all about length of sentence, what you're in for. All that shit. They want to know if you're a chomo or active."

"Or a firebug," adds the blond blob, an eddy of charged particles emanating from his eyes. "They don't like firebugs either."

"What's a firebug?" I ask, aware it is a stupid question. But I really don't know what they're talking about.

"A fucking arsonist," says the blob, giving me an impatient glare.

"Yeah," agrees Porky. "Chomos, sex shit, and arson. Bad news in DVI. But you don't need to worry 'bout that. Just don't say nothing."

"Will they put me in the Hole for two weeks?"

"Who told you that shit?" Porky asks.

"Matt Berg. He said they put you in the Hole for two weeks before they assign you a cell."

"Fucking Berg," says Porky, spitting out the words. "That stutter-boy don't know nothing. They put him in the Hole 'cuz he's a fuck-up." He gives me his serious look. "You don't have to worry 'bout the Hole. You'll be level one or two at the worst." A thought crosses his face. "You going mainline or PC?"

"PC, I guess. That's what Josh told me to do."

"Maybe," says Porky. "I mean, do you want to just lay back, take it easy?"

"Yeah, I guess." I don't really know what to say.

"Then go PC," says Porky, nodding. "Mainline is too risky. That's where all the young punks are. Always fighting and shit."

He glances at Mikey. "Mikey's going PC, right dog?"

Mikey produces a shrill laugh. "PC all the way, dog."

Porky nods portentously. "Yeah, Mikey don't need no trouble. You should go PC. But if you decide to go mainline, be careful. Just keep to yourself. Don't talk to no one who ain't white. Stay away from the gangbangers."

"What about commissary?" I ask.

"When you get there, tell the guards you're a new fish," says Porky. "Ask 'em for a commissary form and write new fish on it."

"New fish?"

"Yeah. Just write new fish on it. They'll let you go to commissary within a few days. Oh, and put on the form how much you want to spend. Like twenty dollars or whatever."

"How much can I spend?" I ask.

"You get ninety dollars a month," chimes in the blond blob.

"Only ninety?" I say. "We get twice that here."

"Yeah, but they rip us off here," says Porky. "You can get a lot of shit for ninety dollars there. Soups are three for a dollar. You can get soda pop, all sorts of candy. Good stuff."

"Soda pop?" I ask.

"Yeah. And all kinds of chips, big bags. Doughnuts too."

"Okay." I try to organize all this information. I don't want to forget anything. "What about mail?"

"Yeah," says Porky. His voice tells me I finally asked a good question. "When you get there, first thing you do is ask for a visitor's form. Shoot it off right away. 'Cuz if you want your fiancée to come visit, she has to be cleared."

"What?"

"They check her out first," Porky explains. "Takes about four weeks to do, so she can't come visit for a month."

"Okay. Can I get books from the library?"

Porky laughs. "Fuck! You can try, but you won't get 'em."

"You mean they don't have a library?" Shock and dismay embrace me. Without something to read, I'll go crazy. I just know it.

"Oh, they got a library," says Porky. "But they don't do shit. Look," he goes on, "the best way to get books is to find one of the handicapped guys, make a deal."

"A deal? What kind of deal?"

"The handicapped guys get special packages," Porky says. "Food, books, mail. All sorts of shit. And it gets right in. So you make a deal. Have your fiancée send books to the handicapped guy. Then he gives them to you."

"What do I have to give him?"

"Usually food," Porky says, as if it's no big deal. "That way you get what you want, and he gets food. It's not exactly legal, but it's the only way to get personal books."

"There's books you can borrow from people," adds the rumpled blob. "Just be careful who you borrow from. No trading outside your race. And never with gang dudes."

"What about mail?" I ask. "Will I get my mail?"

"Takes about three weeks for the letters to get in," says Porky. "But you'll get it eventually."

"Three weeks," I whisper. "I'll only be there six weeks."

"Maybe," says Porky. "Look, it can take less time or more time to process through. They give you these tests, see —"

"Tests?" I interrupt him.

"Yeah, tests. To evaluate you. You take the tests to your cell and just fill 'em in. You won't have any problem with 'em." He gives me a calculated look. "You're educated and all, right?"

I nod.

"It'll be easy for you. It's a good way to pass the time in your cell. Also, don't have any medical problems 'cuz that slows it down."

"Medical problems? Like what?"

"Like be crazy or anything," says Porky. "If you need meds, it screws it up. If you're on a suicide watch, they put you in the Hole for sure."

Jesus, I think to myself. I'll be in there forever.

"But you don't have none of that stuff," Porky assures me. "Once you finish the tests, then your counselor will talk to you, kind of an interview. To find out if you're prison material or not."

"What's prison material?"

Porky guffaws. "Me," he says. "I have a problem with somebody, I just drag 'em in a cell and kick the shit out of 'em. I'm a lifer." He holds his hands out as if to say, "Look at me: what you see is what you see, and what you see is prison material." He goes on, "When they interview you, just tell 'em you read a lot and like to stay to yourself 'cuz you have nothing in common with the rest."

"I was level one when I went in," says the blob. "Now I'm

level four." He sounds proud of this accomplishment, whatever it is.

"Level?" I ask. "How do they assign your level?"

Porky hoists his pants up. "They have a scoring system based on your crime, violent or not. Education and the psych tests they give you. Then they give you a score. You'll be level one, two at the worst."

"Well, what does the level mean?"

"Who you rec with, how much rec you get. What level of security you are," Porky explains. "If you're level one, you rec with mostly level ones."

"Not always," says the blob. "Sometimes level ones end up reccing with max guys."

Porky gives the blob a "Would you just shut up!" look. This adds to my worry level, which is at level four on a scale of four.

"Look," says Porky. "You'll be fine. You ain't no chomo or active. Plus you're an OG. No one bothers the OGs." He holds one hand up, ticking off items on his fingers. "Remember: new fish on the form, shoot a visitor application off, keep to yourself, don't trade, and find a handicapped guy to deal with. Easy."

"Okay," I say. "Got it." Emotion overwhelms me. I put my hand out. Porky shakes it. "Thanks. Thanks a lot."

"You'll be fine," Porky assures me. "Here — gimme a hug."

He embraces me to his chest, squeezing the breath out of me. He smells of tobacco and strength, the effluvium of self-sufficiency. I almost start crying.

They move off.

I enter my cell, sit down on the chair. I wonder if I can do this.

After a few minutes, I wander back downstairs. Bob is walking. I join him, falling in behind him. We walk every rec. Sometimes for two hours at a stretch. It is our ritual. The ostensible reason is for the exercise, but it is so much more. It is conversation, it is bonding, it is sanity. We walk and talk.

We talk about wine, about food, about places we've lived, about our families, about our cell mates, about jail-house gossip, about world affairs, about sports.

Bob is awaiting his trial. Supposedly, he offed his wife one day while they were in his garage. Flipped her life switch from on to off with a pistol. He is tall and thin, gray hair and balding.

"I got a new cellie today," he says over his shoulder.

"That's too bad," I say. "You only got about three days to yourself."

"Yeah. It was wonderful, but it never lasts too long. The longest I've ever gone without a cellie is one week. Usually, one leaves in the morning and I've got a new one by that night." He sighs.

"Who is it?" I say.

"Young guy. Name is Jimbo," Bob says. "He's . . ." He looks around the unit. "He's over there. With Porky." He nods to the tables where the inmates play cards. Porky, Mikey, Slim, and some new guy are seated at one of the tables playing cards.

I look. "You mean the fat blond guy?" I say.

"Yeah," says Bob.

It's the blob.

I laugh. "I was just talking to him. What's he in here for?"

"Car jacking," says Bob. "At least it's a normal crime."

He pulls his pants up so he won't walk on them. He is so thin they keep falling down, so he turns the waistband down for more cinch when he's walking.

"That's good. At least it's not some chomo."

"Yeah," agrees Bob. "He jacked a car, and some guy was asleep in the back seat. So now it's kidnapping and car jacking." Bob laughs, shakes his head.

"What? You're kidding me, right?"

"No. The guy was asleep in the back seat of his Mercedes

when Jimbo jacked it. Then instead of pulling over when the cops gave chase, Jimbo floored it, and a high-speed chase ensued. He hit a couple of cars and finally crashed the thing, ended up upside down in a Mercedes."

I laugh. "Jesus. Is he crazy or what?"

"He's a certified paranoid schizophrenic," Bob says.

"You're kidding me?"

"No. He told me, and then he showed me the psychiatrist's report."

"I'll bet that makes you feel safe, huh?"

"No," says Bob. His voice is fat with gravity.

"Jesus," I say and change the subject.

Rec time, 9:30 p.m. I exit the cell right behind Josh, who is on his way to the yard to smoke. Bob is already downstairs walking. I fall in behind him.

"Hi, Bob. How are you?"

"Good evening, Randy. I'm good," he says.

"How's Jimbo? Is he quiet?"

"Yeah, he's quiet. So we'll probably get along. He likes to read too. But he's ADD and dyslexic, so he reads each sentence twice, forward and backward."

"What?"

"Yeah. He has to read each sentence twice."

"Dear Lord."

"He's married, too," says Bob, looking back over his shoulder. There's a big grin on his face. "Only they're not really married. But he refers to her as his wife."

"What? How can you be married but not married? You mean like common law or something?"

"No," says Bob, still smiling at Jimbo's social and domestic context.

Smiling is contagious, so I find myself smiling too. I wonder why I am smiling, and it hits me: we, two OGs, are walking rapidly, in a single-file formation, counterclockwise in direction, in jail, breathing tired air that smells of disinfectant, wearing standard-issue cunt orange pajamas, discussing the quasi-matrimonial status of a paranoid schizophrenic.

"I mean," Bob says, "he refers to her as his wife but upon specific interrogation admits they are not married. They live as man and wife — she has kids — but they are not married." He laughs out loud, with exuberance; his laugh is like thunder rumbling in the distance.

I laugh with him. "Jesus," I say through my laughter.

"I know, I know," Bob says, grinning like a skunk eating shit.

"And get this," he adds. Then pauses for effect.

"Go on. Tell me."

"His wife is forty-six."

We both bust up, still walking, never missing a step. Jimbo is twenty-three.

After a few moments, I wipe tears from my eyes. "Oh, Jesus," I say.

"Good stuff, huh?" Bob says.

"You bet."

As I keep walking, I keep wondering. At the end of three more laps, I say, "Has he been arraigned yet?"

"Yeah," Bob says. "Right now they're trying to determine if he's competent to stand trial."

"What do you mean, competent?"

"Since he's schizophrenic and paranoid, he might not be legally competent to stand trial. They're probably going to send him to Atascadero for psychiatric evaluation."

"Well, how long does that take?" I say.

"Anywhere from ninety days to three years," says Bob.

"Three years?" I say. "Isn't that kind of long?"

"I guess they can keep him there indefinitely *if* they want to."

"Jesus."

"He's been in and out of jail since he was twelve," Bob says. His smile is gone, his voice is sober. "Twelve!"

"For what?" I say.

"Drugs, car jacking, assault and battery. Mostly car jacking is the way I get it. He likes to boost cars."

"What for? Does he sell them or what?" I say.

"I think he just does it. For the thrill." I can see him shake his head to himself.

"Jesus," I say. That's the only appropriate comment I can think of.

"He told me he's institutionalized," Bob says. "He said he can't handle being on the outside. It freaks him out. He actually feels safe and at home in prison."

"My God," I blurt out. "That's sad."

"It's more than sad," Bob says, "it's pathetic."

We turn left, then left again, always left as we walk and walk and walk. Like we're NASCAR racers.

"His mother was an alcoholic, and his father was a tweaker along with being steeped in the preservative of rum," explains Bob. "And it sounds as if his father was drunk most of the time, when he was even there."

"Did he finish high school?" I say.

Most of the inmates come from the same mold: reprehensible parents or no parents at all, uneducated, angry, with a predilection for violence as a problem-solving device.

"Fifth grade," says Bob, with a note of incredulity. "Fifth grade is as far as he got."

"It's a miracle he can even read, much less wants to," I say.

"Yeah," Bob says. "What a life. What a waste of human life."

ADIOS, AMIGOS

_____

_____

_____

After dinner one night, Josh hurries back to the cell and has a smoke before we are locked down. Once the locks snap into place, we begin our usual descent into boredom. I read. Josh lies on his bunk.

Five minutes later, Porky and Mikey's cell door is opened by one of the COs. He says something to Porky. Sounds like a question. I hear Porky's terse, muffled reply but can't make out what he says.

The CO slams the cell door shut. Then our cell door opens. The CO sticks his head inside and sniffs. "You guys smoking?" he demands.

"No," says Josh in his best self-righteous voice.

"Don't lie to me. I'll ask one more time. You can be a man and cop to it or be written up," says the CO.

He has dark hair, longer than most of the COs. I recognize him. In my opinion, he is a rarity — a racist. Most of the COs display cold professionalism. Most are humane in an automated fashion, like a vending machine. Not this one. His camouflage is jovial, smooth with a fine polish.

(Bob and I saw him slam one of the Mexican homeboys in cell 65 into the steel frame of the bunk bed. "You don't speak English, do you?" he bellowed at the guy. Turning to the cell mate, he yelled, "Neither do you, do ya?")

"We don't fucking smoke," Josh tells him.

I sit up on my top bunk, wanting to tell Josh to cool it. Don't fuck with this guy.

The CO poses in the doorway, one hand on the cell door. Black uniform, black hair, black anger. "Don't plan on this door opening any time soon," he says. He slams the door shut.

"Fucking punk!" Josh shouts from his bunk.

The door twitches open.

"What'd you say?" the CO demands.

Energy crackles in the seven-foot by twelve-foot cell like an evil omen.

Josh leaps up from his bunk, stands three feet in front of the CO. "I said we don't fucking smoke."

"That's what you said, huh?"

Josh's body language fulminates hate. He does not answer.

"Okay, you two," says the CO. "Out of your cell. Now!"

I climb down from my bunk. By the time I get down, Josh is already outside. The CO has him facing the wall, hands up, legs spread. The CO pats him down.

Turning to me, the CO commands, "Back against the railing." He points to the gray steel fence that circumnavigates the second tier.

I obey.

He pats Josh down again. "Stand over there by the phones," he orders Josh.

"Up against the wall," he tells me.

I do the spread-eagle against the wall. His hands move up my legs, squeezing as they ascend. Jamming his right thumb and index finger in the crack of my ass, he gropes my genitals with his left hand. Then he strokes my torso, rubs at my armpits.

"Over with your buddy," he says.

The other CO arrives. They enter our cell. I can hear them opening our drawers, removing our mattresses, ripping off the bedding, poking through the toilet paper wrappers.

The partner approaches Josh and me. "You guys smoking in your room?"

"No!" Josh yells.

He turns to me. "Where's the lighter?"

"We don't have no lighter!" Josh asserts in a loud voice.

"We know there's lighters in this unit," he says.

"I don't smoke," Josh snarls. He punches the wall.

The CO's hand moves to his Sam Browne belt. "You better calm down, son," he commands Josh. He makes a sharp, furious motion.

"Go fuck yourself," shouts Josh. "You punks got no right to search our stuff."

The CO turns Josh a burning glance, turns, walks back into our cell.

"Josh," I whisper. "Cool it, man."

"Fuck that shit," he says to me. His voice is blaring.

We wait. I stand with my back against the wall. Josh walks around, rocking back and forth on his legs, smiling and performing for his cronies as they stare out their cell door windows watching the show.

The CO walks out of our cell, his black widow's peak aimed in our direction. "We didn't find anything," he says to us. His smile is wicked. "Sorry for the inconvenience. You can go back to your cell."

Back in our cell, the CO stands in front of us. I glance around, astonished at the mess. All our stuff is on the floor: bedding, letters, commissary food, books, toilet paper, towels.

"I'll be back in a few minutes," the CO says. There is a harsh edge to his voice. He leaves, slams the door, locks it.

"Fucking punk assholes," Josh says.

I don't say anything. Bending over, I pick up my bedding, toss it on my bunk, begin making my bed.

Ten minutes later everything is back in place, neat and tidy. I think about that. If you can put everything you own back in place in ten minutes, then your life sucks.

The door opens. The CO enters. He has four sheets of computer printout in his hands.

"You gentlemen are being written up," he says. "You need to sign these." He hands each of us two pages.

I glance at them. "If I sign, will I lose my commissary?" I ask.

"I'm not fucking signing," Josh shouts. "I wasn't smoking."

The CO looks at me. "No. But you'll lose morning rec tomorrow."

"Don't sign it," orders Josh, looking at me. "This is fucked!"

The CO, rigid, stares at Josh. "If you don't sign, you go to the Hole," he says in a flat voice.

Shrugging to myself, I sign the second page, hand the pages back to the CO.

"I'm not signing anything," Josh states.

"Roll up your stuff," commands the CO. "I'll be back in three minutes."

The cell door slams.

"Josh, just sign. All you're going to lose is one rec," I plead.

"Fuckin' pussy!" In Josh's round baby face, his eyes glint like blue ice.

"Look," I say. "You were smoking. Just cop to it, and that's the end of it."

"No fuckin' way! I wasn't smoking!"

"What? You were too. Just ask him if you can still sign."

"No!"

I climb up on my bunk, sit Indian style. "What's with you, man? You're getting us both written up. I wanted to call Sharla tomorrow, now I can't."

Josh walks to the cell door window. He shrugs. "I gotta do what I gotta do," he says.

"Sheez, man," I snort. I lie back on my bunk.

The cell door opens.

"Let's go," says the CO. He holds out yellow cuffs. "Turn around."

Josh puts his hands behind his back, turns. The CO cuffs him.

"Where's your stuff?" asks the CO.

"Fuck you!" Josh snaps.

"Okay, asshole." The CO shoves Josh up against the wall, turns to me. "Bag up his stuff," he commands. "I'll be back for it."

Josh is pushed out of the cell. The door slams.

I gather Josh's belongings. Shower thongs, sweatshirt, three books, shaving cream, toothpaste and toothbrush, two pouches of tobacco with attendant rolling papers. I shove it all in a brown paper bag, one of the big ones our commissary comes in.

The CO returns, opens the cell door. I hand him the bag.

He gives me a measured look. "I don't want you to compromise yourself," he says. Translation: I won't ask you to squeal on your bunkie. "But I appreciate the way you behaved," he continues. "Your cell mate calmed down a little, wanted to know if he could still sign." He winks at me. "I told him it was too late."

"Yes, sir," I say.

He leaves with the bag.

Josh spends the night locked down in cell 33, on the other side of the unit. The next day they move him to the Hole, where he languishes for two weeks before he is transported by bus to DVI for his ninety-day op.

SHREK

———————————

———————————

———————————

———————————

Evening rec time, circa 10:00 p.m. Bob and I are walking.

"How's Shrek? He shower yet?" says Bob, grinning. He has heard my complaints for two weeks now.

Josh is gone, baby, gone. He finally got a deal via his public defender. The private asshole attorney his mom hired for him didn't do squat for him. The private asshole attorney was supposed to be some hotshot from San Diego. He turned out to be a $5,000 loser, never came to talk to Josh, never talked to the DA, never bargained for a better deal. Josh's mom fired him.

Josh's public defender got him the deal. And Josh took it: ninety-day op at DVI to determine if he is prison material or not. If not, then he'll get twelve months local time with credit for time served. If so, then he'll get up to twelve months in prison.

My new cell mate is Shawn Speer, but everybody calls him Shrek because he looks just like the ogre in the movie *Shrek*. Except for the green skin color, of course.

Shrek is here for receiving stolen goods and drugs. Seems he bought a stolen car for $800. He asserts he had no knowledge the car was stolen. Yeah, right. And he was high on meth when they picked him up, with more in the car.

"No," I say bitterly, "he hasn't showered yet. Nor has he brushed his teeth, the eight that he has left in his head. And he has yet to wash his hands after using the toilet. And to top it all off, he has not even offered to empty the trash can in our cell, much less cleaned anything."

"That's gross," Bob says, grimacing in disgust. He turns to look over his shoulder at me. "What is wrong with these people? They have no personal hygiene whatsoever."

"Tell me about it."

Jimbo approaches the railing, watches us walk. As we go by him, he makes racecar noises. On the next lap, we stop to talk to him.

"You know," says Jimbo, "I could kick your ass."

He is speaking to Bob. According to Bob, he says that about twenty times a day.

"I know you could," says Bob. He smiles but not convincingly.

Jimbo turns to me. "How's your cell mate?"

"Pathetic," I say. "He's been here two weeks and still has not taken a shower. I've offered him soap, dropped all sorts of hints."

"Well, just tell him to take a fucking shower," says Jimbo.

His hair is greased back with body lotion. His "wife's" name, or its diminutive, is tattooed on his neck in fancy script.

"You gotta be considerate of your cell mate," Jimbo says. His tone is dogmatic, an unwritten law.

"Yeah, well," I say.

"Randy's too polite," Bob says.

Jimbo looks around the unit. "Tell him to fucking take a shower. Stop being nice, and just tell him."

"I'll think about it," I say.

I am embarrassed. I need to become tough. But I don't want to become like these animals. I don't want to be one more item in the Animal Safari.

Jimbo leaves abruptly, which is normal. We watch him walk over to the card tables, where he joins a game in progress.

"I hope he doesn't say anything to Shrek," I tell Bob. "Shrek'll get pissed and kick my ass."

"He won't," Bob assures me.

We begin walking, Bob in the lead with me following along. We dodge inmates as they enter and leave the yard. Some nod to us, others just glare. I never make eye contact with any of them, just look through them, by them, around them.

Ten minutes later, Jimbo is back at the railing. We stop.

"He'll fucking take a shower now," says Jimbo, looking pleased with himself.

"You said something to him?" I am horrified.

"Fuck, yeah," Jimbo says.

Bob smiles. He thinks it is funny. "What'd you do?" says Bob.

"I walked up to him and said, 'You're up there in 52 with my Uncle Randy, right?'" Jimbo says, as if he's telling a bedtime story to two idiot savants. "He says, 'Yeah, I am.' 'Well,' I said, 'you be nice to him, or I'll kick your fucking ass.'"

"What'd he say?" Bob says.

"He got all spooked," Jimbo says. "Said he was always respectful 'cuz he didn't want no trouble. Said he liked Randy. So I told him to take a fucking shower 'cuz the cigarette smell is fucking strong and it bothers my Uncle Randy. And if he didn't take one at least four times a week, I told him I'd kick his fucking ass."

My eyes are wide open. I roll them at Bob.

Bob laughs.

Jimbo gazes at me with shrewd eyes. "If he doesn't take a shower, tell me. And I'll kick his fucking ass." Jimbo turns, walks away.

I look up at the showers on tier two. As if on cue, Shrek stands outside the first shower door with his towel and a plastic red chair. He's going to shower.

"Look," I say to Bob. "It's Shrek. And he's going to take a shower."

Bob looks up and laughs. "I guess Jimbo's threat proved efficacious."

"I guess so," I say. The simple arithmetic of violence, as suggested by Jimbo, is impressive: force generates its own imperatives.

"Jesus," I say to Bob. "Why'd Jimbo do that?"

Bob smiles knowingly at me. "I knew he was going to do it," he confesses. "We were talking in the cell after dinner, and he told me he was going to tell Shrek to shower or else he'd kick his fucking ass." Bob chortles as he says "kick his fucking ass." I can tell he likes the way it feels on his tongue.

"Why is he looking out for me?" I say.

"Because you always give him sweets or oatmeal," Bob says. "And then your fiancée put money on his books. He told me that no one's ever been that nice to him. He had tears in his eyes when he told me."

Sharla had put twenty dollars on Jimbo's books. It was her suggestion. She said that way he could buy his own food from commissary, and I wouldn't have to share mine with him.

"Well," I tell Bob, "that was a purely selfish act on my part. I only get fifty dollars a week, and I was giving half of it to him. This way we both come out ahead. He can order what he likes, and I can eat mine."

"He doesn't see it that way, I guess," says Bob. "C'mon, let's walk some more. They'll be locking it down soon."

Twenty minutes later one of the COs shouts out, "Ten minutes till lockdown. You want water or a last smoke, do it now or fucking forget it!"

Bob and I stop walking. I race up to my cell to get my plastic tumbler. Then back downstairs to fill it with cold water from the dispenser. Bob is there already, filling his twin tumblers: one with hot water for soup, the other with cold water for Kool-Aid. We walk slowly to the bottom of the stairs.

"Good night, Bob," I say.

"See you at breakfast," says Bob.

I go up the stairs, enter the cell, put my ID in the cell door window, place my tumbler on top of my books on the desk.

That way I can reach it from my penthouse bunk without having to descend.

I stand in the doorway, watching as all the orange-clad savages scramble for water, borrow books, scrounge for newspapers, or just plain stall the return to their cells.

"Lock it down! Lock it down!" Three decisive words. The last words heard every night.

I watch Shrek struggle up the stairs. He can hardly move. He's only thirty-five years old, but meth has rotted his joints, ravaged his teeth, ravished his personal life.

His shadow, Justin, is behind him as they mount the stairs. They were "associates" outside in the real world. Not friends. Shrek makes a clear distinction between friends and associates. I am not sure of the separation, but an associate is less than a friend, deficient in some vague way, untrustworthy perhaps. Shrek's meager vocabulary, emanating from his decomposing brain, due, of course, to his *affaire d'amour* with meth, is powerless to supply me with a precise definition.

Shrek enters the cell, pulls the door shut. The hydraulic locks snap into place. Locked down.

"How was your rec?" he says.

"Fine. Boring."

"Mine wasn't good," he says. "I'm not feeling well."

"What's the matter?" I say. I really don't care. I just don't want to catch whatever he has.

"I ache," he says. His voice is an expert whine. He is a whine.

"You need some Tylenol? I've got some if you need it." Tylenol comes in individually packaged capsules.

"No. It's my cancer. I'll be dead pretty soon," he says as he sits on his bunk. There is something vampiric about his words, as if he's sucking sympathy out of me. Shrek claims he has bone cancer, but I don't believe him.

I almost say, "If you *really* have cancer . . . ," but I catch myself. Instead, I say, "Since you have cancer, why don't you transfer to the Med Unit, or Sheltered Housing, so they can do something for you?"

He is now lying on his bunk. I can't see him, but I know he is flat on his back, arms crossed over his chest.

"No," he says. "I can't go back to Sheltered Housing. That's where I was before I came to PC."

"How come you can't go back there?"

"There's some dogs in there I have a hassle with."

"Whaddaya mean, hassle?" I say.

"You know, white power assholes. They think they run the place. Well, I don't do what they tell me to. So they got a hassle with me. I had to beat some shit when I was there. So now they'll jump me. About ten of 'em."

He sounds all bad, as if he's just finished reading *Soldier of Fortune* magazine. The slick zine for will-bes and wanna-bes.

"Whaddaya mean, beat some shit?" I ask.

"You know, guy got shitty with me. So I hit 'im," Shrek says, "Fuck-nuts never got up. So now there's a contract out on me."

"What? A contract? You mean, like to kill you?" I say.

"Yeah," Shrek says.

His voice is nonchalant, as if this is run-of-the-mill stuff for him. He also used to pull down six grand a week repoing cars. And he used to make two grand a week at the local drag strip. His car and he were like Batman and Robin, the unbeatable dynamic duo.

"How come you were there in the first place?"

"Because of my cancer," he says. "Plus I got kinda fucked up when the fucking cops arrested me."

"What do you mean? They hit you or what?"

"No," he says. "I smashed into another car. They had to use those big fucking metal things — whaddaya call 'em?"

"Jaws of Life?" I say.

"Yeah. Jaws of Life — to get me out of the car."

"Wait a minute," I say. "I thought they pulled you over

because you were driving a stolen car then arrested you. Now you're telling me that you had a wreck. How'd that happen?"

"I *was* arrested," rationalizes Shrek, "but only after the fucking cops cut me out of the car. I was all banged up. Had a big gash on my forehead, a broken collar bone, some bruises."

This is the newest, latest version of the story, I guess. Or, I think, could it be that he's a big, fat liar? Hmmm.

"Okay," I say, pursuing him down the dark, twisting alley of truth. "But how'd you have the car wreck?"

"The fucking cops were behind me, tailing me," he says. "I saw them in my mirror. So I tried to lose them."

"So you took off?"

"Yeah, man," Shrek says, a plaintive note in his voice. "I had meth in the car and an expired driver's license. Whaddaya think?" After a moment's reflection, he adds, "Fucking cops. They always pick on poor people. I hate this state. When I get out of here, I'm moving to Texas."

"You have family there?"

"No," he says. "I ain't got no family."

Rolling onto my belly, I look at him over the edge of my bunk. His face is pale with red blotches and pinched up. I know him well enough to realize something is chewing at his mind. "Yes, you do!" I snap, then roll onto my back. I adjust my orange sweatshirt over my upper torso because I'm cold. "You have a wife and a kid. And what about your aunt?"

"My wife is a fucking cunt bitch, and I haven't seen my kid in four years, and my aunt just wants me to die and go away," he says.

His voice is that of a philosophical orphan. In his mind, he is dead to these people or wishes he was or, more probably, enjoys feeling sorry for himself — a kind of addiction in itself.

"I'm sure you miss your kid," I say. "And your aunt writes to you, which means that she cares about you. Otherwise, she wouldn't even write."

I roll over, look down at him. "By the way, it's none of my business, but did you ever write her back?"

I gave him a stamped envelope to that end and have encouraged him to write to her so she will, perhaps, put some money on his books, so I won't have welfare Shrek withdrawing from the Randy-the-Sucker Food Bank.

He's already stolen from me. I know for a fact. He knows Sharla visits me every Sunday afternoon. Last Sunday, after my visit, I came back to the cell. Shrek was asleep on his bunk. I opened my drawer and counted my Star Crunches. Two were missing. I looked in the trashcan, and there were the wrappers. Not even a smart thief.

Josh stole from me too. Candy bars, usually Baby Ruths or Reese's Peanut Butter Cups. I was shocked and dismayed that my own cell mates would steal from me. Then I laughed at myself. Whaddaya expect, as Josh would say, it's fucking jail. Everyone in here is a criminal.

"No," says Shrek. "I started a letter to her, but I didn't know what to say. Just go fuck yourself, you fucking dried-up old cunt."

I have seen his attempts at letters. He can barely write his own name.

"That might not be the most tactful thing to say," I admonish him. "Why don't you simply thank her for writing to you, ask her to think about putting some money on your books? So you can get some tobacco?"

"Fuck it," he says, pouting.

I don't say anything. You can't argue logically with a depressed, self-indulgent, angry tweaker who is more than likely the missing link.

Five minutes later he says, "You got any of those white kites?"

"On the desk," I say. "Help yourself."

He struggles to a sitting position. "Can I borrow a pencil?"

"Sure."

He has nothing except the orange pajamas he wears. He fills out the kite.

"It's none of my business," I say, "but what are you doing?"

"I'm going to go to the Med Unit. I'll just die there, in jail. At least no one will bother me."

His last statement opens entire new vistas for speculation, namely that someone is giving him shit.

"Who's bothering you?" I say.

"No one," he mutters.

"C'mon, Shawn," I say, "someone's bothering you. Who is it?"

"Johnnie."

"I thought Johnnie was your associate," I say.

Johnnie is a short black homeboy, in here for some sex-related crime. He's a mooch, which means he has no money on his books, and he's sure-thing bizarre, even for this place. Always singing some hip-hop ditty, talking to himself, or doing this jive-ass clap and stamp dance, where he slaps his shoulders, knees, and feet, rapping out ebonic-lingo lyrics. And there's this odor that surrounds him like a cloud, a combination of overcooked broccoli and dogshit.

"*Because* of Johnnie," Shrek amends. "You know Chuckie, right?"

"Yeah."

"Well, Chuckie came up to me in the yard, told me to stop hanging out with the blacks, stop giving them cigarettes, eating at their table."

"Sounds like Chuckie," I say. "He's full of hot air. He won't do anything."

"He told me straight up to stop it."

"Yeah, well, Chuckie thinks he's the hall monitor or something," I say. "Like he's all bad. He's not. He's harmless."

"Everybody's always getting all fuckin' in your face. They'll kick your fuckin' ass if you don't do this. I don't want any trouble. I just wanna do my time, move to Texas." He pauses, thinking. "If the bullshit bastards'll let me. Probably have to stay in this fucking place until my probation's done. Or I could just fuckin' go. Nobody's gonna care. I'll be dead soon anyway."

"Of course someone will care," I say. "What about your kid? Wouldn't you like to see him again?"

"I guess. Yeah," he mumbles. Thinking about his child and ex-wife lights his fuse. "The fuckin' cops and the fuckin' women are why I'm here. Cops won't leave me alone, and don't marry no mean-ass bitch. They just want your money, then split. She sold my motorcycle, my car, all my shit."

I jump back in time a couple of minutes to when he quoted Jimbo: "they'll kick your fuckin' ass." "You take a shower tonight?" I say. "I mean, your towel's hanging on the hook. Usually, it's your pillow."

"Yeah," he says. His voice is heavy with "I don't wanna talk about it" resonances.

"I'll bet you feel better, huh?" I say, smiling to myself.

"Yeah. Except my joints hurt me. I need to get out of here, over to Sheltered Housing." Remembering the white power pure boys, he changes his destination. "Probably the Med Unit," he says.

"Whatever you think is best," I say. I'm bored with him, with the conversation. Anger and self-pity are his default emotions.

"Does aching have two cees or one?" he asks, scrawling on the kite.

"Just one," I say, lamenting to myself.

Two days later: rec time, 9:00 a.m. Walking with Bob.

"So Shrek is waiting to go to the Med Unit?" Bob says.

"Yeah. The nurse told him he'll be transferred sometime this week. He's ready to roll it up anytime. I'm supposed to give his tobacco to the guy in cell 32," I say, almost treading on Bob's ankles as he loses his rubber slipper. "Pit stop," I say as I come to a stop.

"Yeah," laughs Bob. "Mechanical problems."

He retrieves the slipper with his foot. We're off again.

"Why is he transferring to the Med Unit?" asks Bob.

"Because of his cancer. At least that's his explanation. In reality, it's because Chuckie told him to stop socializing with Johnnie. You know, that weird black guy with the Crip haircut?"

"Yeah," Bob says.

"But his main motivation is because Jimbo threatened to kick his fucking ass. I'm pretty sure of it."

"Really?" Bob says.

"Yeah. For all his badass posturing, he's pretty meek."

"Maybe you'll get a few days all by yourself," says Bob. "Perhaps even a week."

"I hope," I say. "I just don't want a chomo. And I'd really rather not get another tweaker."

"Hey," says Bob. "Get this. Jimbo is tracking all the meals."

"What?"

"He's writing down every meal that we have, what it is. He's going to do it for a whole month. So he can predict what we'll have at any meal on any day."

"Why?" I ask. "What purpose does it serve? It is what it is."

"Ahhh," says Bob. "That's why you and I don't fit in here." He pauses. "You know," he continues, "if this were a prisoner-of-war facility rather than the county jail, these guys" — he spreads his arms to encompass the orange multitude in the unit — "would survive. You and I would probably die."

I think about that. "You're probably right," I say. "Which is pretty scary."

"I know," nods Bob, turning left. "Anyway, Jimbo has an agenda. Of course he does!"

"What?" I say. I see no advantage in predicting meals. But I am intrigued.

"He's going to start a betting pool," Bob says, grinning at me over his shoulder.

"You mean betting on what we're going to have for, say, dinner?"

"Precisely. And since he has tracked it, the odds are in the house's favor. Just like Vegas." Bob's voice is full of astonished admiration.

"And people will actually bet on this?" I say.

"They'll bet on anything," states Bob.

I shake my head. "You're right." I think about the enterprise involved in this scheme. "You know, Jimbo's a pretty talented guy. He ought to be working for some Fortune 500 company. Give the guy a problem, and he'll come up with a unique answer."

"Yeah," says Bob. "He just needs to be channeled in the right direction."

We keep walking. After another ten laps, Bob says, "Remember when I told you about how Jimbo goes grocery shopping?"

"Yeah?" I say.

Jimbo's audacity is overwhelming. He walks into the local Safeway, grabs a cart, and proceeds to shop. He fills the cart to the top with food. But rather than going through the checkout lane and paying for it, he simply pushes it out the automatic doors. He walks to his car, where he unloads the contents of the cart into his trunk, returns the cart to the cart depot, and drives home. The simple brazenness, the sheer creativity of it, almost blow my mind.

"Well," Bob says. "I've decided that I'm gonna try it sometime."

"You are?"

"Yeah, just as an experiment. When I'm ninety and they tell me I have terminal cancer or something, I'm going to try it. Just to see if it works."

I laugh. "You should. It probably will work. I mean, when you stop and think about it, it's ingenious. Because if they stop you, all you have to do is say you forgot. You have so much on your mind, you forgot."

Bob nods. "Yeah. I wouldn't have thought of it in a million years."

"Me either."

JEFFERSON STILLWELL III

It's 4:25 p.m., and afternoon rec is almost over. I enter my deluxe cell. Disappointment envelops me because my privacy is now over. An orange-clad body occupies the lower bunk. I sigh.

Turning back to the cell door, I push my ID into the rubber molding around the window. Below it resides another ID. I snap it out, read it. Jefferson Stillwell III. I note the year of his birthdate, do the math in my head. He is forty.

I climb up to my bunk, lie down. Movement below, accompanied by a muttering groan.

The hydraulic locks snap into place with an echoing finality.

"Fuck," says a voice.

He stands up, leans against the opposing white wall. A tall figure with curly gray hair, his face is curiously still and composed. Like his hair, his skin carries a gray hue, a kind of ash-colored pollution.

"Hey, man," he says.

"I'm Randy," I reply.

"Jefferson Stillwell — the third," he says, smiling.

I nod. "I'm here for embezzlement," I say. "And, yes, I did it."

"Okay, man," he says, rubbing his hand over his face. Heavy gray stubble sprouts on his face.

"I know I'm not supposed to ask, but what are you in here for?" I say.

"Probation violation," he says.

"Well, what are you on probation for?"

"Drugs, grand theft," he replies. He shrugs broad shoulders.

"And what did you do to violate your probation?"

"Supposedly I stole some copper wire." He laughs. His laugh is lithe and supple, as if it gets a lot of exercise.

"What?"

"There was a bunch of copper wire missing," he explains. "I was standing in a park, and this cop comes along and arrests me. I had nothing on me but my wallet and clothes and my bike."

"Well, how can they arrest you because some copper wire is missing?" I ask. I remember reading something in the paper about millions of dollars worth of copper wire stolen in Stockton.

"I found a roll of wire. It was behind a tree in the park," he says.

"So they arrested you?" I don't get it.

"Yeah. But I didn't have it on me, so they got no case." He begins pacing back and forth like a tiger in a zoo.

"Well, is it worth anything? The wire, I mean."

"Shit, yeah." His eyes glitter with knowledge. "Seventy-five dollars for a twenty-foot length."

"Really?"

"Yeah."

"Well, where does it come from? I mean, how do you get twenty feet of copper wire?"

"You know those light poles on the street?"

"I guess so. I don't live in Stockton."

"The wire is underground. You just pull it out and take it to the recycling center. Seventy-five bucks," he says. "Easy money."

"And that's what you do?"

"Sometimes."

"How do you get it out if it's underground?"

He makes a clenching motion with his right hand. "With wire cutters. You cut the wire at the base of the pole, then pull it out. You gotta use gloves 'cuz it'll cut the shit out of your hands, yanking it out of the insulation." As he tells me, he is showing me, making pulling motions with his hands and shoulders.

"Jesus," I comment.

"It's not so bad," he brags. "Couple hours of work will get you maybe $500. Then score some white, spin out for four or five days." He nods, smiles, adds, "The good life, man."

"What's white?"

His head darts back in disbelief. "Crystal meth, man." He smacks his lips.

I look at the ceiling, then back at him. "You like it?"

He gives me a huge grin. "I love it, man. It's the juice."

I think about this for a minute or two while Jefferson Stillwell — the third — takes a piss. He pisses like a horse, a long, powerful stream. After the toilet sucks it all down, I ask, "Got any kids?"

"Five," he says.

"Oh, so you're married."

"Divorced, man. Can't live with 'em, can't live without it. You know, pussy, man."

I nod, as if he's just delivered some magnificent truth. "You live in Stockton?"

"Yeah. I used to own two houses. But I sold one to buy white, and the other I gave to my son " He's still pacing back and forth. He looks over at me. "Hey, man. When do we get out?"

"We just came in," I tell him. "We won't get out until tonight, around 9:30."

"Fuck! I could really use a cigarette." He stops pacing. "You know, we used to be out all day long in this place."

"You mean here, in PC?"

"Yeah, man. Out all day. Cell doors open and everything, man."

The pacing renews; the big cat on the prowl.

"You've been here before, then?"

"Oh, yeah, man. Three, four times. Back in" — he lays his head back, looks at the ceiling, thinking — "'94 and '95."

"That was ten years ago," I say. "I guess things change."

"Yeah, man. I worked in the kitchen. Baker's helper. I wound up practically running the place."

"What was that like?"

"Pretty cool, man. Except for the early hours. Getting up to bake shit about two in the morning."

"You mean they actually bake the shit they serve?" I ask.

"Yeah, man. Anyway, they used to. I don't know about now. You could eat all you wanted too. Whenever you wanted, man. But only if you worked in the kitchen."

"That sounds cool," I say. "What were you in for then?" I ask.

He stops pacing, looks at me. "Assault and battery," he brags. "Twenty-nine assault and batteries."

"What? How do you get twenty-nine assault and batteries?"

"I was a collector for some drug dudes," he explains. "Somebody'd owe 'em money, I go round and collect." In a sad voice, he adds, "Sometimes they didn't want to come across."

"So you?" I ask, leading the witness.

"So I'd have to get mean about it." A superwicked smile blooms on his face. Lots of white teeth gape at me. "One time I had to use a baseball bat on a guy." The memory pleases him. He swings an invisible bat, down low, as if at someone's legs.

"Well, twenty-nine assault and batteries probably carry some stiff sentence, doesn't it?" I say.

I am horrified. This man is bragging about this stuff as if he's proud of it. As if he won a Nobel Prize.

"No, man. They couldn't ever prove anything. Just arrested me. I'd be out in a few days, sometimes a month. It was a nice vacation from the old lady, if you know what I mean." He laughs.

I think about this. "Well, where do you live now? With your son?"

"No, man. I gave the house to him so I wouldn't have to pay my old lady any child support. All legal like and shit." He pauses. "Now I just crash wherever, man."

"You mean you don't live anywhere?" I say. I don't get it — again. This is a lifestyle beyond my comprehension.

"Right now, man, I'm living with Angie. My girl. She works at the docks. Makes good money. Twenty-two dollars an hour." He makes the lip-smacking noise again.

"You gonna marry her?"

"No, man. Well, maybe. She's really nice. Takes care of me. Cooks for me. Cleans. Does the wash. Buys me new clothes." He looks at me with a strange intimacy. "I'm not sure I love her, though. She's a good fuck and all, but I like to fuck a lot of different chicks, ya know, man?"

He gazes at me for affirmation. So I nod, as if I agree.

"I got another girl, Crystal, that I like too," he tells me. "She's hot, man! Twenty-two years old. Tight body. Great piece of ass." His face falls. "But she might be pregnant."

"Is it yours?"

"Yeah, man."

"Well, then, maybe you should marry her?" I say, tossing it out to see if it's caught.

"Maybe," he nods. He throws himself on his bunk. "This shit is giving me a headache, man," he says to me.

I hear him roll over.

"I'm gonna take a nap, man. That's what I need. A nap."

I lie there, staring up at the ceiling, thinking about copper wire that goes for seventy-five dollars per twenty-foot length, twenty-nine assault and batteries, a pregnant girlfriend, five kids, two houses. I can't explain. In the end, I just shake my head to myself, begin reading.

KICKING ASS

_____

_____

_____

Later that night, during rec, I'm behind Bob, walking, turning left.

Bob looks back over his shoulder at me, says, "Did you hear about Jimbo?"

"No. What'd he do now?" I'm already smiling in anticipation.

"Dragged Chevy into a cell, where he proceeded to kick his fucking ass," Bob says.

"What? Why?" I say. I have this vision of a crazed heavyweight boxer pummeling a frenetic welterweight.

"Because," says Bob, in a "what-else" tone, "Chevy disrespected him."

"Who told you that?" I say.

"Jimbo."

"Well, how did Chevy disrespect him?" I say. I want a precise definition of jailhouse respect, both in its lexical form and in its function.

"I don't know," Bob says. "All I can get out of Jimbo is that Chevy didn't show him respect."

"Well, were they playing cards or what? I mean, I don't think they occupy the same social circle, do they?"

Bob turns left. I cut the corner to close the gap. Todd, the trustee, is now standing at the railing. Bob and I nod to him as we pass.

"Seems Jimbo was playing cards with Gene and company,

and Chevy was watching. Chevy said something, I don't know what. And Jimbo jumped up and had words with him. Whatever he said, it pissed Chevy off. So Chevy pushed him."

"Oh, yeah," I say. I shake my head from side to side, like a wily horse. "That would not score points with Jimbo." I laugh, just picturing it.

"Correct," Bob says. "Jimbo grabbed him, pulled him to the nearest cell, shut the door, and they went at it."

We pass Todd. "You talking about Jimbo and Chevy?" Todd asks.

"Yeah," Bob says.

We keep walking.

"I guess Chevy held his own," Todd says, speaking just loud enough so we can hear him.

"Jimbo said Chevy's quick," says Bob, "but he punches like a girl. Jimbo said he couldn't even feel it."

"Well, who won?" I say.

"Jimbo had Chevy backed up against the wall," Bob says. "Then Chevy jumped up on the desk and was kicking at Jimbo's head. Otherwise, Jimbo would've killed him."

"I heard that too," Todd says as we pass him. "Chevy was all cut up. His face looks like Jimbo took a knife to him." Todd laughs.

"Blood was everywhere," Bob says. "Jimbo had blood all over his oranges, and it was on the walls in the cell."

"Who stopped it?" I say. "The guards?"

"No," says Bob. "It was Thomas Herbert's cell. He asked the guard to pop his cell door. When he did, Gene Davis went in and grabbed Chevy, hustled him out."

"You mean the cell was locked?" I say. I am impressed by the size of Jimbo's balls: dragging another inmate into someone else's cell, shutting the cell door, which locks. Like gladiators in the Roman circus, only reduced to eighty-four square feet.

"Yeah," says Bob.

"That takes balls," I say.

"Or paranoid schizophrenia," laughs Bob. He laughs so hard drool slips out of his mouth. He wipes it with the back of his hand.

Bob stops walking when he reaches Todd. I stop, cross my arms.

"Chevy's pretty banged up," Todd says.

"So is Jimbo," says Bob. "He's got a pretty good shiner. That's why he's wearing his hair parted down the middle, to cover his face."

"Won't the guards notice?" I say.

"They already did," Bob says. "On rounds, one of 'em looked in the cell and saw Jimbo lying on his bunk reading. The guard opened the door, asked him if he was okay."

"What'd he say?" I ask.

"Told the guard he banged it on the metal step on the bunk, you know, that little piece that sticks out?"

I nod. "Sounds plausible," I say.

"Yeah," agrees Todd.

"Yeah," chuckles Bob. "That Jimbo's always got all the angles covered."

"Are they gonna go at it again?" I say.

"No. They shook hands," says Todd. "The drama is over." He pauses, thinking. "Only in jail," he adds, like a philosopher.

"Yeah," Bob says, "never a dull moment."

CIAO, MAN

_____

_____

_____

_____

Jefferson Stillwell — the third — receives a sentence of two years in prison for probation violation: failure to report to his probation officer. All of the other charges are dismissed for lack of evidence. Three days after he is sentenced, unscheduled, the bus arrives to transport him to DVI, where he will be processed.

It is 8:30 a.m., and I am lying in my penthouse bunk, not thinking, just being linear — killing time. In jail, there is no later, only now. And what they will do to you. How much more "now" they will give you.

Jefferson snores below me.

Machine gun pops of our cell's door locks shock my linear now. Jefferson rolls over, goes back to sleep. I jump down from my bunk, push the door open, peer down at the podium.

"Stillwell?" yells the CO. He is at the podium, at the computer.

"No, sir," I say. "I'll get him."

"Tell him to roll it up. His ride is here," says the CO

"Yes, sir."

"Jefferson. Jefferson," I say. My voice cuts into the armor of his sleep.

"Yeah, man. What?" he mumbles, tightening his crossed arms across his chest.

"Get up! The bus is here to take you to DVI," I tell him. "Roll up your stuff."

He jumps up, naked from the waist up. He dons his T-shirt, his orange blouse, his sweatshirt. His shaved head wears a fuzzy gray skull-cap, where the hair is growing, like a bonnet on an old lady. "Fuck," he says. "I didn't think they'd come so soon, man."

Slipping his jail-issue white socks into his jail-issue rubber slides, he reaches for his stuff. A small plastic bag sits on the desk. It contains the totality of his personal property: a four-inch toothbrush, two jail-issue lozenges of Colgate toothpaste, a black plastic comb, two letters, his pink copy of his court papers.

The court clerk retains the white and yellow copies.

He looks at me, wearing a distinctly soft expression.

My insides in the grip of a full winter, I am scared for him.

"Gotta go, man," he says. "Be sure to give my property release forms to the guard. So Crystal can pick up my things."

He couldn't decide to whom he should release his property, the clothes he had on when he was booked. It hangs in a green mesh bag in the jail property room, along with two thousand other bags holding relics from another existence. Like artifacts from an archaeological site. Initially, he released them to Sharla. Then changed his mind for the umpteenth time. In the end, last night, gripping his pencil like a five-year-old boy, he scribbled Crystal's name on the blank line.

"Stillwell!" booms the guard from the podium. "Hurry it up. They can't wait all day."

"I will," I say.

"Thanks, man," Jefferson says. "Thanks for everything."

My hand is engulfed by his. Grabbing me, he hugs me, forcing me to exhale. I smell his smell. Stale tobacco, fermented sweat. Jefferson Stillwell — the third — effluvium.

I hug him hard. Emotion swells my organs. I know I will not see him again. I will not hear from him. Compatible as cell mates, we are incompatible in the real world. Yet shared suffering has made us friends.

"Stillwell! Move it!" yells the co.

"See ya, man," Jefferson says.

"Take care of yourself," I say.

He is gone.

The hydraulic lock plunges into place. I watch out the cell door window as he bounds down the steps, a smooth, gray figure with a small plastic bag.

SOLITAIRE

_____

_____

_____

Three days later, I greet a new cell mate. Chris Murphy. Tall, dark hair, forever bouncing his leg. Like a nervous chicken.

"Hi," Chris says, entering the cell.

I nod.

"How long you been here?" he asks.

"Five months," I say.

"What for?"

"Embezzlement. And, yes, I'm guilty," I say in a direct tone. It is a challenge.

He tosses his bedroll on the lower bunk. "You got any paper? And a pencil I could use?" he says.

Another mooch, I tell myself. "I guess so," I say. "What? You wanna write a letter?"

"No. Make cards."

"Cards?"

"Yeah, playing cards. I play solitaire. It's my thing," he says.

"Okay. Let me get 'em." I open my drawer, take a pencil from my white Styrofoam cup, my pencil holder. Holding my yellow legal tablet, I turn to him. "How many pages?" I say.

"Three or four," he says.

I tear off four pages.

He seats himself on the red plastic chair at the desk, begins folding and tearing the pages into three-inch squares. After counting out fifty-two of them, he stacks them. One at a time, rapidly, he numbers them then assigns suits to them.

As he concentrates, I interrogate him. "What're you here for?"

"A bullshit probation violation," he says.

"What does that mean?" I ask. "What're you on probation for?"

"I don't know," he says in a whining, tinny voice, one he's familiar with.

"C'mon," I say, "what'd you do to get put on probation? I mean, they don't just put you on probation."

"Really," he says. "I didn't do anything. This chick, her name is Jessica. She's crazy, man. She got this restraining order put on me. For talking to her."

"Who is this chick?" I ask. "Your girlfriend?"

"No, just a friend, a chick from school."

"What school?"

"Delta College," he says. "She goes there too."

His homemade cards are done. He moves to his bunk, lies on his side, takes his new cards for a test drive. After shuffling them, he fans them out in a pattern, starts playing some game.

"Okay," I say. "So you attend Delta College. What're you majoring in?"

"I wanna be a teacher," he says. A bitter note enters his voice. "Only that won't happen now 'cuz they won't hire a teacher with a felony."

"What felony?" I say. "You're on probation, not parole. So it must be a misdemeanor. And most probation violations turn out to be misdemeanors too."

I look at him. He looks at the cards.

"What'd you do to this crazy chick?"

He turns a card over, puts one down. "I told you. She's crazy. She does this to people — gets them thrown into jail. She thinks it's fun."

I don't get it. "How do you know this chick?" I ask.

"From school. Lots of my friends know her friends, so we all know each other, sorta hang together," he explains.

"Is she good looking?" I say.

"Yeah, man. She's hot," he tells me, glancing up at me. Rolling onto his back, he puts his hands behind his head, stares at the gray steel bottom of my bunk.

"So are you in love with her?" I ask.

"Yes," he says. "No," he amends.

"Yes or no?"

"Well . . . I guess so," he says. "She wants to marry me, have kids with me."

I feel like a gaudy old whore at a sorority party: mislaid. "She told you this?" I say, my brow furrowed.

"Yeah. Marched right up to me and said she wanted to marry me," Chris says.

"And she's somehow responsible for you being here?"

"Yeah. She got this restraining order against me. And I sent her an e-mail telling her I loved her. And they arrested me."

He rolls back onto his side, shuffles the cards, laying them out.

"Do you think they can trace the e-mail? Use it against me?" Chris says.

"Easily," I say. "I mean, you sent it, right?"

"Yeah. But it was from my mom's computer. I don't think they can access her computer, can they?"

"Look," I say. "They can do anything they want. And tracking an e-mail is kid stuff for them."

"Shit," he says, laying down a card.

"How come this crazy chick got a restraining order against you?" I say.

"She said I was following her around," he says. Picks up the cards, shuffles, starts anew.

"You mean like stalking her?" I say.

"That's what she said. Only I wasn't. And it wouldn't have worked except her father is some rich guy. Some kind of big businessman, involved in politics and shit."

"So you're stalking this chick, or at least that's what she

maintains. And then she gets a restraining order against you. And then you send her an e-mail telling her you love her. Is that right?" I say.

"And then they arrest me," he says. "But I didn't do anything. This Jessica, the crazy chick, just wants to fuck with me 'cuz she's crazy." He jumps off the bunk, walks to the toilet, spits. Then spits again.

As he's going back to his bunk, I say, "You been in jail before?"

"Once," he says.

"What for?" I say. "And when?"

"About a year ago. I was driving this Jeep I just bought and crashed into another car."

"Why is that a jail offense?" I ask. "People have car wrecks every day, and none of them goes to jail for it. They just call their insurance company."

"I didn't have a license, or insurance, and the car I hit was parked," he tells me.

I shake my head. "You don't have a license? How old are you?"

"Twenty-three," he says.

Twenty-three years old, just like Josh, just like Jimbo. I don't get it. "How come you don't have a license? Most kids get them when they're sixteen."

"I'm kind of not a very good driver," he says, embarrassment skimming along his features.

"Okay," I say. "So they tossed you in jail for no license and no insurance? That doesn't seem right."

"I know, man," he says earnestly. "I didn't do anything wrong. They just showed up at my mom's house and arrested me."

"Why were you at your mom's house?" I say.

"After I hit the car, I left," Chris says.

"What do you mean, left? You mean you left the scene of the accident?"

"Yeah."

"You just took off? Without trying to find the owner of the car you hit?"

"It wasn't damaged that bad," he says. "Besides, I didn't do anything."

Now I get it. "So how long were you in jail then?" I ask.

"Three months. I got core-capped out after three months," he says. He thinks about that for a second. "Maybe they'll core-cap me out?" he says, looking up at me expectantly.

"Maybe. Anything is possible. It's not a violent crime. So you never know," I say.

My words energize him.

"Have they been core-capping people out of here?" he says, rolling onto his back.

"Every day," I say. "The place is running over maximum capacity."

"Every day, huh?"

"Yeah," I say.

"Cool. Then I might be out in a week or so, maybe less."

"Maybe. Like I said, anything's possible."

"Cool. Because I need to work on my scooter."

"Your scooter?" I say, imagining one of those two-wheels-with-a-handle gizmos that kids ride.

"Yeah," he says, excitement in his voice. "It's my thing."

"What kind of scooter is it?" I ask.

"A Vespa," he says. "A 1983 Vespa, with a 200cc motor." Pride balloons his voice.

"Oh," I say. "I've seen those. In fact, I rode one once, in the Bahamas. They're pretty cool."

"Yeah," he agrees. "I don't like the new ones. I like the old ones. The new ones look gay. But they have more power."

"So you bought one, huh?" I can't think of anything else to say.

"Yeah. It was in terrible shape. I fixed it up. Went through the motor, all the electrics, painted it."

"Huh," I say. "So you're a mechanic?"

"No, not really. But I like to tinker with things, figure them out. Fix 'em up. Like I like old bicycles too. I've got this really nice one. Painted it candy apple red."

"Kinda like what's his name? Pee Wee Herman," I say. "That funky bike he rode in the movie?"

"Mine's better than that," he says, disparagement in his voice. "It's even older and has sleeker lines to it."

"So you like old things?"

"Yeah. Don't ask me why. There's just something about 'em. More style, I guess." He shrugs as if it doesn't matter.

"Well, then," I laugh. "You ought to get along with me, 'cuz I'm an OG."

"Old gangster," he says.

"Old guy," I correct him.

"Either way," he says. "It can be either old gangster or old guy."

I think about this. "What's your mom think about all this?" I ask, holding my hands out to indicate our cell, the jail.

"She's gonna be pissed," he says. "She thinks I'm a loser."

"Will she bail you out?"

"No. She doesn't make much money. And even if she did, she wouldn't."

"What's she do?" I say.

"She's a secretary at an elementary school."

"Any other brothers or sisters?"

"A sister," he says, grimacing.

"Older or younger?"

"She's twenty-one," he tells me. "She's a bitch. Only interested in her car and clothes and partying."

"Nothing wrong with that."

He leaps off his bunk, goes to the toilet, spits. Then spits again. "Yeah, there is," he says. "She's got nothing but her car and her clothes."

"Well, what's your ambition?" I ask.

"I was gonna be a teacher," he says. "Now I'll probably work construction."

"Pays good," I say.

"Not really," he says. "I did it for a while. Worked for a roofer. All I did was haul stuff up a ladder all day long."

"You quit to go to school?"

"No. I quit 'cuz it sucked. Just stopped showing up. They called, left a message I was fired."

"Uhhmm," I say.

"What'd you embezzle?" he asks me, plopping down another ersatz card.

"You know," I say, "if you have any money on your books, you can buy some real cards from the commissary."

"I know," he says. He shrugs. "I'll just take some from downstairs. They cost too much. I can use the money for a pouch of tobacco."

"If they find 'em in the cell, they'll write you up," I tell him.

"They won't find 'em," he says in an assured tone. Laying down two cards, he looks up at me. "So. What'd you embezzle?"

"I sold some property that didn't belong to me."

"Like what?"

"A house. A commercial building," I say.

"Shit, man." He pauses his shuffling, glances up at me. "How much?"

"How much what?"

"How much did you get for 'em?"

"All together?" I ask.

Chris nods.

"Around $750,000."

A whistle escapes from his pursed lips. "Shit, man! And you're still here?" He leans his head back, thinking about all that money. "If I had that kinda money, I'd be long gone," he says.

"I didn't actually ever have the entire amount in my hands," I tell him. "Most of it was recovered when they seized my accounts."

"How much did you actually spend?"

"Over time, around 300 grand," I say.

"Still," he says. "You should've taken off for Europe. Or invested it." He sits up, Indian style. "Yeah, you should have invested it."

"Stolen money? I didn't embezzle it to make investments. I wanted to spend it."

Lying back down, he shuffles once more. "Yeah, I guess. But still. You shoulda just split. You could go pretty far on 300 grand," he tells me.

"Look," I say, a little irritated that a Vespa-riding, solitaire-playing stalker is now advising me on the nuances of fraud, embezzlement, and the distribution and allocation of derived funds. "Three hundred grand is not — ." I stop, think about it. "Let me rephrase that: even if I'd had the entire amount — the whole $750,000 — in cash — in my hands — which I didn't — that is not very much money in today's world. I could buy a nice middle-class house and a nice middle-class car. And that's it. I couldn't even afford to furnish my middle-class house with bargain-basement, kitschy furniture.

"And if I'd run — which I did, during a brief moment of insanity — not only would the money have lasted — at best — maybe two years — but I'd also be looking over my shoulder for the rest of my life. Plus I wouldn't even be able to get a job at McDonald's.

"So," I say, cherishing my little spark of preaching, "it was a bad idea, which was poorly implemented."

Unimpressed, Chris plops a three of hearts down on his bunk, jumps up, walks to the toilet, and spits. Twice.

Back on his bunk, his white-stockinged foot begins flapping against his other foot, like one of those flippers on a pinball machine.

"What's with your foot always bouncing around?" I say. "You nervous?"

"No," he says, looking up from his cards. "It's bouncing leg syndrome."

"You're kidding me."

"No. That's what it's called," he asserts.

I shake my head to myself. "Okay," I say.

He rolls over onto his back, gazes up at the bottom of my bunk. "Now that I think about it," he says, "I don't think they can produce anything against me but that e-mail. And since it's my mom's computer, I don't think they can get it." He nods to himself. "So I don't think they can hold me very long. Either that or I'll core-cap out in no time."

"Maybe," I say.

Back on his side, he shuffles his stopgap cards. "You have a private attorney or a public defender?" he says.

"Private," I say. "If I had a public defender, I'd probably be looking at four to six years."

"Yeah? How come?"

"'Cuz public defenders are so overworked they can't spend any time on your case," I say. "Besides which most of them suck, although I have heard of some good ones." I shrug. "Mostly, though, they don't care 'cuz they don't have time to care."

I look at him as he concentrates on his cards. "You got the money to hire an attorney?" I say.

"No," he says.

"What about your mom?"

"No way," he laughs with a scoff. "How much you pay yours?"

"So far, around twenty thousand," I say.

He laughs. "Fuck me, man. That's a lot of money for an attorney."

"Yeah," I nod. "But it beats prison for six years."

Chris leaps up, spits in the toilet. This time three times. Back on his side, feet dancing, he shuffles. "I'll have to go with a public defender," he tells me. "But since I didn't do any-thing — and they can't produce any evidence — they'll probably just cut me loose in a few days."

"When is your arraignment?" I say.

"I don't know," he says.

"You don't know?"

"They told me, but I can't remember," he says, laying down four cards. "Sometime next week."

"Umm," I say.

Bored, I climb up to my penthouse bunk. Lying on my back with my eyes closed, I wish I were anywhere but here. Every few minutes I hear the rustle of an orange-clad body rising off the bottom bunk, followed by the double-splat of saliva spanking toilet water.

IRISH SNOW

Later that night, evening rec, Bob and I are walking, giving wet fellatio to our sweet and sour suckers.

"What's going on with Snow's case?" I say.

Bob knows everything, hears all the juicy gossip, for two reasons: one, his bunkie is Jimbo, a bottomless pit of data who, since he is always on the make, needs to know everything about everybody; two, Bob does homework packages for all the inmates, mostly the gangbangers, who are trying to get their GEDs but are too ignorant, too lazy, and too busy doing nothing to actually do the work themselves.

One candy bar per package is Bob's fee. In the jailhouse economic system, Bob is a rich man, pulling down ten to twenty candy bars per week.

"They offered him a deal," says Bob around his sucker. "Twelve months local time. But he has to take a strike and hand over his passports."

I nod. "Well, how long has he been here?"

Bob pulls his sucker out of his mouth, one of the blue-yellow-green ones. They're the best. Next best are the orange-red-yellow ones. Or maybe the red-yellow-white ones, or the green-white ones, which taste like sour granny apples. The worst are the blue-white suckers 'cuz they're too sweet. They begin by being cloying and eventually become asphyxiating.

"Eight months," Bob says.

"Then if he takes the deal, he'll be out tomorrow," I say, thinking half of twelve months is six. He's already done eight.

"Almost," says Bob. "But his crime involves violence, so he has to do eighty-five percent."

"Yeah," I say. "I forgot."

We turn left, dodging orange-clad bodies as they move in and out of the yard door.

"I'm sure Snow has a problem with it, though," I say.

"Of course," laughs Bob. "He doesn't want to take a strike, which everybody knows. And he doesn't want to give up his passports."

"Well, I thought he could get another Irish passport pretty easy," I say.

"So he says," Bob says. "But you know Snow. The whole thing just makes him angry. Just like everything does."

We jog to the left, pass the phones. As we're about to make a hard left, I see Snow waddling down the ramp.

"Speak of the devil," I say to Bob.

Travis Snow is a twenty-eight-year-old Pillsbury doughboy. With an anger problem that makes a rabid dog seem like a cute little puppy. In here for some kind of sex crime, no one knows precisely what he did. Maybe Todd, but he's not saying. Bob and I suspect he molested one or both of his step-daughters. And he had a gun on him when they arrested him.

Born in Ireland, he lived in San Bernadino, where he worked for the railroad. Made good money, about $75,000 a year, according to him.

"Hey, Bob," Snow says as he stops.

"Travis," Bob acknowledges and keeps walking.

I follow in Bob's wake.

"You make a decision yet?" says Bob.

"No," says Snow. Anger leaks from his voice like water from a sieve. "The whole thing sucks. I didn't do it, and they want to strike me. And my fucking attorney says it's a good deal. That I should take it. I told her she's a fucking stupid cunt. I'm gonna fire that cunt."

"Well, Travis," Bob says around his sucker, "it is a pretty good deal. You'd be out in no time. Then you can get on with your life. Go wherever you want."

"I don't see it that way," snarls Snow. "If I take a strike, I won't be able to work again. Fuck! I didn't do anything anyway."

"Look, Travis," Bob says in a soothing, logical voice. "The important thing is to just get out of here. Then you can decide what you want to do." Bob bites into his sucker with an audible crunch. "You can go back to Ireland, or maybe — like the guy told you — you still might get your job back."

"Not with a fucking strike I won't," Snow whines. "The fucking railroad said they'd try but couldn't guarantee anything — if I take a strike. Without a strike, I'm guaranteed to get my job back." Snow is becoming visibly disturbed. The black inferno of rage surrounds him.

"I thought you wanted to go back to Ireland anyway," I say.

"Yeah, but they want me to give up my passports," Snow says.

"So take the deal, then just leave," I say.

"I could," Snow says. "But it just pisses me off. I didn't do anything, and they keep hitting me with shit. And that fucking bitch took all my money, so I can't even get a plane ticket."

The "fucking bitch" is his ex-wife, who divorced him, emptied his bank account after he molested one or both of her daughters. Go figure, right?

"I read your story," Bob says, changing the subject. "It's really good. I like it."

"What story is that?" I ask.

Snow stands in the middle of the anteroom, which leads to the yard, turning in a tight circle as we walk around him.

"He's writing a story, kind of a fairy tale for his daughter's birthday," Bob says.

"Yeah?" I say, looking at Snow.

"Yeah," says Snow. "It's got dragons and knights and trolls and shit."

"Cool," I say. "How long is it?"

"Twelve pages so far," Snow tells me. "I'm drawing pictures and shit too."

"You really like it?" I ask Bob.

"Yeah, I did," Bob says. "And — don't take this the wrong way, Snow — but I didn't expect to. But it's very well written. A real story."

Snow smiles. "When you're done with it, give it to Radic," he says. He looks at me. "Maybe you'd like to read it too?"

"Sure," I say.

"Oh, I'm done with it," says Bob, looking over his shoulder at me. "I'll give it to you tonight before we're locked down."

"Sure," I say, not looking at him because I don't really want to read it.

"Just be sure to give it back to me," says Snow.

"Okay," I say, turning left behind Bob.

"Fucking shit is what it is," barks Snow, coming back to his legal predicament. "It's not a deal. It's a fuck you! I'm not gonna take it."

Bob looks over his shoulder at me, rolls his eyes. "C'mon, Travis," Bob says, "just don't think about it. Let it ride in the back of your mind so it grows on you."

"Fuck that shit!" says Snow. "Fuck 'em all!" He stands there, turning in place, immersed in monomaniacal fury.

"You going out to smoke?" I ask, reminding him of his ultimate goal.

"Yeah," he says. He waddles out the yard door.

"Whew," I say. "That is one angry man."

"I know," Bob says. "He can't see past it. He needs some kind of therapy. Antidepressants or something."

"Yeah, but he won't get it in here," I say. "Therapy, I mean," I add. "He's probably already on antidepressants. Hell, everybody else is."

"I know, I know," Bob says. "Ya know, he kinda reminds me of Mike Wilson."

"Mike Wilson? I don't see any similarities."

Mike Wilson was one of Bob's former cell mates. He was here for about six weeks, just before Christmas. A talented artist, he'd draw you a card, birthday or Christmas, in return for a soup or candy bar.

He was visiting our plush facility because of drugs, attempted murder. He tried to run over his ex-wife and her new husband with his car. Of course, the crystal meth spiraling through his brain cells made it seem like a really good idea at the moment.

Unfortunately, Mike had tried the same maneuver before, fifteen years earlier. Not on his wife, though. On a police officer, who had almost died. So Mike was looking at a second strike. And a long sentence.

"I see many," Bob says. "They're both manic-depressive, or whadda they call it now? Oh, yeah, bipolar. They're both bipolar, with only high school educations; both feel betrayed in some sense by their wives; and both of them sustain anger at truly subterranean levels. Anger which erupts like Krakatoa at the slightest provocation."

"They're really fucked up is what you're saying?" I deadpan.

Bob laughs. "That's another, valid way to state it."

We continue walking. After ten more laps, I ask, "How's your trial going?"

"So far, so good," Bob says. "The DA is still calling witnesses. After she finishes, then it's our turn. And my attorney has fifty-two witnesses lined up and ready to go."

"Fifty-two!" I exclaim. "That seems like an awful lot."

"I thought so too," Bob says. "But more than half of them are either police officers who were at the scene, rescue personnel, like ambulance drivers, or emergency room doctors and nurses."

"Oh," I say. "Well, are you getting nervous? I mean, what does your attorney say?"

"He's already planning a victory celebration," Bob says, smiling.

"He's that confident?" I ask.

"Yeah," says Bob. "Our forensics team is the best in California, and my attorney assures me that the evidence they have gathered is irrefutable."

Bob looks over his shoulder at me, anxiety in his eyes. "But the DA is out for blood. She keeps distorting everything. I can't believe how she lies. Out and out lies." He shakes his head in amazement. "I always thought they were after justice. But it's not about that," he says, waving his hands. "Remember that book you loaned me? *The Bonfire of the Vanities?*"

"Yeah."

"It's just like that," he says. "It's all about her career. How many convictions she gets so she can look good in the papers. She doesn't care whether I did it or not."

Bob dodges around Jimmy Benson, who plows toward the phones like an ebony supertanker.

I stop rather than get in Benson's way. I do not mess with homies. Charged with triple murder, Jimmy Benson is Crips or Bloods — has cryptic, cursive tattoos on his neck and face. He neither reads nor writes, can't tell time.

Cutting the corner, I fall in behind Bob.

"This is my life we're talking about," Bob declares earnestly. "And the DA is only concerned with managing her career."

"Like what is she saying?" I ask.

"She says I planned it all out," Bob says, looking back at me. "She says I killed my wife then turned the gun on myself to make it look like she shot me. Like I actually shot myself in the side. That all of that was premeditated."

"Well, that's bullshit," I say. "Who in their right mind is going to do that? If you missed, just a little, you'd end up killing yourself."

"I know. I know," Bob pleads. "I just can't grasp it. The way she lies about me, makes me sound like all I did was abuse my wife, like I was some kind of supercontrolling monster." He waggles his head in dismay. "I cannot believe this is happening to me."

He looks gray, a waxy gray color presses out from him, and hollow. One of the hollow men.

A desperate, chaotic hum enters his voice, sudden, radical, irrational. "I loved my wife. We had our problems, I admit. But I never struck her, never abused her. I gave her everything she wanted. And now this."

I don't know what to say.

"It's utterly unbelievable," Bob chokes out.

"Well, the forensics should disprove that, shouldn't it?" I say.

Bob says something, but I cannot make it out because Benson is rapping into the phone — some original gangsta rap song of his. He calls his mother, sings his rap songs to her. As he sings, he thumps out a bass beat on the wall. And no one, not even the CO, has the nerve to tell him to shut the fuck up.

Bob stops, turns around to me. "Let's move over here so we can talk." He glares at Benson's jiving hulk — 350 pounds of dancing, illiterate, mean-ass meat.

We walk to the corner, near the ramp.

"What were you saying?" I ask.

"I said that the DA keeps emphasizing to the jury the size difference between my wife and myself. That I weigh 220 pounds and that she only weighed 110 pounds. That she was five foot two, and I'm six two."

"That's not relevant to anything," I scoff. "Just because you're the size you are doesn't mean you killed her."

"I know," Bob says, a crabbed look across his face. "God! I cannot believe this is happening to me. I mean, I was gainfully employed, paid my taxes, raised two children, never broke the law. And now I'm in here."

He looks around the unit, as if he's living in an orange-hued version of Dante's *Inferno*. Again, this place has the potential to ravage you, to make you less than you are. It's as if by merely being here, by seeing it, some part of yourself vanishes from you. And you can't get it back.

"Not exactly paradise, is it?" I say.

"What?" says a deep, mellow voice. "This? Not paradise? And here I thought I was on vacation at Club Med."

Todd, the trustee, stands by the rail, two feet directly above us.

I smile. Bob grimaces.

"More like *Paradise Lost*," says Bob.

"Just look," Todd says, indicating the rapping Benson, "free entertainment and the finest cuisine."

"Just think," I say.

"Yeah," Bob says sourly.

"What's up?" Todd asks. "How come you OGs aren't walking?"

"We're discussing Bob's trial," I say.

"I've been wondering about that," Todd says. "I read about it in the paper when it started. But they haven't had anything since then."

Thomas White arrives. "Buk, buk, buk," he clucks, standing five feet behind Todd.

Todd turns. "Go away."

"Buk, buk, buk," clucks Thomas.

"Look, Thomas," Todd says, "I don't have time for you right now. Whatever you want, talk to me later."

Thomas moves off. The chicken sounds fade.

Todd rolls his eyes at us. "What about your trial?" he asks Bob.

"Nothing," Bob says. "I'd really rather not dwell on it anymore."

"Not going well?" Todd asks.

"About as expected," Bob says. "Only I can't understand why the DA is so vindictive."

"That's their job," Todd says. "Face it, Bob, the system is the way it is. Good, bad, or otherwise. And once you're in it, it's hard to break out. Just look at me," he waves his hand toward himself. "I been wrestling with this now for four years — what with all the time in and out of jail."

He gazes at something far, far away, himself maybe. A few moments later, he returns, "That's long enough. I'll be out of here and done with this in one more month. Then back to my family, my business, my life."

"Buk, buk, buuuk," clucks Thomas White, returning from wherever it is he goes during rec.

Todd rolls his eyes. Arms crossed over his chest, he turns and looks at Thomas. "Go away."

Thomas sniffs, making a noise like a Shop Vac sucking up water from a garage floor. "Buk, buk, buuuk, buk," he clucks.

"Go. Away. Thomas."

"Uh huh. Uh huh," says Thomas. He is scrawny, all of him: his hair, his lank pencil mustache, his body — everything. Scrawny and unkempt. He snorts up another wad of mucous, swallows. "This heren T-shirt ya gave me is torn and thin," he says, pulling at the neck of his white T-shirt. "I want anothern."

Todd smiles graciously. A practicing Christian, he always does what he thinks Jesus would do. "No, Thomas," he says. "Not until laundry. Which is tomorrow. If I got something for everyone whenever they wanted it, I'd never stop. You'll have to wait until tomorrow."

"Uh huh. Uh huh," says Thomas. "This heren one is in sad shape. You need to be more'n careful how you hand 'em out."

For all his what-would-Jesus-doism, Todd doles out the good laundry to the inmates he likes, who are mostly white or supercool gangbangers whom Todd likes to pal around with. The chomos, like Thomas White, get shit.

Todd is a partial racist; he learned how to be one when he did his ninety-day op at San Quentin Prison. He told me that at San Quentin a black trustee would come along with a cart full of clean laundry. Todd told the guy what he needed. The guy just passed him by.

As he did, Todd said, "Now I see how it is."

The trustee nodded and said, "That's how it is."

The next day at San Quentin, a white trustee came along with the laundry cart. The black inmates told the guy what they needed. He just passed them by. When the guy got to Todd, well, Todd got the best because Todd's white.

As Todd got his clean laundry, he said to the trustee, "Now I see how it is."

The trustee nodded and said, "That's how it is."

And that's how it is.

Todd nods to Thomas White. Todd oozes patience. "I will, Thomas. I'll be more careful from now on. Thanks for bringing it to my attention. I'll get you a new one — brand new — tomorrow at laundry. Remind me."

He turns back to us. "Everybody always wants something," he says. "I learned to draw the line a long time ago. Unless it's an emergency, they can wait."

"Coo, coo, coo," gurgles Thomas White from behind Todd. His head bobs like a pigeon. "Coo, coo, coo."

Just now Thomas doesn't want anything, he's just there, cooing.

Todd turns to him. "Thomas, why don't you and Duane do me a favor?"

"Coo, coo, coo, coo," he trills, looking at Todd.

I look at Todd too: his clean-shaven head, literally smooth as a baby's butt; the blond imperial sprouting from his chin, like an Egyptian snake.

"Why don't you and Duane go up to the storage room and stack the toilet paper, clean the place up for me? Whaddaya say?"

"Coo, coo, coo," Thomas warbles as he moves off to find Duane.

"I thought he was still in the Hole," Bob says.

"Who? Thomas?" Todd asks. "Yeah, I guess he was — for a week or so. Now he's back."

Thomas is a pack rat as well as a collector of photographs.

He hoards everything: sugar packets, food, newspapers, kites, toothpaste, Tylenol — everything. And he collects photographs of little boys, cuts them out of the Penney's ads in the newspapers. Or the Target ads or Macy's or Gap for Kids, whatever. So does Duane Smith, his one and only friend. They collect and exchange photos like other people collect baseball cards.

A while back, during a random cell search, one of the COs discovered Thomas's stash of sugar, about five pounds of it, and a stack of extra oranges and whites (jail-issued underwear, T-shirts, socks). The CO confronted Thomas with it. Thomas got shitty with the CO, started making noises like a spitting cat. So they threw him in the Hole.

Bob gives his head a sad shake. "How's your wife?" he asks Todd.

"Good, good," Todd says. "In fact, I'm about to go up and call her. Find out how the business is going."

Todd owns a shutter and blind business in Manteca. He reads the daily *Wall Street Journal*, which he subscribes to. Checks on his stocks and shit. He talks like he's wealthy. I don't know, maybe he is. In here, it doesn't matter. Jail is the ultimate equalizer. In here, everybody is shit.

Todd's here for buying, growing, using, and selling marijuana. According to him, "a lot of marijuana." Anyway, that's what he tells everybody. It's true, but like one of those icebergs there's more to it. The more is this: he's here for a sex crime, having sex with an underage female. She was seventeen. Of course, he doesn't talk about that part because the Surenos would never accept him as a trustee. They'd try to kill him the first chance they get.

Todd told Bob. Bob told me. I don't say anything to anybody.

"Didja see what Google's doing?" Todd says to Bob.

"Yeah," Bob says. "Maybe I'm just old, but I don't see how they make money. I mean, they don't *make* anything."

"I don't know either," admits Todd, "but their stock is kicking butt. I told my wife to sell ours a while back. I guess I should've waited."

"It's always a gamble," says Bob.

Bob holds an MBA from Ohio State University, has a bunch of stocks, mostly stock options in his former company, Orkin.

"Gentlemen," announces Todd, "I am gonna go call the old lady."

"Say hi for us," Bob tells him as he leaves. "Let's walk," Bob says and strides off in the lead.

"You feeling less tense now?" I ask.

"Yeah," he says. "I get too intense about stuff."

"No wonder," I exclaim. "I mean, we're talking murder here. I'd think you were dead if you didn't get stressed about it."

"Yeah," Bob says.

Two minutes and thirty left turns later, "Do you think Todd is as wealthy as he makes out?" I say.

"No. He probably invests, but he's a salesman at heart. So he's selling an image, an idea. I'm sure he makes a good living, but I would guess that most of it's just talk."

"He talks about how he's got it all planned out, how he's going to do this, that, and the other when he gets out," I say. "But I don't know. . . . I think Todd likes the way he used to live."

"I know," says Bob. "He told me he's worried about it. Wonders if he can stay straight. That's why he's so vocal about Jesus and religion. He thinks that will do it for him."

"He's kidding himself," I say. "That's not what —"

Thomas Herbert arrives, leans over with his elbows on the railing. He's looking down at me, got that smug smirk that he wears, as if he just butt-fucked Madonna and she liked it.

"Radic," he says to me as we pass him.

"What?"

He holds up a small beige envelope. I know what it is.

"You need any?" Thomas asks.

"Is it Tylenol?"

"Not the regular," he says. "The prescription strength. I got ten of 'em."

I think about this.

"Whatcha want for 'em?" I ask next time we pass him.

"Two nutty bars," he declares. His tone indicates take it or leave it.

I think about it.

"Well, Thomas," I say as we pass him again, "it's a pretty good deal, but I don't think so." I look over my shoulder at him since we are well past him by now.

"How come?" he says.

"I already got about fifty Tylenol. I don't need any more."

"Yeah, but these are the prescription ones," he reminds me.

"I know. But no, I don't need 'em right now."

The smug smirk remains as he leaves.

"Do you really have that many Tylenol?" Bob says.

"Yeah. Everybody's got Tylenol, all the welfare guys, and they all want sweets. So who do they come to? The guy with sucker on his forehead." I laugh at myself.

"They all know you're a nice guy," Bob says, admonishing me. "You need to be tougher."

"I know. I know," I say. "But I don't want to be like them. Always trying to screw everyone for a candy bar."

"I know," agrees Bob. "I find myself becoming so cynical." He shakes his head. "God! I hate this place."

We walk.

PIMP ROLL

Aaron Woods comes in through the yard door, singing some hip hop ditty. King Kong Pimp Roll, that's what they call his walk. A kind of arrogant, rocking sway, which only some of the blacks can do. Woods is a virtuoso at it. It is at once disdainful, insolent, and intimidating.

Woods stops in the middle of the foyer, twitching his hips obscenely, singing in his high, clear falsetto.

I nod in approval. "Woods," I say. "Man, I'm telling you, you can sing. When you get out, look me up. I'll be your manager for only fifteen percent. We'll both get rich."

Bob walks in front of me, looking down at the gray carpet. I've never seen him speak to anyone of color in here except when answering a direct question.

"Fuck you, OG," says Woods. Then smiles like Jack Nicholson with eight too many teeth. "Fifteen percent of nothing is what you'll get." He performs a sinuous pirouette.

Anyway, that's what I think he says. Woods' jive-molly-boy ebonics is all but incomprehensible to me.

"C'mon, Woods," I say. "With your talent and good looks, I'll make you a superstar, man." I hold up my hands as if reading a marquee. "Snoop Dog and Fifty Cent can kiss the money good-bye."

Woods laughs. "Fuck you, mo'fucker!" He King Kong Pimp Rolls up the stairs to the quad, singing.

"Too bad," I say to Bob. "The guy can really sing. And he looks like Sidney Poitier."

"He's not bad," Bob agrees. "What's he here for?"

"I'm not exactly sure. But Josh said it was for armed robbery. And he oughta know 'cuz he used to hang with him."

"Does he ever go to court?" asks Bob. "I mean, I never see him go to court. He's always just here."

"Josh said Woods is holding out for a better deal," I say. "Josh told me he's been here a long time."

"Too bad," Bob says.

"Yeah. Ya know, there are a few of these guys that have some talents. They just need to redirect them," I say.

"Maybe," Bob says, "but most of them don't know anything else. They sleep all day in here and probably outside too. No jobs, no education, no ambition. Just sleep all day and go out at night. You live like that for a while, and you're bound to get in trouble."

"You're right," I say.

We walk another few minutes, turning left, always left.

Bob stops. "I'm going to go watch the news. You want to join me?"

"No," I say. "I think I'll just keep walking. Then go get some water, beat the rush."

He nods. "See you at breakfast."

"At breakfast," I say.

I walk.

SHARK

April 25, 2006

Intake 2, Rec Time

9:00 p.m.

It's an absurd color of orange. An angry, howling cunt of an orange. The eyes above the orange are flat black, all alone and dead, like those of a great white shark. The face the eyes inhabit exudes energy, a streaming, cutting flow of hideous indecency. Roy Smith. He has a supercilious expression on his face. He gazes off to the side, as if wishing he were somewhere else or reflecting on some inner puzzle.

The mouth below the eyes rumbles, "You guys remember Lane Silva?"

I hesitate, rummaging through my memory files: short, approximately fifty-five years old, Hispanic, but he looks almost white because of his complexion; he cuts hair for a candy bar or soup, in here for some violent crime. I can't remember what, though.

I nod. "Yeah, I remember him. Whatever happened to him?"

I couldn't recall the last time I saw him — then a memory bulletin is received from my brain: Lane, wearing handcuffs, a plastic bag filled with his property over the shoulder of his fireplug body, being escorted to the Hole. Black-clad correction officers on either side of him, their Sam Browne belts bristling with nonlethal weaponry: mace, pepper spray, zap guns, long shiny black flashlights of unbreakable plastic, which double as billy clubs.

The other guy of the "guys," plural, in the question looks

bewildered. It's Bob. He reminds me of a balding bassett hound, with his sad eyes and hanging jowls. "Who?" asks Bob.

"You know," I say, plop-plop, fiz-fizzing with instant memory relief. "Short guy, cut hair. An OG like us."

"Oh, yeah," Bob says, crossing his arms over his chest. "I remember him." He looks expectantly at our shark-like interrogator, a voiceless "What about him?" expression smearing his visage, as if trying to condense fact from the vapor of nuance.

"He went to DVI," growls Roy in a dry, brittle voice birthed in the dungeons of his solar plexus. "My attorney told me he tried to make a deal with the DA, rat on me. But the DA decided he wasn't a credible witness. Somebody in the PD over in Tracy told my attorney about it."

As the words *rat on me* flee from his mouth, an energy of fear tingles through my limbs. It starts in my stomach and radiates outward at a steady pace, thrumming and humming in my bones. I feel nauseous. I want to throw up. Instead, I erase any expression, any emotion, from my face. Or try to.

"Can you believe that?" A thick reality settles in Roy's voice. "The little fuck was willing to rat on me? He didn't hardly even know me. Cut my fucking hair once."

Roy pauses for a second, as if his brain is performing informational hygiene, which I doubt because he is pretty much a supersubmoron; more probably, he is just running through his mental dictionary to see if any other nouns besides *rat*, *shit*, and *fuck* are available for immediate usage. But the lexicon is depleted, so he turns and swims off, like the shark he resembles. Moving through the door into the yard, he quickly lights up a hand-rolled cigarette, inhales deeply, consuming a third of the cigarette's length.

Bob turns to me, his eyes wide. He looks like one of those old white men on the TV pundit powwows, where somebody has just insulted somebody. "That was a warning." He gazes intently at me, searching my face for agreement.

"What?" I say. Despite my fear, I don't want to believe it.

It's not for me. He was just talking about what Lane had tried to do.

"It was a slap across the face is what that was," says Bob, his face pale with concern. So now he resembles an albino, balding bassett hound. One that is terrified. Uncrossing his arms, he flutters his hands as he continues, as if he is trying to speak to someone, namely me, who is mentally and aurally impaired, dumber than shit and deaf as a nail: hoping I can read lips but in case I can't using sign language too. "He knows that we know."

"You think so?"

"Yeah, I think so," says Bob. "If we open our mouths, we're dead." He peers down at me from his six-foot-two-inch altitude, a stealthy smile on his lips. One of those biblical, Laodicean smiles, ya know? Lukewarm, halfhearted. As if he's smiling but only because his brain is making him do so, because it believes that a protective smile ensures survival. Somehow.

All I know is this: I want to get out of jail. I don't want to go to DVI and live in the jungle with all the beasts. And I don't want Roy and his vague death threats looming over me. To do this, I must become a snitch. I can hardly wait for tomorrow so I can squeal.

Roy has just made up my mind for me. Sharla and I have discussed the dangers of snitching on the phone. We don't talk about it much during her visits because the conversations are recorded. Sharla thinks I should do it, simply because it's the right thing to do. So do I.

But the danger is real. In the subculture of jail, snitching is a sin unto death. Snitching carries the death penalty. And not just from the guy you rat out but also from anyone. Any inmate will try to kill a snitch, because a snitch has violated the criminal code of muteness. Though of course it goes on all the time. Criminals are notoriously self-serving and will do anything to reduce their time in prison.

My sister and my mother advise me against it. I call them collect from jail during rec time and talk with them about it. I don't give them any details because there's always someone around. So I use a kind of double talk. They understand me because I wrote to my mother, providing the details.

"I don't think you should do it, Randy," says my sister on the phone. "Word gets around in jail. And a snitch is about as low as you can go."

"I know that. But I don't think there's that much danger if I just keep quiet."

"Don't kid yourself," says my sister. "They'll find out. Rumors and gossip circulate at the speed of light. Remember when I was at High Plains?"

Once upon a time, she taught at a low-security detention facility in Colorado. A juvenile prison for teenaged drug lords was what it was. One seventeen-year-old in there was pulling in $35 million a year running a small drug empire. He was from Illinois and was sent to Colorado because Illinois contracted out a lot of its juvenile criminals to save money. Whereas Colorado made money from the deal. Everbody was happy, except the drug lord. Nobody cared what he thought.

One day in class my sister reminded them that they needed an education so they could get a real job when they got out.

The millionaire from Illinois raised his hand. "Miss Radic, I got a question."

"Okay," said my sister.

The millionaire stood up and said, "You mean I need to get educated so's I can get a job where I make $36,000 a year?"

"Yes."

"Well, that don't make no sense," he said, looking at her askance. "You're telling me to be happy with $36,000 when I got my whole family — my mom, my three brothers and five sisters, and all my aunts and uncles — to take care of. I can't do that on no $36,000. They'll all starve to death."

My sister just looked at him.

The millionaire from Illinois smiled at her. "Right now I make $35 million a year. So you're telling me I ought to give that up so I can make $36,000?" He sat down.

My sister didn't know what to say. He had a point. After a few seconds, she said, "Yes, but what you were doing is illegal."

The whole class just laughed.

After a while, the detention center began accepting lots of teenaged twcakers, many of whom had AIDS. Female teachers at the facility risked being raped. So my sister resigned.

"I don't think being raped would bother me that much," she told me one time. "But I don't want to get AIDS as a bonus prize. I don't want to die that way."

"Yeah, I remember," I tell my sister on the phone.

"Well, rumors flew around High Plains," she says. "And if they even thought someone was a snitch, they'd hurt him. Hurt him bad." Dread enters her voice. "And I don't want my brother to get hurt. They could kill you."

"I know, I know," I reply. "Mother, what do you think?" She's on the extension, listening.

"I don't think you should do it, Randy. You only have two months before you're out. Just do it and don't put yourself in danger."

"Yeah," I protest, "but what about the right and wrong of it. Should I just stay mum even though I know it's the wrong thing to do? I mean, I know something!"

"Yes, you do," says my sister. "However, you have to protect yourself, because if word gets out that you're a snitch the guards might not be able to protect you. Even if you're in solitary confinement, they can find ways to get to you."

"Yeah," I admit, deflated.

"And remember," adds my sister in a cautious tone, "lots of people don't like snitches. Not even guards."

"Yeah, there's that." I pause. "Okay, I'll think about it.

When I decide what to do, I'll let you know."

"I don't want you hurt," says my sister. "I just want my brother back in one piece."

"Okay. I need to go. I'll call sometime next week."

"We love you," says my mom.

"I love you guys too. Bye."

RED MAN

April 26, 2006

6:45 a.m.

Next morning: the door lock pops rapidly, like a machine gun with no bullets. Pressing the steel door open, I look down at the podium. "Radic!" bellows the voice. "Court!"

I snap my ID out of the window insulation, clip it to my orange top, where the neck vees. Walking around the corner to the stairs, some black guy in cell 56 gestures to me to turn on his lights. I just walk by. Fuck you.

As I go down the stairs, I focus on the white tackies on my feet. I march quickly to the railing that stands twenty feet in front of the podium. Behind the podium stand two black-clad COS. They stare at me. Their faces have no expression. One of them, the corporal, is frail, sallow, with dank gray hair and a long lumpy nose. The other is a man of great girth with bulging black eyes and a short brush of coarse black hair at the back of a pale receding forehead. I recognize them but have never spoken with them, couldn't begin to tell you their names, which reside on gold-colored tags above their left chest pockets.

I refuse to make eye contact. Making eye contact with a guard draws attention to you. Attention usually leads to mal-treatment. Instead, I stare at a point twelve inches above their heads, on the wall. The wall is pale yellow, without texture or ornament.

To the left of me, there is a heavy popping sound. A large

steel door opens; a CO enters, carrying a computer printout in his right hand. He stands tall and erect, an elderly gentleman with a ruff of gray hair, a notable nose, narrow blue eyes under shaggy eyebrows. He's dressed in black, three sets of handcuffs dangle from his Sam Browne belt. Two of the sets of cuffs are silver, the third set is yellow. He wears white latex gloves on his hands in case he has to touch me.

He marches straight over to me, raises his left hand, greeting the two COs behind the podium. "Radic?" he says.

He doesn't expect an answer, but I respond anyway. "Yes, sir."

He doesn't hear me, just looks at my ID, matches the name and the booking number to those on his printout. He never looks at my face or the photo on the ID.

He turns and walks back toward the door. Automatically, I follow, five feet behind him. He stops at the door, pushes a silver steel button above a silver mesh square. A closed-circuit camera stares at him; at the other end of the camera, a female CO examines him then hits an electronic release. The door pops; he pushes it open, holding it for me. The door slams shut behind me. We are in a keep, facing another door. Automatically, I move to the right-hand wall, staying five feet behind him. Once again he pushes a silver button, a camera stares at him, he is scrutinized, the door pops. I follow him through it.

We walk down a long, wide hall. We pass a scanner, like going through security at an airport. But I don't walk through it. On the way back, I will. I remain five feet behind him at all times, three feet off the side of his left shoulder.

At the end of the hall, the door routine takes place again. Above this door in black three-inch letters is the word TRANS-PORTATION. We enter, walk across a green-and-white-checked floor, like a huge chessboard. Four rows of molded blue plastic seats are off to the right. Orange-clad inmates occupy eight of the seats. Two female inmates sit in the first row, wearing yellow.

Both of them are untidy, hard. They look bored. Waiting.

"Across there," my CO says, pointing with his latex-ensconced hand. "Number 11." I enter the cell. In it are two metal benches, which face each other, a stainless steel toilet, a stainless steel sink, one roll of toilet paper. The floor is cement. The walls are cinder block. I shiver. I'm scared. I'm lonely.

I'm a six — level six. Level six is the highest security level, which means I am never allowed to mingle with inmates from the general population (mainline) for fear they might try to kill me.

The guard slams the steel door shut behind me. I sit down on the steel bench. I feel goosebumps rise on my legs. Nothing but cold and waiting. Never just one or the other, they always come packaged together, like sleep and nightmares.

A key grates in the door, which swings open. The guard enters. In his hands, he has yellow handcuffs, silver leg shackles. Familiar with the routine, I stand, turn, and place my knees on the steel bench, my palms on the yellow wall three inches in front of my face. He snaps the shackles around my ankles, adjusts them for fit, locking them with a small black screwdriver-like tool.

"Down and hands out," he says.

Turning, I face him, extend both hands, thumbs up. He cuffs me. He leaves, slamming the door. I sit, shiver, and wait.

To ease my wait, I read the inside of the cell door. Crudely scratched in many layers of yellow paint are names, slogans, affiliations, endearments. The names are usually Hispanic: Juan, Nacho, et cetera. Brief slogans such as "notorious dog" or "bad motherfucker" are there, along with a few endearments, things such as "Jeffe loves Rita." But most prolific are the affiliations: Surenos followed by XIII or Nortenos accompanied by XIV or NorCal Woods or SWP or a swastika-cum-Low Riders. Gang shit.

Gazing through the twelve-inch by twelve-inch window of

the door, I see eight orange-clad figures walk by, two by two. They are cuffed to each other; all wear shackles. The two female inmates walk by, JAIL in six-inch letters on the backs of their yellow blouses. Normally, they would be in orange too; the yellow signifies they are inmates who work in the laundry.

After they pass by my cell, the guard opens my door, gestures to me to step out. I exit the door, stop. I know the routine. He stands three feet from me; we watch the inmates leave the building. Two by two they awkwardly scale the steps into a waiting bus. I feel the shackles hurting their ankles because I know my turn is coming. Twenty-four inches of steel chain links one ankle to the other. Walking is take a step, have it stop short, take another step, have it stop short. As the chain stops the step short, the ankle cuff is jerked into the ankle bone — a brilliant biting sensation.

The bus is brown, black, and dingy white. The windows have steel slats welded over them. On the side of the bus, I read "San Joaquin County Sheriff." Underneath that, in huge letters, "SHERIFF."

As the last woman struggles up the steps of the bus, my guard says, "Go." I walk toward the wide, open portal, where another guard stands. When I am five feet from him, he holds up his hand. I stop. Twenty feet from the bus. Another guard stands in the doorway of the bus, on the top step.

"This is a six," says my guard.

Taking a look over his shoulder, the guard on the bus step makes a come-hither motion. "We're ready," he says to my guard.

"Go," says my guard.

I walk across the twenty feet of tarmac, the shackles biting with each step. I know my ankles are already bruised; by this evening, they will be black and blue. Clenching my teeth, I grab the handrail, pulling myself up as well as climbing the steps. There are five rubber-covered steps. I am in the bus. It smells of old urine, desiccated rubber molding, sweat, and tension. Inmates piss in the bus, on the floors of the holding cells, everywhere. It's how they attack the system. They piss on it. They think it's funny.

A guard stands behind a half-open cage door. It looks like the door on a chain-link fence but stiffer, stronger. It is painted royal blue. I enter the cage, sit down on a padded seat. The guard shuts the door, locks it. Sixes always sit alone, in cages.

Two guards enter the bus. One is the driver, the other available for inmate collision avoidance duty, which, in translation, is keep the animals under control. They unlock a box behind the driver's seat, take out two automatic pistols, holster them. Seating themselves, the driver starts the engine, and the bus circles around, turns left, then left again, then straight ahead for fifty yards. It stops in front of a gray-green building that has "Administration Building" mounted on it in neat metal letters.

Sounds directorial, a place where secretaries sit in front of computer screens, answering phones, collating important data. And in the back, in austere offices, ranking officers pore over vital documents, make important decisions. It's not. It's "administrative segregation," a euphemism for "the Hole." You fuck up, they throw you in the Hole. The Hole is your own private cell in hell. Seven feet by seven feet, stainless steel toilet (no seat), stainless steel sink, bunk with one sheet and one thin blanket, no pillow. Even while you sleep, the lights are on. A very efficient HVAC system keeps your cell at sixty-five degrees. And it is loud beyond belief, as there are no ceilings on the cells, so all conversations are carried on by shouting to other inmates.

The inmates in the Hole become so bored they need to be loud. So they bang on the steel doors with their hands, their arms, their heads, anything they can find — all night long. In the Hole, you get out of your cell for one hour three times per week, to shower or walk. You are cuffed and shackled while out. You eat in your cell.

The bus picks up two inmates from the Administration Building. One male, one female. Their ankles are shackled, and their hands are cuffed, but their handcuffs are tethered to a chain around their waists.

The male is dressed in dark crimson. A "red man." He is a murderer. A black pressure emanates from him. I feel it, I see it. Death is his companion. As he walks by my cage, I look straight ahead. No eye contact with the red men. They are psychotics; I can see it in their eyes if I look. I don't want to see it. It frightens me. *They* horrify me.

The female is in orange. She is tall, with large bones, meaty shoulders, strong legs and haunches. Her coarse brown hair is cut short and straggles unflatteringly down around her square face. The overall effect is porcine.

The red man is locked in the cage behind me. I feel his eyes boring into the back of my head. The female is caged across the aisle from me. Instantly, she yells at one of the females in the back of the bus. "Madie! You bitch! Where are you?"

"Intake 3," screams Madie from the back of the bus. "Where you, girl?"

"The Hoooole," hoots the piggy-looking one, "47-A. Richard's in 60-B."

"Richard?" says Madie. "You one lucky beeatch, got yo' man in witch'ya."

"Fuck!" yelps piggy. "Asshole chewing up some other pussy. So I got on his ass, told him to bite down and stop. Or I am gone! Think I'm putting up with that shit? Hell no!"

She pronounces "hell no" as a kind of vocal heterodyne: the production of a low frequency from the combination of two almost equal high frequencies. So as it leaves her mouth, it sounds something like "hail no," with special emphasis on the "hail." Additionally, there has to be a certain nasal-bimbo-box screechiness to your voice to do it right. And she has it.

I tune her out.

"Randy!"

I hear my name, shake my head, wonder if I'm losing it. No one else from PC is on the bus, so no one can know me.

"Randy Radic!"

I turn to my right, look back two cages. Matt Berg. With a mustache and goatee. He is tanned, healthy looking. Looks as if he's been pumping iron at Gold's Gym.

"Matt?"

He was in PC with me just before Christmas. In for drugs and credit card fraud to support his habit, Matt's been in and out of jail and prison for the past ten years.

"Radic!" he says, his voice a happy howl. "I thought that was you."

"What are you doing on this bus? I thought you were down south, at CRC?"

"I was. Th-th-th-they shipped me up to DVI last week, th-th-th-then over h-h-h here at five-fucking-a.m. this morning. I'm going to Manteca Court and don't even kn-kn-kn know why."

Matt stutters. He has one of those personalities that you just can't help liking. Fizzy with excitement and enthusiasm, the stuttering seems a necessary adjunct to his picturesque antics.

"Hey," he yells at me, "is Chuckie still in I-2?"

"Yeah," I say.

"We'll be in the tank t-t-t-together," says Matt, fidgeting in his cage.

"Yeah, I guess so," I say.

"Cool. W-w-w-we can t-t-t-talk in the tank." He shakes his head and laughs, whether at himself or to himself I don't know. "I don't even know what charges I'm up-up-up-up on in Manteca," he says to no one in particular.

"They'll be glad to inform you," I say.

"Yeah," he says, then becomes introspective, which in Matt's case means he's tired of screaming at the top of his lungs so I can hear him. Settling back in his cage, he tries to peer out at the world. Through the welded slats, he sees some girls doing that female hip-roll thing. They are young Hispanic *fashionistas*, walking down Matthews Road, about seventy-five yards away, just outside the jail perimeter fence.

"Radic!" he says, making a sexual ululation of my name.

"Yeah," I respond. He doesn't pick up on the weariness in my tone.

"Whoo! Pussy, man! Look, right over there!" He raises manacled hands to point.

I squint. All I can see, through the slats, is horizontal puzzle pieces of a Taco Bell. Which, right now, I'd rather have than pussy.

"Tasty," confides Matt at full vocal volume.

The bus, at the urging of the driver, whips a U-turn in front of ad-seg. Right turn, then another, and behold — a thirty-foot wall composed of cement, faced with ersatz brown rock. And in the wall resides a steel gate. It is twenty feet tall, thirty feet long, and five inches thick. Pale green in color, it stands motionless. The driver stops the bus beside a control panel, swipes his card in the slot. An electric motor engages, the pale green monolith rolls open.

The bus driver floors the gas pedal, the bus lurches forward with only two or three inches clearance on either side. A stop sign, then a left turn onto Matthews Road. I peer out the narrow slots between the steel slats that cover the windows. The world is horizontal and hazy but the world nevertheless. I suck it into my eyeballs, reveling in its authenticity. There is no beauty, for French Camp is dull, gray, and brown: dilapidated houses, most of them white, but somehow they look gray. Bare trees reach without reservation to an overcast sky, and a blanket of moisture covers everything, like a sweating piece of fruit. It sucks, but it is real. The real world. Out there. Not jail or a bus that smells of old urine and sweat.

The bus merges onto Highway 99, goes past Delicato Winery; as we pass, the bus engine roaring stridently because the driver knows only one throttle setting, floored, I dream of Chardonnay and Cabernet Sauvignon, their sarcastic smell, their sweet fruit sachet as they flood over the taste buds. But that is out there. I am in here. The bus is an extension of the jail. An invisible, surreal kind of umbilical cord attaches them.

Now on Center Street in Manteca. The sand-colored courthouse will be visible soon. The back of it, that is. The bus turns into the parking lot behind the courthouse, jolts to a stop. The driver leaves the engine running, puts the vehicle in park, stands, removes his pistol, places it in the lockbox. His partner performs the same routine. They lock it, pull it twice to make sure the weapons are secured. The bus doors open, one of the guards picks up a large plastic bag full of puffy brown paper bags. Lunch.

He throws the plastic bag through the open door. It lands with a flat, whacking sound on the black tarmac. The guard descends the steps, grabs the neck of the bag, and, dragging it behind him, leaving a rasping wake, moves toward the entrance.

The back door of the courthouse is already open, like a giant vagina. Standing beside the orifice are four bailiffs. My cage is unlocked first, then Matt's, then the female's. I struggle down the steps, metal shackles waging war on flesh and bone, walk toward the door. I squint and blink rapidly as the sun peeks out from behind the clouds. Warm white, traveling at 186,000 miles per second, caresses my head, my face, my shoulders. I sigh ecstatically. I forget myself, and where I am for just a moment, thinking to myself, "Now we're living. Outside, walking in the sunshine. This is really living."

Reality impinges: "You got any contraband on you?" asks one of the bailiffs. I recognize him. Hispanic, vascular muscularity, the kind where the blue veins stand up like filigree, the kind you get from unsmiling time in the gym. A blue sheriff's T-shirt stretches over his hypertrophied magnificence. Fucking bad.

"No, sir," I say. "I don't smoke."

"Neither do I," he says. "Except maybe a good cigar every now and then." He grins at me.

"Me too." I turn, face the wall, place my hands on it, spread my legs.

"Thank you, Mr. Radic," he says as he pats me down: shoulders, armpits, then runs his hands down my legs, making squeezing motions with his hands. Reaching around my hips, he quickly brushes his hands over my genitals, feeling for anomalies. He is looking for cigarettes.

READY TO DEAL

April 26, 2006

Manteca Courthouse

7:45 a.m.

"One leg up, please," says the bailiff.

I comply.

He removes my tacky, a kind of white canvas tennis shoe that slips on, pounds it on the floor, shakes it to loosen anything I might have in it. It is empty. So is the other.

"This way," says the bailiff.

Down a short hallway, past a bench that has funny-looking rings welded to it, looks kind of like one of those gynecological examination chairs, with the stirrups and all. It is where they restrain the major fuck-ups. They chain them to the bench through the stirrups so they can't move.

"To your left," he says.

I turn left, and I am happy, because this holding tank has a thermostat on the wall outside the tank. On the thermostat is a digital clock. I will know what time it is. Knowing the time is a wonderful thing

Entering the holding tank, I turn and look at the bailiff. "Thank you," I say.

"You're welcome, Mr. Radic," he says. Looking at my handcuffs and shackles, he adds, "Sorry, but I can't take them off."

"I know," I say, sitting down on the bench as the door slams shut. The heavy banging is a vocalization, a mechanical voice, a metallic sound that condemns. I hear the key turn in the lock.

Thirty seconds later the key scrapes, the door opens. Matt Berg shuffles in; he is talking nonstop to the bailiff. "I-I-I don-don-don't even kn-kn-kn-kn — no one told me why I'm here," he says. "They just slap my ass on a bus, sh-sh-sh-ship me to DVI, th-th-th-th-then wake m-m-m-m-me up at five this morning and bus me over to j-j-j-jail. See if y-y-y-y-y — find out why I'm h-h-h-here, will ya?"

"I'll check with the clerk," says the bailiff, "but I can't guarantee anything." He slams the door shut.

"F-f-fuck!" says Matt. Placing his orange-clad ass against the wall, he slides down to the bench. He is ten feet from me, directly in front of me.

I don't understand, so I ask. "Are you at DVI still? Or at CRC? Chuckie told me he got a letter from you, from CRC."

"CRC," he says. "I w-w-was at DVI last night f-f-f-f-for f-f-f-four hours, then in the t-t-t-t-tank at jail."

"How's CRC?"

"Plump, dog. Plump!" he says, grinning at me. "Look at this," he says, pointing a tanned finger at his feet. "Fucking N-n-n-n-nikes, dog," he says, his voice high pitched with excitement. "I g-g-g-got four pair."

It's an indicative statement, backed up by a flat stare. But he knows that I know that he knows that he's got it made, in jail terms that is. No one in jail has Nikes. Only tackies and standard-issue rubber sandals.

"Dog!" I say, with appropriate amounts of envy, respect, and awe in my voice.

Really, I don't care. But Matt is a friend of mine, so I play along. I pretend. Pretending is all Matt has. It's all Matt has because he'll be at CRC for the next three years. And when pretending is all you have, it becomes reality in a make-believe kind of way, like Peter Pan or Santa Claus. They're not real, and everybody knows it.

A smug glow emanates from Matt's eyes; he smiles. His color, his aura, goes from brown to blue. He sits straighter, flexes his tanned forearms, admires the trenches formed by hardened tendons and muscles. He is satisfied with my respect. I am satisfied that he is satisfied because that means I am safe.

"Where did you get *four* pair of Nikes?"

"M-m-my mo-mo-mo," he pauses, willing his mouth to enunciate. Sheer willpower. "My mother," he says. "I got a portable DVD player," he says, making a ten-inch box with his hands. "And a CD player."

"Music? You get to listen to music?" I say. There is no pretend in my voice now. I haven't heard *any* music in six months. No classical, no western, no rap-crap, no hip-hop, no rock, no pop, no hyphy. Nothing. I miss music. And Matt has a CD player. He can listen to the music of his choice.

"Yeah, dog," Matt says, as if it's no big deal. "I work out every day. With weights. S-s-s-s-sometimes two times a day." He flexes his biceps for me, and up pops a small mountain of muscle fibers and blue veins. "Then I shower a-a-a-and hang out w-w-w-with Fester, who is a bad dog, dog. Don't nobody do nothing o-o-o-o-on the block without Fester's s-s-say s-s-so. Some Pure Boys started messing with me. G-g-g-giving me shit a-a-and all. Fester hears a-a-a-about 1-1-1-it and throws out a-a-a-a word. Next thing some of th-th-those w-w-w-w-white crackers jump me, kicking the shit o-o-o-out of m-m-me. Fester shows up like in a m-m-m-movie, fucking R-r-r-rambo — got a b-b-broom handle. Tat, tat, tat. One, two, three, dog!"

Matt's head tilts back, I can see down his throat as he laughs. His laugh is harsh with the violence he remembers, but there's a zone of thrill there too. The thrill of immediacy — being there, participating, seeing it happen.

"Pure Boys are down! F-f-fester's got a franchise on fuck-k-k-king f-f-f-force. An ear off. Five teeth from another fucker, and he p-p-put the fucking b-b-b-broom stick through a cheek. Broke the guy's jaw, dog." He laughs again. A short laugh, without the thrill because he can see it again, and I can see him seeing it. I sit motionless, shocked by the violent reality I perceive he has perceived.

Matt's face is a picture of shadows cast on a sensitized surface by encounter, the grays of brutality on a light-colored background of humanity. His eyes are negatives. He is somewhere else: a place of ever more dreary phases.

"What's CRC like?" I say.

His eyes become dual positives, focusing back in on the here and now, as he says, "Cool. Sun. Out all day, sh-sh-sh-shower w-w-w-when you want, pump iron. O-o-o-only my mom can't v-v-v-visit, it's too far from M-m-m-modesto. I m-m-m-m-miss my mom." His eyes shine with welling tears.

I remember reading once that tears are the overspill of human emotions. There is so much emotion that is so strong that the human body can't contain it. So it spills out of our eyes, like coffee over the edge of a cup. I believe it.

CRC stands for California Rehabilitation Center. It's located in Norco, California, near San Diego. It's prison for tweakers is what it is. They're all drug addicts. The idea is to get them off drugs while at the same time punishing them for being stupid enough to become addicted to drugs in the first place. A kind of double retribution.

I stand and shuffle over to the small window in the holding tank door. Peering out at the thermostat, I announce to Matt, "It's 9:15." Soon now, I think to myself. My attorney told Sharla, who told me, that he would arrive around 9:20 or 9:30. I'm getting very nervous.

"Look at this," says Matt, extending his forearm for my examination. A black-flame design decorates his upper forearm, as if he's stuck his arm into black fire inside a wind tunnel.

"A new tattoo," I say. It's a good one, well done.

Tattoos don't impress me. What impresses me is the psychology behind tattoos: why do people get them? I read once that tattoos are a search for the sacred, a kind of affiliation adventure, as it were. Maybe. They're everywhere in jail. Jail symbolism. Another book said tattoos are simply a form of art, body art, which would mean that they're just a form of self-expression.

All I know is this: ninety percent of all inmates sport tattoos, and eighty percent of all asylum inmates have tattoos too. Those numbers and their demographics scare me.

"It's a good one. I like it," I say. If I said I didn't like it, it would be disrespectful. Showing proper respect is vital in jail. Not showing respect results in violence. Which sounds simple enough on the surface, but it's not, because there is no clear definition of what "respect" comprises. "Did you get it at CRC?"

"Yeah, dog," Matt says, admiring it under the fluorescent light.

The harsh scraping of the key in the holding tank door interrupts us. I stand, ready to go. "Berg," says the bailiff. "Let's go."

Matt stands, shuffles out, his leg chains provide cold accompaniment.

"Good luck," I say, sitting back down, feeling half cold, half warm bite my butt from the steel bench. I missed the spot I'd been sitting on, so I scoot over until the half-cold teeth go warm. Waiting. Wondering what's going to happen. I'm scared that they won't make me a deal, that I won't get out, that I'll have to go to DVI for two months. Fear grips my mind, my breathing rate accelerates, my arms won't move, some gush of fluid is migrating down my intestines. Diarrhea. No! I tighten my bowels, and the feeling of jetting urgency subsides.

A few minutes later I hear the metallic scrape of the key. The piss-yellow steel door opens, and in shuffles Matt. Back already. I look at his orange clothing. It's exactly like mine, only his says CDC-PRISONER, where mine says JAIL.

"What happened?" I say.

"Fucking nothing," Matt says, sitting down with a rattle of chains and cuffs. "The j-j-j-judge doesn't know why I-I-I-I'm here either. There's a w-w-w-warrant out for me in Modesto, but n-n-n-n-no one knows why or wh-wh-wh-what for." He shakes his head and laughs. "Fuck!"

"You mean to tell me they hauled you all the way up here . . . and now they don't know why? And they took you to the wrong court to boot?" My face and my voice squinch in disbelief.

"F-f-f-fuck yeah, dog!" says Matt.

DIRTY LOWDOWN

April 26, 2006

10:00 a.m.

As I sit in the bubble looking at the DA and his investigator, I know what they want: the dirty lowdown. So I give it to them.

"The first conversation occurred sometime in March, late in the evening, when we were out on rec. Bob Gay and I were out talking, and Roy G. Smith came out of his cell with a copy of *Entertainment Weekly* magazine, asked if I wanted to look at it. I said yes. Then someone else came up — it may have been Gene Davis, I can't remember — and wanted to know if he could look at it when I finished. I said go ahead and take it, but give it to me when he was finished with it. Then someone else came by and handed Roy a copy of *O* magazine. He gave it to me also. Later I gave it to Bob because I didn't think I would like it. After getting *O* magazine, I asked Roy, 'How's it going?'

"He said, 'Pretty good. It looks like my case will be dismissed soon. It's just a waiting game now.'

"He always says that — that 'it's a waiting game.' That and 'I don't want to talk about it,' which he obviously does 'cuz he always starts talking about it.

"Then he continued, 'They have no evidence, regardless of what the media say.'

"I said, 'Like the body in the tub?'

"Roy squatted down, like some Jewish woman giving birth, said, 'Yeah. 'Cept it wasn't in the tub. It was in the shower.

And I showed my coworker how I strangled her.' He had both his hands out front, as if around her neck, his face happily demonic.

"Bob said, 'Well . . . if there's no body. . . .'

"Roy chimed in, 'Yeah. They said I threw her body in a dumpster.' He sneered. 'Like I'm stupid enough to get rid of her body like that.' Then he smiled slightly. 'All they found was a dead dog. I could have told 'em they wouldn't find anything. That's not where it is.' He laughed.

"I glanced at Bob, and Bob stared at me. We both had our eyes wide open in disbelief. This guy had just, in effect, confessed his guilt. Roy went on.

"'Yeah,' said Roy, 'it's just a waiting game now. I think they'll pin it on that friend of mine.' He laughed softly.

"By 'friend of mine,' I think he meant his coworker, whom he has mentioned before, but not by name.

"Then he went on about the Rolling Stones, because he had been reading something about them in a copy of *Rolling Stone* magazine, which he has a subscription to, but most of the time they won't let it in. I didn't follow what he was saying because I was too busy being stunned by what I'd just heard.

"He was arrogantly confident, which explains why he talked so freely.

"When he said, 'That's not where it is,' I got shivers up my spine because his tone, his face, his projection all said he *knew* where it was.

"Also, when he corrected me, saying, 'in the shower,' he *knew* where she was."

Through the smell of disinfectant, stale urine, and tired air, I see satisfaction register on faces: the investigator looks even puffier; Babitzke nods his approval, lips turned down and pouched out, as if he's tacitly saying, "See, I told you so." And the district attorney, standing behind the investigator, rises to his tiptoes then right back down, looking like the advertisement for C to C cigarettes: "for satisfaction."

"Where did you hear about the body in the tub?" asks the investigator, shattering the lull of rumination.

"From Sharla," I say. "She read about it in the newspaper and related it to me during one of our phone conversations."

"Umm . . ." hums the investigator, scouring his notes. "Do you speak with her often?"

"At least once a day, sometimes twice," I reply.

"And she read about the body in the paper, you say?" says the investigator.

"Yes, sir."

"Has Roy made any other reference to the body in the tub?" he asks.

"Yes. He told me that his wife made the statement to the police — that she had seen a body in the tub. But he said that it was coerced out of her. Roy said that his wife is meek, easily manipulated — that's why he moved her down south — anyway, he told me that when the police arrived to arrest him, they wanted him to make a statement, and he was going to, but he didn't because they had taken his wife into another room to question her, and he divined somehow that something was going on — something wrong — like he has superpowers or something — and he told them that he wanted his attorney. He said they manipulated the statement out of her. Then they took him to the police station to book him, and he told the one officer that he knew what they had done, and he said the officer became verbally abusive, so Roy told him to fuck off."

"So Roy maintains that the statement was coerced?" queries the investigator.

"Yes, sir."

"And he told you that he had moved his wife and family south?"

"Yes, sir. I assumed down in the LA area, but he never stated a specific location. Just down south."

"And you think that Roy knows where the body is?" asks the investigator.

"Yes, sir."

"Why?"

"Because you don't know where something *isn't* unless you know where it is," I explain, proud of my logic.

The district attorney inches closer, says, "You said that he demonstrated to you how he strangled her."

I nod.

"Could you show us exactly how he did that?" asks the DA.

I extend my hands out from my body, at a forty-five-degree angle, making talons of my hands, saying, "He put his hands out, like this, and kind of shook them, like he was choking her."

The investigator scribbles in his notepad. I watch blue ink wrinkle across thin, bleached wood pulp, the tracks of an animal on white snow. Insidious imprints that will doom a man of doom. I recall children reciting the limerick: "Sticks and stones can break my bones, but words can never hurt me." My words carry life — life imprisonment, even death. *I have become death, the destroyer.* Siva. Oppenheimer. Roy. Me.

"He was demonstrating to his coworkers how he killed her," I add.

"You said 'coworkers,' plural?" repeats the investigator, hissing the sibilant out on the word *workerssss.*

"Yes. I'm sure he said coworkers. Although every other time he used the word, it was in the singular. I cannot explain the disparity," I tell him, shrugging.

"Okay," the investigator says. He glances over his shoulder at the DA. Some telepathic-like exchange takes place, some swap of real body language, such that he proceeds to the next topic. I know because he turns to a clean page in his notepad.

"Mr. Radic," he says, "could you please relate the second conversation to us? And once again, please, take your time and be as lucid as possible."

Silence. The silence of strange attractors, the kind of silence you can fold and squeeze out of the rag of hush. I remain afraid but saddle up for another campaign. I clear my throat, which feels the way rusting steel must feel: stressed and cannibalized.

My hands rest in my lap, fingers interlaced, my shoulders curl as I slump forward, my legs crossed *à la femme*. Cold churns about my ankles as I begin.

"The second conversation also occurred in March. I can't recall the precise date, but it's on the copies Mr. Babitzke has and on the originals that my fiancée has.

"It was around 3:30 or 4:00 p.m., near the end of rec time. Bob and I stopped walking and were talking. We were both leaning against the railing, inside the area where we walk. Roy Smith stopped by on his way out to the yard, on his way to smoke a cigarette. We asked him about his case, how it was going, 'cuz he's always having conferences with his attorney or his investigator.

"'Looks good, looks good,' Roy said. 'It's just a waiting game. They haven't got anything. The problem is my mother-fucker coworker, who called me and asked me to help him with a stolen car.'

"He continually referred to his coworker as 'fucking motherfucker' because Roy says the 'guy is trying to set me up.'

"Anyway, later on in the conversation, Bob deliberately asked, 'Did you know the car was stolen when you agreed to help?'

"Roy said, 'No. I didn't know it was stolen.'

"So first he said his coworker called and asked him to help with a stolen car, then he told Bob he didn't know it was stolen.

"'Have they done much discovery?' said Bob.

"Roy said, 'Some, but not much.'

"Then Roy provided more details about the stolen car. 'It had a purse and a cell phone in it,' he said, then added, 'I didn't know the purse had $327 in it.'

"Roy left us, went out to smoke.

"Bob stared at me, one of those goddamn looks, as if 'Can you believe this shit?' 'Did you catch it?' he said.

"'Catch what?'

"'The discrepancy,' said Bob, a fat note of satisfaction in his tone, like Sherlock Holmes explaining the obvious to Dr. Watson. 'First he said that his coworker told him on the phone that the car was stolen. Then when I asked him if he knew it was stolen, he said no.'

"'Yeah, you're right,' I said. 'I heard both statements but didn't catch it.' Beginning to smile, I peered at Bob. 'You set him up,' I said, bulging with respect for Bob's manipulation.

"Bob smiled. 'Yeah. I was waiting for just the right moment in the conversation to pose my question.'

"'You should be an attorney,' I said. 'You're good.'

"'Yeah, well,' said Bob, pregnant with pride in his abilities, 'based on that discrepancy, to me it's clear he did it.'

"'You think so?'

"'Of course. He can't even keep his story straight. Any good prosecutor is going to shred him in court.'

"'Yeah,' I said, 'not very shrewd, is he?'

"'Also,' said Bob, his elbow propped on the railing, one leg up on the ledge, 'the authorities would not have released the dollar figure of $327. Even if they knew, they wouldn't reveal it to the press. The only way he could know is because he went through the purse while he was in the car.'"

"So he knew the amount of money in her purse?" asks the investigator.

"Yes, sir."

He glances at the DA, a pensive squint to his eyes. "And he initially said that his coworker informed him that the car was stolen?"

"Yes, sir."

"Then, later on, your friend Bob asked him if he knew it was stolen before he went over to help?"

"Yes, sir, that is correct."

"Did he say anything about where the stolen car was?" the DA asks, with a note of eagerness in his voice.

"Yes, sir. He said that he went over to his coworker's house, and then they drove to an orchard, where the car was parked under some trees."

"Did he use the word *orchard*?"

"Yes, sir."

"Did he tell you where he was taking the car?" says the DA.

"No, sir. But from other remarks he has made, I assume he was on Highway 120 at some time."

The DA nods. He is in a cocoon of thought.

"Did he say anything else about the purse or the cell phone?" the investigator asks, reading his notes.

"Yes, sir. He said that it was late at night. When he first got into the car, he couldn't see anything because it was so dark. Then, while he was driving, he noticed the purse and cell phone on the seat next to him. It pissed him off, he said."

"Why?"

"Because he realized then that his friend had gotten him involved in a lot more than just a stolen car," I say. Then I add, "I wondered why he was telling us all this, so I asked Bob. Bob said he thought Roy was 'trying his story out'; if he could convince us, then he could convince a jury."

"Which would explain the discrepancy," remarks the investigator, his pen at his lips, as if he's about to kiss it.

"And both you and Bob heard this?" asks the DA.

"Yes, sir."

"Do you think Bob would testify to this?"

I hesitate. "I'm almost positive he would," I say. "I have not asked him, but I know Bob would testify, too, as long as he is safe. Roy is a very angry man. Deep rivers of rage despite the placid performance. Bob and I have talked about that — that there's a lot of anger in Roy." I pause, then add, "He scares me."

As I wait for the next sequence of events, I glance at my attorney. He sits as still as a fern, just soaking it all in. I survey my side of the bubble of privacy: it's a filthy shithole, replete with stains of vomit, food, snot, spit, probably urine, and maybe even feces. The door is gouged, scraped, and scratched with names, gang logos, fuck yous, arcane gang numerology, some of which I recognize and understand, others I have no clue. Cold tension fills my side of the bubble.

"Okay," states the investigator. "Please tell us about the next conversation you had with Mr. Smith." He appears relaxed, but that's his business, I tell myself.

"The next one took place near the end of March, about a month ago. It was during evening rec. I was walking by myself, as Bob was watching *American Idol* on television. Roy G. Smith came out of his cell and started walking behind me.

"'What's up?' he said, making that little stoic-head movement of his.

"'Just walking,' I said, uneasy because he and his radioactive eyes were behind me.

"'Where's your partner?'

"'His show is on,' I said, motioning toward the benchchairs in front of the television. I could see Bob. He had a front-row seat.

"Walking slowly, almost side by side, Roy was a little behind me, off my left shoulder. 'Any more court dates coming up,' I said, 'other than your trial?'

"He said, 'A readiness hearing in September. The trial in October.'

"I nodded. 'You still think it will be dismissed prior to trial?'

"'My attorney's working on it,' he said. 'And I have an appeal filed in Sacramento.'

"'An appeal? For what?' I didn't understand how you could appeal if you hadn't been tried.

"'To get the whole case dropped. The DA who's prosecuting me is a little faggot-motherfucker, with one of those voices.' Here he inserted his imitation of the DA, speaking in a soft, high falsetto, 'Well, your honor, we . . .'

"He stopped his imitation, shaking his head in severe criticism. 'He's got nothing on me but won't let me go 'cuz he doesn't want to admit it. They're holding me only on the statement of an officer.'

"Again I didn't understand. 'How can they — ?'

"Roy interrupted me, said, 'If an officer has five years of experience, or more, they can hold you over based on his statement alone.'

"'Yeah,' I said, half a statement, half a question. 'But I thought you said they were holding you on the basis of what your coworker said.'

"'No, my attorney destroyed all the witnesses at the preliminary hearing.' As he spoke, he moved his left hand back and forth across his neck, as if cutting off someone's head.

"'All of them?'

"'Yeah. That motherfucker's gonna be taken care of when this is over,' he said softly, a wolfish grin on his face. Then he said in a rasping whisper, 'Soon.'

"He was referring to his coworker.

"'Whaddaya mean?' I said. 'You mean they'll bring charges against him?'

"'I mean he won't be around,' Roy said, and again he slashed his hand across his throat, adding, 'I'll take care of him.'

"I just kept walking, not daring to say anything, afraid to even exhale.

"'I knew him for fourteen months,' said Roy. 'We ate lunch together. Then the fucker sets me up.'

"He was instantly very angry. A black rage exuded from him, almost palpable.

"'You think he did it?' I said, going along with his perennial stance of innocence.

"Roy shook his head; his eyes unfocused, the thousand-yard-stare look, as if he was somewhere else, seeing something else. His hands out front of his stomach, down low, he whispered, 'No . . . I took her and . . .' His hands clenched around something. I assumed her neck. I felt nauseous and scared to death. 'I did it,' he said, very softly. And I don't think he knew he said it, he was somewhere else, a different time and place.

"He came out of his reverie. Then asked me, 'When they arrested you, you didn't make any statements, did you?'

"'No. I was all set to, but a friend told me not to. Told me to get an attorney.'

"'Good for you,' he said. He smiled. 'They took me in, and I knew. . . . I had this feeling they had done something to my wife, so I turned to one of them, said, "I know what you did." The cop told me to shut my fucking face, so I decided to not say anything. Right then. I decided, fuck you. I want an attorney.'

"'Good thing you did,' I said.

"'Yeah,' he said.

"'Sounds like you got a good attorney too,' I said. 'King Arthur, you call him, right?'"

The DA smiles at this. One of those quirky smiles, as if there's a private joke here.

"He smiled. 'Yeah.' He stared directly at me, said conspiratorially, 'Bob paid big bucks for his, right?'

"'Two hundred grand,' I said. 'Of course, that includes a forensics team and everything. Supposedly the guy's one of the best.'

"'What's his name?'

"'Randy Thomas.'

"'I been following Bob's case in the papers — the gun and all. First they questioned him, then they left — the cops — and then came back a few days later to arrest him in the hospital. That doesn't look good,' he said.

"'Bob doesn't say much about it,' I said. 'His attorney put an unofficial gag order on him. And Bob sticks to it.'

"Then Bob showed up and started walking with us. His show was over. After a few more minutes of walking, Roy left to grab a cigarette before lockdown."

SAY AMEN

No one says anything. I sit on the bad guy's side of the bubble, they sit on the white hat side — the good guy's side. My side feels cold, full of decay and solitude. The decay of warehoused prisoners. The solitude of glacial loneliness swells around me, like a bloated iceberg.

The DA shines a smile at me. "Thanks for your time," he says. He leaves the bubble, taking his power with him.

"Is that everything you can recall?" asks the investigator. He switches off a small black microrecorder, which I had not noticed.

"Yes," I nod. "There are probably other things, little things, that I'm forgetting. But that's the gist of it."

"Well, okay," he says, rising. "Thank you for your information." He leaves too.

I turn to my attorney. "Do you think it will get me a deal?"

"We'll see," Mike says. "I'll go speak with them in just a moment. But I would imagine it might. Maybe house arrest for the rest of your time." He walks to the door, spins to gaze at me, adds, "I'll be back in a few minutes."

I give myself a melancholy shrug. Wait. Cold. I pull my legs up to my chest, hugging my thighs to myself, my white tackies gripping the edge of the chair. I don't think, don't hope, don't imagine. It takes too much energy. My worry is now a physical thing. My body worries for me.

The good guy's door opens, Babitzke comes in, sits down. I cannot perceive any smile, any positive body language, any overt favorable signals.

"Well, what did they say?" My emaciated ass is perched on the edge of the chair now.

"They're going to release you on your own recognizance," he tells me. Now he smiles.

I hear but do not understand. "What?"

"They're going to release you on your own recognizance," he repeats.

"No home detention?"

"No. You'll be on your own recognizance, return on the 18th of September for sentencing."

"Well, what will the sentence be? I'm not going to get out and then go back, am I?"

"No. More than likely, the sentence will be reduced to time served," he says.

"What about parole?"

"Parole will not begin until you've been sentenced."

"So I don't have to report to a parole officer?"

"Not until you've been sentenced."

The information worms its way into my fuzzy mind. I should be ecstatic; all I feel is creamy relief, like a soft sigh leaving my soul, oozing out the pores of my skin.

Babitzke stands up, says, "I'll be back in just a few minutes. They're preparing the agreement. You'll have to sign it."

"Then what? How soon will I be released?"

"One week," he says. "You'll be released on May 2nd."

"Why so long?" A warbling whine presses from my voice.

"That's how long it takes," he explains. "It's a process."

"But I *will* be released in a week? You're sure?" My relief is gone, replaced by a stream of gasping fear.

"Yes. I'm sure," he states. He has no doubts.

I have many. "Okay," I say.

My body wants to scream, jump up and down in front of

the DA because he won't just let me go now. Wait, cautions my inner boss. Wait. I count the days off on my fingers, like a child. Six days: Thursday, Friday, then the weekend (Saturdays are the worst, but Sundays go fast), then Monday, then out on Tuesday. I count them again, just to be sure. My whole being needs to be sure, to know, to anticipate — to wait.

Okay, okay, I can do this.

Babitzke comes back through the good guy's door. He carries a folder in his hand. He sits down, reaches into the inside pocket of his suit jacket, retrieves a fancy silver pen. "You need to sign and date this agreement," he says as he pushes the document through the paper pass hole. The pen sits on top of it. The paper startles me with its whiteness, like milk in the noon sun.

"What am I signing?"

"That you'll be released on your own recognizance. As long as you cooperate and the judge doesn't think you're lying, your sentence will be reduced to time served."

My hand cramps as I take the pen, my fingers feel dry, as if they're made of old dry sponge, not flesh — they won't work. I wonder if I can sign. I see the DA's signature on the page. Below his line is another line — mine. That's where my name goes. Mind over matter kind of thing. I will my hand to work. I sign a miserable scrawl of my name. But at least I sign. I will be free . . . in six days. I count them off on my fingers again as Babitzke signs his name.

"I'm scared. If Roy hears about this, even a hint, I won't be safe in there."

"The DA knows that," says Babitzke. "They've done this before." He folds the pages back, places them in the folder. "They're going to transfer you."

"I don't want to go to the Hole." Which is worse? The Hole or Roy?

"They won't send you to the Hole." He puts his pen back in his pocket.

"Where will they put me? Not in mainline?"

"No. They have lots of units over there. They'll put you in another one."

"But not the Hole. I don't want to go to the Hole."

"They won't put you in the Hole," he repeats, trying to reassure me.

"Okay. I just don't want to go to the Hole. How soon will they transfer me?"

"Within the next twenty-four hours, I suspect. It will be quick."

"Okay. As long as it's not the Hole."

He stands. "I'll tell the bailiff we're done in here. They'll put you back in the tank, and I'll see you in the courtroom in about forty-five minutes."

"Okay," I say. "And thanks. Thanks very much for doing this."

Gratitude floods out of me. I hope he can feel it because my voice is a monotone, a mirror image of my mind. Six days. Six days.

A few minutes later the bailiff unlocks the door, and I shuffle out. As he escorts me to the tank, I think back to last night when my decision to become a snitch took on a new eagerness.

OUTER VIEWS

April 26, 2006

Holding Tank, Manteca Courthouse

11:00 a.m.

Back in the tank with Matt, after making my deal and signing the agreement, I discover a refined repast residing on the metal bench, my lunch in a brown paper bag: four slices of anemic wheat bread (kind of like Wonder Bread that's been dyed brown); two slices of synthetic meat, which claim the double distinction of being both odorless and tasteless; one slice of processed cheese, not Kraft, that's for sure; one small orange, the kind with the thin skin you can't peel, instead you kind of flake it — they always taste partly fermented, as if they popped out of someone's intestines halfway through digestion; two sugar cookies of tectonic density; one small, squeezable packet of mustard, one of mayonnaise.

"What h-h-happened, dog?" says Matt, his tongue peering around a massive bite of sandwich. He chews with his mouth open, those large, elliptical chews, like a rambling wreck redneck in the movies.

"Nothing yet," I say. This is a lie, and I don't want to lie to Matt. He is my friend. I like him. The lie is necessary. I will not, cannot, tell anyone I just made a deal — that I am a snitch.

"Y-y-y-y-y-y," says Matt, then stops, alters his consonantal direction for easier articulation. "Didja see the judge yet?"

"No. I just talked with my attorney."

"W-w-w-what'd he say?" says Matt, jamming the last of his sandwich in his mouth with three fingers.

"He says I'm supposed to be sentenced today, but it'll probably be continued again because of determination of restitution." Another lie. "Hey," I say, "you want my lunch?" I hold the Saran-wrapped mass out to him, like a pagan tendering a sin offering.

"You d-d-d-d-don't want it?" Matt says.

His face betrays his lust for it, yet jailhouse etiquette demands he politely confirm my offer: do I expect anything in return, because if I do that means he will owe me if he accepts it. Owing leads to violence and/or the hated nickname of "mooch." Matt is not afraid of me. His confirmation is not emblematic of his respect for me; it is reverence for jailhouse tradition, myth, culture. Jail is Matt's surrogate mother, a kind of Industrial Lovely Lady Lump — a cement teat at which he suckles. Matt is institutionalized.

"No," I say shaking my head. "I don't want it. I can't stand this shit." I thrust it toward him.

He extends his arm tentatively. "Y-y-y-you sure? Really don't w-w-want it?"

"You take it," I say, giving a silent motion "take it" with my head, rearing my chin a half inch, an insistent motion. "If you don't, it'll just go to waste."

"Thanks," says Matt as he releases the uninspiring mass from its Saran-wrap prison. He snarls the condiment packages open with his teeth, spreads the yellow and white pastes over the fake meat, which rests on his orange knee, with an index finger, sucks it clean, centers the cheese with microscopic precision, traps it inside a two-sided sandwich, like a clit in a vulva. He eats half of it with a cavernous bite. With a vast swallow, Matt says, "You think th-th-th-they'll send me back to DVI or let me go back to the jail?"

"You want to go to the jail?"

"Yeah," he says. "Kind of a holiday, ya know? DVI, they'll just p-p-p-p-put me in the Hole while I wait." Then adds, because of my questioning frown, "'Cuz they won't b-b-b-bother assigning me since I'll be transport-t-t-ted in a f-f-f-few days."

"Probably the jail," I say. Another lie, but the one he wants to hear.

"Are there any empty bunks in PC?" he says then snaps a sugar cookie in half. "Jesus," he snorts. "B-b-break your fuckin' teeth on this, dog."

"Yes, there are two or three bunks available, now that I think about it. Ed Ventura's bunk is available and a couple downstairs."

"So there's room?"

"Yes."

"Then they'll probably take me to the jail rather than DVI. I mean, if there's room and all. That way I could have a vacation — kind of. I want to see Chuckie again." A smile rises on his face, like the sun coming up, as he muses over Chuckie. "I miss 'em, dog," he says. "M-m-m-m-me and Chuckie, we're like th-th th th-this."

He demonstrates their closeness by holding up his hand, crossing his index and middle fingers. It's as if he's saying that's how close we are, so close it's physical, so close it's like two fingers side by side on the same hand, controlled by the same brain, which encompasses the same spirit.

Matt chortles contentedly, rolling his head, twisting sideways, clasping his hands in his lap, as the happiness ripples and morphs down into his body. "He's my dog!" His energy is yellow; a yellow energy, a nice energy, radiates from him. "I sure hope they take me to the jail," he says.

"They more than likely will." I shrug. "Just makes sense. They have room, and they have to put you someplace." Comfort words, that's what I'm doing, trying to comfort him by telling him what he wants to hear. Kind of like comfort eating.

"I hope so, dog." He's now lying down on his metal bench with a roll of toilet paper as his pillow. His ankle shackles shake, rattle, and roll with every minute adjustment of his body. "I'm gonna take a nap." His eyes snap shut. "Hey, dog," he says, eyes still shut, "if they don't take me to the jail, be s-s-s-sure to t-t-t-tell Chuckie for me. Tell him, I l-l-l-love his l-l-l-l-life. Yeah, I love his l-l-l-life. And tell him, 'What's up, dog?'" He turns his head, his blue eyes examine me. "You'll tell him, r-r-r-right, dog?"

"Sure, Matt. Sure, I'll tell him."

"Whattaya s'pposed to tell him?"

"That you love his life. And ask him, 'What's up, dog?'"

"Right," says Matt, like a teacher to a student. "That's right." Satisfied, he closes his eyes and does that old man thing with his lips, as if he has no teeth and needs to arrange his tongue and his lips just so, like a jigsaw puzzle.

I stand. My feet tingle with beginning numbness from the cold cement, lack of movement, poor circulation. Positioning myself beneath the vent on the ceiling, I hope the furnace will kick in, giving me a warm-air shower. I cross my arms on my chest, start to do the Radic mambo, swaying my hips in a circular motion. It brings thoughts of scrubbing bubbles, the commercial on TV, where the little cartoon brushes scrub away with rooster tails of bubbles trailing them. As I sway, I am scrubbing away time, bubbling away the boredom, keeping myself warm.

Fifteen minutes later the key rummages in the locked door. A bailiff peeks in, tall, with a craggy face, a face wrinkled with compassion. I've seen him before too. He's not an industrial bailiff, the kind that comes off the assembly line: standardized, quantified, categorized.

"Mr. Radic," he says. "Time to go to court, see the judge." He leads me out. Because of the shackles, the cuffs, I'm sure I look and walk like a penguin. We turn right, through a wooden door, into the warmth and light of the courtroom.

My eyes locate Sharla. She smiles. I try to smile back, it's more like a sick grimace because my face is stiff. Doe is there too, her long blonde hair, her fluorescent green nails, surreal in their real worldliness.

Doe is a good friend. She's the bartender at Tony Roma's, where Sharla and I used to eat often. She comes to all my court hearings to give Sharla emotional support and show me that someone cares.

"Take a seat," says the bailiff, pointing to the third seat in. I sit down. I am in the jury box, which is where they seat the criminals, unless there's a trial. Some tarty-looking assistant DA is telling the judge something. She is brunette, thin, waspish.

Babitzke is standing in front of me. To his left and farther out is Phil Uri, the DA prosecuting my case. Babitzke rounds to face me, leans in close, whispers, "What are you planning on having as your first meal when you get out?" A little smile caresses his face, one of those impish, spontaneous grins. It's really very cute, almost endearing.

I feel a surge of delight. Six days. I'll be out in six days. "Grilled salmon and coleslaw and some wine at Tony Roma's," I whisper.

"Sharla told me you had it all planned out," he says, the smile expanding.

"She knows?" I say.

He nods.

"Everything okay?" I'm worried about the DA or judge shutting the deal down.

"Yes," says Babitzke.

"The State of California versus Randall Radic," reads the clerk.

The judge peers at my attorney. Judge Valvianos. He is immaculately mustachioed, amen good looking.

I hold my breath.

"Mr. Babitzke?" says the judge.

"Yes, your honor. I have spoken with the DA," he says, nodding formally toward Phil Uri, "and I am requesting that my client, Mr. Radic, be released on his own recognizance."

"Do the people have any problem with that?" the judge says to Uri.

"No, your honor, the people have no objection."

I exhale.

Judge Valvianos peers at my dossier on his pulpit-like bench. "I think it necessary to add one restraint," he says.

Fuck! I think to myself. I knew something would go wrong.

"There should be unrestrained search and seizure," says the judge. He looks at me. "Do you understand what that is, Mr. Radic?"

"No, sir."

"It means that any officer can search any vehicle or residence that you occupy — without a warrant. Is that clear?"

"Yes, sir."

"Mr. Radic, I am ordering you released on your own recognizance. Your sentencing is set for September 18, 2006."

Inhaling deeply, I almost rise and start singing. Instead, I glance at Sharla. She is grinning like the proverbial skunk eating shit. She dips me a knowing nod. She knows. I know. My attorney knows. The DA knows. The judge knows. No one else knows.

"Bailiff?" says the judge. "Is there an agreement on file?"

"Yes, your honor," says the bailiff, "there is an agreement on file."

That is my deal, I realize. Anyone who knows anything about court procedures knows what was just said. If not, they are wondering, 'What the hell?' Like the two ladies from my church who are sitting in the back of the court. Two vultures. Two bemused, distant bitches who came to hear me sentenced to prison.

"This way, Mr. Radic," says the bailiff.

I shuffle along out the door, into the tank area, like the dark side of the moon. He hands me a copy of the court order: it is pink, it asserts that I am released on my own recognizance, that I am susceptible to unrestricted search and seizure.

Six days, just six days, and I will be out. Thursday, Friday, Saturday (which sucks), then Sunday, then Monday, then out. Six days.

"Good news," says the bailiff. He sounds sincere, as if he is happy for me.

"Yeah," I say. "Finally."

He agrees. "Yeah, finally. Now don't come back," he adds with a grin.

"Count on it," I say emphatically.

In the holding tank, Matt is awake, sitting upright. "Dog!" he says. "What'd they s-s-s-s-say?"

"Postponed again," I say. Not only a necessary lie but also a "word of wisdom." By snitching, I have just taken on a new persona: alienated loner Steppenwolf.

"C-c-c-c-cool, dog," says Matt. "If they keep stalling long enough, they'll send you to DVI, probably release you after two weeks 'cuz your time is so short."

"Maybe," I say. "Maybe."

Matt stands, says to the bailiff, "How soon does the bus come?"

"In about fifteen minutes," says the bailiff, having checked his watch.

As the door clamps shut, Matt says, "Man, dog, I hope they take me to the jail."

"I'm sure they will."

I feel like a eunuch in a porno flick, misplaced; I'm not an inmate anymore, but I am — for six more days anyway. But I'm not out either. I'm a snitch.

BACK TO JAIL

April 26, 2006

12:30 p.m.

The bus arrives. I am happy to hear it, to see it, because it means I'm going home — back to jail. I concede I think of jail as "home." This is toxic thinking; it scares me. Jail is not home. It is hell.

My system of ratiocination is becoming insane. I am participating in what Bob calls adaptive behavior. And that is the beginning of institutionalization, where one way of thinking replaces another. I am replacing the idea of home with jail. This is sick! I am sick!

As Matt and I board the bus, our shackles scraping over the tarmac, I wrestle with my just-detected insanity: to think of jail as home! Jesus.

Matt is in the cage behind me. He keeps going on and on about Chuckie, about going to jail instead.

"Do you think they will take me to DVI? Or do you think they will take me to the jail?"

"I'm sure they'll take you to the jail, Matt," I say. "They have room."

The mainline crowd in the back of the bus are yelling and laughing. They brag about their sentences, either how short or how long they are. If their sentence is short, they brag because they got away with it. If their sentence is long, they brag because now they are somebody "bad" in the jail/prison subculture. They brag about what they said to their judges.

248

I feel sad for them. They are seeking status. Even in this shithole, they are worried about their status. It is all they have.

Piggy woman is in the cage next to me, to my right. "Fucking three years that bitch judge gave me," she boasts to her friend, who shares her cage. Their shoulders rub, their hips press, their thighs polish each other as Piggy's voice spews hate. "Fucking three years for some fucking crack. Fucking bitch judge. I knew they were coming, so I took off. Sheeeit! Who wouldn't? Fucking bitch judge said probation violation, possession, resisting arrest. Three years! Goddamn, I'm already getting fat. In three years, I'll be your mama's cow, all teats and ass."

She whinnies. Her friend laughs, too, then lows like a cow. This sends them into hysterics.

"Hey, Radic," says Matt. "Do you think they'll send me back to DVI? They'll probably drop me at the jail, huh? I mean, don't you think?"

"Sure," I say, "they'll more than likely hold you at the jail for a while then transport you from there. It just makes sense."

Three years. Jesus. And she's laughing about it, swanking, as if she's Britney Spears or somebody, as if she's Jessica Simpson in the back of that limo, saying to her siliconized Barbie friends, "I wanna be so famous. . . ."

I glance at her. She's right, she is fat. Chub-a-lub-dub. Post-tweaker syndrome, I call it. The tweakers come in all skinny and stupefied, barely able to mumble their names through the few teeth crystal meth has grudgingly left them. Because they can't feed their habit in jail, they clean up. And as they do, they do two things: sleep and eat.

Thinking about tweakers reminds me of Howard. I'm sure he has a last name, but to me he is just Howard the tweaker.

HOWARD

Six of us at the table: me, Bob, Snow, Ed Ventura, Luke, and Howard.
Howard the tweaker. He was here about a month ago for crystal meth, possession, sales, using — the hat trick of drugs. Now he's back for . . . crystal meth. Bob told me all this.

Howard looks like a hairy, gray shadow. He needs a shave, a bath (Jesus, he stinks!), and some teeth. He shovels the food from his tray into his mouth with his hands, which are spiderwebbed with black filaments: crystal meth residue embedded in his pores and wrinkles, along with filth.

Finished, he peers around the table, seeking more food. Pointing at a piece of corn bread on my tray, he mumbles something. I can't make it out because, one, he has no teeth; two, he suffers from the lingering effects of drugs; three, he is a numbskull, most of his gray matter deep-fried by heroin, crystal meth, coke, and marijuana.

"What?" I say. I know what he wants, but I don't like Howard, so I play stupid. I'm not going to eat the corn bread, but I'm not going to give it to him.

"Rrrrrrmmmmmbbbrddd," he says. As if he's fucking gargling.

"He wants to know if you're going to eat that," says Snow.

Snow hates Howard too. I can hear it in his voice, a sarcastic sneer. Of course, Snow hates almost everybody. Snow has severe anger management problems, at least that's what his therapist would say. Mostly, he's an asshole, child-molesting, fat boy who sees his expectations and his life's Quicken-generated bar graph dwindling. But I kinda like Snow, because he can chat (not quite converse) for about two minutes on semi-normal subjects, such as cars or books or Ireland.

"Yeah, I am," I say. I try to vaporize Howard with my look. He knows jail etiquette: you don't ask other inmates for the food off their trays. If they offer, you certainly may take, but don't ask. So uncouth.

Howard grunts and does that old-toothless-man thing with his lips, like a cow chewing cud.

I stare right at Bob, point to my corn bread. "Bob, would you like this corn bread?"

"Sure," he says, reaching for my tray. Scooping the corn bread off, he asks, "Do you want the butter?"

"No," I say.

"Thanks."

"You're welcome."

I turn to Howard, who glares at me. I smile. Howard looks away.

Mike Brown stops by our table on his way back to his cell.

"Taking all bread," he chants. "Taking all bread." Within seconds, he has eight slices of wheat bread.

Howard is pissed. He gargles something, "Rrrddddm-mmnnqqq."

I look at Snow, the interpreter.

"He wanted the bread," says Snow. "He's starving to death. And he wants something sweet too."

I know what that means. Howard has no money on his books and thus can't buy any commissary, which means he's on welfare, which means he is a mooch.

I stand, pick up my tray. "Fucking tweakers," I say to no one in particular.

BACK IN JAIL

Three years. I would die if I was looking at three years. I feel sorry for her. How can she laugh about it? Brag about it? I look over at her, careful not to meet her eyes. It's like she's a carbon-based female space invader. She doesn't care, or at least is pretending she doesn't care, which is worse, because it lays bare denial.

The bus lurches to a stop in front of ad-seg. Red man is the first to get off, a kind of crimson royalty as the COs give him room to pass. In keeping with his royal status, he acknowledges no one, simply looks through them.

Next Piggy and her friend waddle down the bus steps. Back to the Hole.

The bus pulls a giant U-turn, travels two hundred yards to the transportation compound.

"I hope they take me off," says Matt.

"They will," I assure him.

I'm the first off the bus.

"This one's a six," says the driver. The CO at the intake door nods.

As I pass him, he points to tank 11. I look at about twelve inmates sitting in the row seats. They are waiting to go to afternoon court.

"In there," he says. "I'll be back in a second." He slams the door.

I know the routine. He will remove my cuffs and shackles after the twelve inmates are on the bus. He cannot risk my person being compromised by some supreme white power Neanderthal Nazi Low Rider who imagines I'm a child molester or some ambitious Mexican Mafia banger, with XIII tats decorating his body, who decides to gain some "respect" by taking me out.

Sitting on my shiny steel bench, I am frightened for my physical person. Not from the twelve inmates awaiting transportation, not from the Surenos, and not from the Low Rider skinheads. But of Roy G. Smith. If he even suspects I've made a deal to snitch, he'll kill me. And CNN is sluggish compared to the news delivery rate of the jailhouse gossip machine.

I hope they will have me transferred within twenty-four to forty-eight hours. I remind myself to say nothing about anything, especially to Bob. Not a hint, not a smile, not a degree of jauntiness, only the same old same old.

The CO returns, the ubiquitous white gloves protecting him from my cooties. "On your knees, hands on the wall," he says.

I obey. He removes the leg shackles then the handcuffs. Usually, it is the other way round, cuffs first then the shackles. I turn, expecting him to motion me out.

Instead, he says, "Sit down."

I obey. Matt is not taken off the bus. If he was, he would be in the tank with me. Two sixes together, on their way to PC. He is on his way to DVI.

Sixty seconds later the door opens to the key of a different CO. Sloping shoulders, around sixty years old, with white hair; I recognize him. He's okay.

"Radic?" he says, consulting the laser-printed page in his hand.

"Yes, sir." I stand.

"They're moving you." He glances at the page again, a bemused frown on his lips. "I don't know why," he says. He shrugs, motions me out. "Let's go."

I just got off the bus, and I am being transferred. Like a sharp knife entering my brain, I wince at the power of the DA. Himmelblaugh is a high flyer. I am impressed by the dynamic velocity of his authority.

We stroll down a long hall painted a very pale green, with ugly-sister gray tile. I stay next to the wall, five feet behind and three feet to the right of the CO. I say nothing; he says nothing. This is the central hall that interconnects the various appendages of the jail.

Protective Custody, my previous unit until about five minutes ago, is Intake 2. We pass it, moving down the hall to Intake 3. I have heard of it, along with Intake 4, but I assumed they were mainline or general population units. Maybe I will be in GP, with lots of rec time. No. They wouldn't do that. GP would be even riskier than Intake 2.

The CO pauses before the massive steel door, presses the silver button, waits as he is scanned by the camera. The door pops, sending deep reverberations, semiotic sound signals of restriction shimmering through the machine-scrubbed air. The echo says, "We are in control."

I glance around as we walk in; except for a distinctive new look and the Mr. Clean sparkle about it, it's the same as Intake 2.

The CO leads me over to the podium, where one of the unit's COs stands. Déjà vu. He is tall and muscular, with a shaved head, Eurasian looking in that God's elect handsome way. This is the CO who was on duty my first day in Intake 2. Here he is again, on my first day in Intake 3.

"Got a transfer for you," says my escort. He gives him the page and leaves.

The CO checks the computer screen in front of him. "Okay, Radic," he says, "grab a bedroll and a towel. Cell 23." He points to it.

I grab a bedroll, which consists of a thin blue blanket and two coarse sheets. I already miss my pillow in Intake 2. Only six days, I tell myself. Spotting an extra sheet next to my bedroll, I snag it too.

I turn to the CO. "Excuse me, sir. May I ask a question?"

"Sure. What is it?"

"What about my personal property, sir? Will I be allowed to get it from I-2?"

Reaching for the phone, he says, "I'll check on it."

"Thank you, sir." I stride to cell 23. As I approach the blue door with the big white 23 on it, it pops. I enter, banging the steel door shut behind me.

Appraising my new luxurious quarters, I note no toilet seat, unlike Intake 2, where we had porcelain toilets with plastic seats. Cell 23 has a stainless steel toilet and stainless steel sink with timer-regulated hot and cold water buttons. Press cold and receive a fifteen-second stream of cold water. Then press hot and receive fifteen seconds of warm water. But that's it. I must now wait two minutes before the faucet will reset, allowing me to obtain water again. The toilet functions on the same principle. After each flush, I must wait two minutes to flush again.

I quickly make my bed: bottom sheet, two top sheets, blanket. Taking my sweatshirt off, I fold it into a makeshift pillow.

Six days. Only six days.

I check the toilet. It is disgusting. There is green algae growing inside it, with a putrid reddish-yellow layer beneath the green. A heavy brown scum ring resides at water level, like burnt cheese around a casserole pan. Jesus. A rotten odor wafts up to my nostrils. I almost vomit.

Walking to the cell door, I peer out the window. Both COs are now behind the podium. The Eurasian and a shorter blond CO. I recognize him. He, too, is okay. I will wait for one of them to make his rounds. Patience is not difficult when there's nothing else to do.

I see two trustees sitting at a table folding towels. Then I see two female trustees. One black, one Mexican. They are both obese. But women? Maybe Intake 3 runs the kitchen differently, I tell myself.

The blond CO begins his rounds. As he nears my cell, I say, "Excuse me, sir."

He stops and stares in at me. His expression tells me he recognizes me. "Yeah?"

"When it's convenient, sir, would it be possible for me to get some cleaning supplies so I can clean my toilet?"

"Sure," he says, moving off.

"Thank you, sir."

I lie down. It is around 1:30 p.m., I guess. Over in Intake 2, they are out on rec. I wish I was walking with Bob, talking. I wish I could call Sharla, talk to her about what is happening. How excited I am becoming about getting out, that I've been transferred, about how vile the toilet is, how cold the steel rim will be when I sit to defecate. Just to hear her voice, to know someone exists outside this absurd setting.

I begin to pray: dear Lord, deliver me from the pit of my life. Confound the minds, stir up the hearts of those involved in my case, my deal. Let me get out of here. I pray this same prayer ten to twenty times a day. Deliver me from the pit — this pit — of my life.

Thirty minutes pass. I feel it. The CO will be back around shortly. Every half hour. I rise and stand at the door. He nears my door, slows, uses his master key to open it. Behind him is a trustee, pudgy, one of those pale-skin types with lots of dark, coarse, curly body hair. He hands me a bucket that contains an agent orange spray bottle, a toilet brush, and a ragged white towel.

"Thank you," I say.

"You're welcome," says the trustee.

The CO shuts the door, locks it with his key — a key that descends from his Sam Browne belt; it's attached to a reel, like one of those retractable dog leashes people use to walk their foo-foo dogs. This device precludes loss by either accident or theft. Whenever the COs use their keys, as they whip them out on their tethers I feel like they're exposing themselves — like the key is the glans of their penis and the tether is the shaft, albeit a thin one, and that they have just deliberately revealed their genitals to me.

I spray agent orange disinfectant on everything, the sink, the exterior surfaces of the toilet, the cement floor. I clean. Cleaning is therapeutic in jail, perhaps even a form of rehabilitation, because it is something to do. A job, a function, an action, one that presents immediate results: the thing being cleaned becomes cleaner.

After cleaning, disinfecting, sanitizing, I sit down on the stainless steel toilet bowl rim to pee. Sitting is the only way to keep the seatless toilet free from pee splatter. The steel is uber-cold on my ass, causing my sphincter and balls to pull back in wrinkly protest. As I flush the toilet with my white-socked right foot, the door pops. I push the door open, peer out.

The handsome Eurasian CO says, "Come get your stuff." He points at a large plastic bag in the middle of the commons. My personal property has arrived. He had to walk down to I-2, where my cellie, Chris Murphy, bagged it up, per orders, and drag it back.

I drag it to my cell, saying, "Thank you, sir," to the Eurasian guard as I do. It is heavy. Too many fucking personal books.

I begin to unpack my shit — my personal property — allocating it to either one drawer or another. I am the proud owner of two drawers, which are pale green steel drawers underneath my bunk. They thunk, clunk, and squeal as they are opened and closed. No matter, they are mine, and the stuff in them is everything I own.

Personal books; tea bags; tumbler; bowl; sweets; Planter's peanuts; toothpaste; toothbrush; letters from Sharla, my mom, my sister; some personal photos from Sharla and my soon-to-be ex-wife, Traci. Parked underneath the drawers, on the cement floor, are my thongs and my jail-issue rubber slippers.

Before I am half done, the door pops, sounding like somebody dropped a sack of steel bolts in my cell.

"Radic," the blond CO says in a flat-projectile voice, one that smacks your cheek but is not a bellow. He stands behind the podium, turning the pages of some newspaper in mechanical fashion.

"Sir." I stand in the doorway.

He looks at me. "You've got one hour to shower, exercise, smoke. Whatever you want to do. One hour only," he says. He turns back to his newspaper.

"Yes, sir."

I move rapidly. Put my white tackies on, pick up the cleaning supplies, walk across the open area, put the supplies back on the rack, pick up four rolls of toilet paper, return to my cell.

I pick up my shower thongs, my towel, my soap in its opaque plastic dish, dumping them all on my red chair. Grabbing the chair, I move quickly to the showers. Knock, just to be sure, although it is already evident that I will be recced alone because of my protective status, at least until the classification officer speaks with me. Once he speaks with me, I hope to be allowed out with the other inmates. Not because I miss normal human interaction but because I will be out longer. Eighty-four square feet gets claustrophobic and as boring as Theravada Buddhism (you know, previous lives, self-salvation, all that shit).

I shower in my thongs, because of athlete's foot infection in jail showers, while trying to keep the shower spray from my clothes, which are parked on my red plastic chair, my one and only piece of furniture (and for that reason I cherish it), behind me, in the shower.

This is because inmates must enter and exit the showers "fully dressed." Fully dressed means T-shirt (tucked in), underwear, orange top, orange bottoms, socks, rubber slippers or tackies, and ID tag. Failure to do so results in a loss of privileges, usually no commissary for two weeks.

I exit the shower fully dressed. Returning to cell 23, I put everything back in its place, grab my plastic tumbler, drop a tea bag in it, walk across the open area to the kitchen, where I fill my tumbler with hot water from the dispenser. While swirling the tea bag in the tumbler, I walk to the phones. The water's heat oozes through the plastic tumbler, almost burns my hand. The almost pain stimulates, soothes, reassures, all at the same time. Because I can feel pain and be miserable — this is good, for it means I'm alive.

I want to call Sharla. I miss her. I dial her number, wait for the connection. "Thank you for using Evercom," says the female voice.

"Hello," I say.

"Hi," says Sharla. She extends the iota vowel, her tone descending so the aggregate is pure sexy sexiness.

My blood jets through my body in response. "They moved me," I say. "I'm in Intake 3 now."

"I know," she says. "Babitzke told me. I was hoping you would call."

"Yeah. I was hoping I'd get to. However, I don't know when I'll be able to again. I think I'm locked down for my protection."

"That's good," she says.

"Yeah, but bad too because I'm going to go crazy with only an hour out every other day. Jesus."

"I know it will be hard. But you can do it. And it's for your own safety. And you'll be out in six days I can hardly wait."

"Me too."

"I love you, Randy."

"I love you. More than you'll ever know." I hesitate. "Listen, call my mom and tell her I was moved, so I don't know how soon I'll be able to contact her. Okay?"

"Okay. I'll do it. And call me whenever you can."

"I will. I'd better go now, I have only a few minutes left, and I need to do some things. I love you, sweet girl."

"I love you too."

"Bye. I love you."

"I love you. Bye," she says.

I walk toward the yard, out the door, into the warm, my eyes squinting because of the glare. Looking up, I begin to walk in a counterclockwise direction. Up because that's where the sun is, although I can't see it. But there is the blue sky at the top of the thirty-foot cement walls that ring the yard. I feel as if I'm tumbling in a kaleidoscope, one made of cement, with a chain-link fence supported by four-inch steel bars instead of a viewing lense.

This is only the second time I've been "outside" in six months. The first time was at the end of the hunger strike in Intake 2.

INTAKE 3

_____

_____

_____

_____

After my hour of rec time, during which I have the whole fucking unit, basically, to myself, I return to my cell. Lock it down.

I expect the other inmates in the unit will now be blessed with rec time. I am wrong.

One of the COs comes by on his rounds. As he passes, a voice in cell 22, next door, shouts, "Getting out on rec soon?" The voice is black, or rather the speech pattern is black: thick and ropey, like strands of mucus hanging from a nose; geometric intonation rather than linear.

"Not right now," says the CO, rapping his knuckles on the steel door. He is walking swiftly, yet his attitude is mellow.

"Why not, man?" shouts the black voice.

But the CO is gone, unperturbed.

"Fuckin' A!" the voice whines. He thumps his cell door once — loud but not loud enough to draw attention to himself. "Goddamnit. Motherfucking assholes," he says to no one in particular; maybe himself, maybe God. I don't know. I empathize with his desire to desert his cell for a while but retain no sympathy for him. I think to myself, "If you want more time for rec, my advice is this: organize a hunger strike." I laugh.

I gaze out my cell door window, watching two trustees setting up tables for dinner. In the kitchen area, I see two women. They are moving plastic crates of milk cartons into the refrigerator. I wonder if this unit is co-ed. Maybe they just have two female kitchen workers who come in for meals. One is black, the other is white. Both are hugely obese, with great, magnificent bosoms and grand hips, protuberant buttocks. They move ponderously, like twin T. Rexes. They finish their preparations, join the two male trustees at one of the tables. All four sit playing cards, gossiping.

The black voice next door begins shouting. "Vince! Vince! Hey, Vince!"

Hearing his name, one of the male trustees turns his head. He grimaces and shrugs his shoulders, the indications of "What?"

"Hey, Vince!" continues the voice. "C'mere, man! Vince! C'mere!"

Vince shakes his head, turns back to his cards. The other male trustee, a pudgy Mexican, says something to him. Reluctantly, Vince rises, walks to a point fifteen feet in front of cell 22.

"What?" says Vince.

"Hey, man," shouts 22. "How come we ain't getting out for rec? We need to get out, man."

Vince shrugs, which is his way of saying, "It ain't up to me, dog. Talk to the COs, you wanna know why."

"Fuckin' shit, man!" complains 22. "Didn' get out this mornin', didn' get out now. Why we ain't getting out, man?"

Vince shrugs, makes a cool-it motion with his hands out front of his body, as if he's patting dough. One more shrug, and he returns to his card game.

The guy in 22 thumps his bunk, kicks his drawer, muttering something I can't understand.

Today, Thursday, Friday, a boring Saturday, Sunday, Monday, and then Tuesday. And I'm going home, I tell myself. I can do this. I can do this.

I open my drawer and select a book to read. Neal Stephenson's *The System of the World*, volume three of his baroque trilogy. Sharla has been sending them to me. Thank God for Sharla and books.

Lying on my bunk, my head propped on my folded sweat-shirt, which is propped on the two-and-a-half-inch steel brace of my bunk, I read. My yellow legal tablet and my commissary pencil are on the desk beside me. As I read, I make notes of interesting words, phrases, sentences. Mental stimulation, a kind of mental masturbation.

Lists. I make lists of words to look up in my dictionary. Lists of wines I want to try from the Wine Section of the *San Francisco Chronicle*: cabernets, pinot noirs, nutty chardonnays. Lists of books I want to read. Lists of places I want to travel to when I get out. Lists of foods I want to eat: a bag of dough-nuts, baby back ribs, BLT sandwiches, real eggs, bacon, Burger King Double Whoppers, In-N-Out Double Doubles with three rafts of fries and Thousand Island to dip the fries in. Lists of ideas for books I want to write: this memoir, gang-bangers, supreme white power dudes, (dis)organization, status, the concept of beauty (volume two).

I wonder what Bob is doing right now because he, too, makes lists. Lists of cities he wants to visit. Tennis tourna-ments he wants to attend. Lists of every major ballpark in the United States, as he wants to see them all. Lists of foods and wines he wants to enjoy upon his release. Lists of books he wants to read, mostly classics such as *Dracula* and *The Count of Monte Cristo*. Lists of all the national parks he wants to visit. Lists.

I cherish my lists. They are little sparks of sentience, mini glimmers of hope, small coruscations of "out there." It is probably pathological, but I don't care. I remember a quota-tion from Carl Jung: "People will do anything, no matter how absurd, in order to avoid facing their own souls."

They will even make lists. Lists of the future. Lists of *a* future. Lists of life yet to come, life yet to be lived, life that wants to be lived. Lists of Life.

The crump of heavy steel dock doors invades my reading. Jumping up, I move to the cell door window. The beef trust, the trustees, are wheeling in the cart upon which resides dinner. It is Wednesday. What will it be? I think of Jimbo's meal betting pool. I guess sloppy Joes.

BEEF TRUST BEAUTIES

It's still Wednesday. Six days; actually, less than six now — depending on how one counts. I stand at my cell door window. It is circa 5:30 p.m. Feeding time at the zoo.

The two beef trust beauties, the female trustees, are in their plastic caps, aprons, and gloves. Their male counterparts are seated in front of crates of milk and oranges.

"Ready?" says one of the COs to the trustees.

"That's a big affirmative," cackles the black female trustee.

This indicates to me she is the big cheese, the head trustee.

She places three trays on a small stainless steel cart. Adds three milks, three coffee cups, three oranges, glances at the COs, both of whom are women. One of the COs is fifty-something. I recognize her from Intake 2. The other is in her late twenties, long dark hair wrapped atop her head in a bun-like contrivance.

The young CO walks down the ramp toward my cell. The black female trustee follows her, pushing the stainless steel cart. They arrive at cell 23. Inserting her key, the CO opens my cell door.

I know the routine. Standing back two feet from the cell door, I wait for her instructions.

"Dinner," says the CO. She steps back, allows the trustee to approach my door. The trustee hands me my tray. I hold it before me, as if it's a religious artifact. She places one cup of coffee, one small milk carton, and one orange on the tray.

"Thank you," I say.

"You're welcome," says the trustee.

The CO slams the door shut.

My tray contains two taco shells, greasy synthetic meat, corn, shredded iceberg lettuce, soggy white rice. As I look at the food, my stomach yields an involuntary heave.

I place the tray on my desk then drink the coffee while it is lukewarm. I set the orange aside. Three times I plunge the spork into the corn, devouring it. Carrying the tray to my toilet, I use the spork to ladle everything else into the toilet, which I then flush. The toilet sucks it down with a whoosh.

I peel and eat the orange, leaving the peels on the tray. Then I pour the milk down the drain of my sink. I place the tray on the cold cement floor next to the cell door.

I know the routine. First the lockdowns, of which I am one, are fed in their cells. Then one side of the unit or the other is released to eat. They have fifteen minutes to pick up their trays and eat. After they are locked down, the other side of the unit is released to eat.

The loud popping of door locks tells me my side is first. I push at my cell door just in case the COs make a mistake. It remains locked. I sigh to myself.

Then I watch from my cell door window as the orange-clad inmates line up for their trays. The usual suspects: tall, short, thin, fat, shaved heads, a few long-hairs. Most are young, a few OGs. Just like Intake 2. But fewer Mexicans and more blacks, most of whom are tall and slender.

Minutes later one of the COs shouts, "Wrap it up, gentlemen. Dinner's over."

Trays are dumped, stacked on the cart, where the trustees strap them down.

"Lock it down!" yells the older CO to the stragglers.

Hydraulic locks snap into place with pops, sending shudders through the steel skeleton.

The other side is released. Women!

I watch as they line up. All in jail orange, they look like shabby replicas of those floor mannequins in Macy's, showing the season's latest fashion trends. Half of them are twenty-to-thirty-year-old white women, the other half Mexican or black.

Most are stout fireplugs in physique, with big bottoms and ponderous thighs. Their hair hangs straight, without style, and looks parched. Their dull faces speak a harsh language: boredom, guttural apathy, the bar-bar-bar of female barbarians. High-pitched voices float in the air of the unit as they prattle to one another.

Once the novelty of tits, asses, and wombs dissipates, I sit on my bunk and compose a letter to Sharla. It is short since I am sharp, like a newly honed knife, with excitement. My singular environment and my forthcoming release from jail furnish a physical edge, a hyperawareness.

I finish the letter, insert it in a prestamped envelope, slide it between the cell door and the steel door jamb, where it hangs like a white tombstone in a perpendicular world. One of the trustees will eventually see it, pluck it from its steel cemetery, drop it in the mail slot.

Lying down on my bunk, I read George Orwell's *Essays*.

Around 8:00 or 9:00 p.m., the explosion of hydraulic locks rattles the unit. Evening rec. The zoo animals are let out for showers, cards, hand-rolled cigarettes, the anesthetic effects of television and its parade of things they could have, places they could go, if they had a life and money.

I don't even bother to rise off my bunk and watch. I read until sleepy. Moving to the door, I look out the cell door window. Not six feet from my door, like zombies peering at *Playboy* centerfolds, sit six orange-clad inmates watching television. The volume on the television is loud, so I can hear the dialogue. They are watching the *Dukes of Hazzard*, with Jessica Simpson and her high-res blonde hair, her uber-tits, her redneck pastiche outfits. One of jail's top-ten requested movies.

Rapping sharply on my cell door, I motion to the nearest zombie. He looks at me with haunted eyes. I rap once more, gesturing to him. With vicarious energy, he rises, walks to my door. "Yeah?" he says. He is young, maybe twenty-two or twenty-three. His jaws sprout three days of scraggly beard.

"Hit my lights, please," I shout through the steel door.

"What?"

"Would you turn off my lights, please?"

"Turn off your lights?"

"Yeah. Please."

He hits the switches.

"Thanks," I shout to his receding back.

I climb under my two top sheets, my blue coverlet. My head rests on my carefully folded sweatshirt — my pillow.

SHOPPING A COP

It is midnight. My cell door opens, waking me instantly. Standing in the doorway is CO Moore. Average height, buff upper body. His immaculately shaved head gleams in the dim tier lights. "Radic," he says.

"Yes, sir?" I say, sitting up on my bunk.

"Get up. Make sure you're fully dressed, come to the podium," he says. His voice is low.

"Yes, sir."

He walks away, leaving my cell door open.

I put on my white tackies, wondering what the hell is going on. This is flat-out weird. I put on my ID.

I walk across the quad area to the podium. The two duty COs stand behind it. Officer Moore stands to the right of the podium waiting.

I know the routine. So I stop ten feet from the podium. "Yes, sir?" I say.

"Step in here, Radic," says Officer Moore. He points to an open door behind him. Above the door, black letters read "Mental Health Interview."

I enter, move to the side, wait for instructions. Inside the room is one white steel desk, two chairs. Officer Moore enters, closes the door. He does not turn on the lights. He sits down behind the desk. "Sit down, Radic," he says.

I seat myself across from him — the interviewee's chair.

"I want to talk to you." His tone is conspiratorial.

"Yes, sir."

"I don't want anyone in this unit to know I'm here or that I'm talking to you."

"Yes, sir."

"You were in Intake 2. Now you're here, in Intake 3," he says. He pauses. "When you didn't come back to Intake 2 after your court, people in Intake 2 started asking questions."

"Yes, sir."

"Why are you here?"

I gaze at him blankly. I don't know how to answer. I will not lie to a CO. But to tell the truth is dangerous.

"Nothing will leave this room," he says.

He knows, I tell myself. "I made a deal when I was at court," I say. "So they moved me for my own protection."

"Does the deal involve Roy Smith?"

"Yes, sir."

"The reason I'm asking is because, when you didn't come back, Bob Gay and Roy Smith came to the podium, started asking questions. Roy Smith started acting all weird."

"Yes, sir."

"Did you agree to testify against Roy Smith?" he asks. He looks thick behind the desk.

"Yes, sir."

He regards me curiously, then he makes a delicate gesture. "Do you know where the body is?"

"No, sir, I don't."

He stares straight at me. His eyes are black holes in the dim light. "What do you know?"

"Everything except where the body is." I cross my arms over my chest, a defensive gesture. I am beginning to feel as if I'm on trial, as if I've done something wrong.

"He confessed to you?" says Officer Moore.

"Yes, sir."

"A jailhouse confession," he says out loud to himself. He

taps his right index finger three times on the desktop, as if counting down to blast-off. "Look," he says. "When you didn't come back to Intake 2, Bob Gay came to the podium and asked if we knew where you were, where you had gone. We stalled and told him we'd check and let him know. Then Roy Smith came to the podium, really acting weird, and wanted to know where you were."

"May I ask a question, sir?"

"Yeah, sure." He gazes at me expectantly.

"What did you tell Roy Smith?"

"We knew you were in Intake 3," he says. "But we didn't know why exactly. But we suspected.

'Cuz they don't transfer inmates that fast unless there's a behavior issue. So we told Bob and Roy that you'd been sentenced and that they had immediately sent you to DVI."

"And they believed you?"

"I think so," says Officer Moore. "Bob Gay started telling other inmates that's what had happened to you."

"And Roy?"

"I don't know for sure if he bought it or not." He pauses. "He's pretty weird. He might suspect what's going on." He shrugs. "Anyway, that's what we'll keep telling people. We call it 'shopping a cop.' We misdirect them with plausible information. And we will continue to do so in your case." He places both hands squarely on the desk, a sturdy, final gesture. "This might be your chance for redemption," he says.

I nod.

He knows my crime, my former status as a pastor. They all do. In fact, most of them still refer to me as "the preacher."

"Maybe that's why all this happened to you from the get-go," he says. He makes an approving sign with his hand. Rising from behind the desk, he adds, "God works in mysterious ways."

"Yes, sir," I say. "He certainly does."

He escorts me to the door, opens it. "You can go back to

your cell now," he says. "I'll be on duty here in Intake 3 on Friday. We'll talk again then."

"Yes, sir. Thank you, sir."

I walk across the quad to my cell. Only the tier lights are on, providing a yellowish, parasitical lighting, as if trying to suck the evil out of the sleeping inmates.

I enter my cell, lie down on my bunk. I think about Officer Moore. The untiring resources of Christians is a continuing wonder to me. In the godforsaken environment of jail, he has evolved a philosophical system in which God works in god-lessness.

I think back to my first encounter with Officer Moore.

JESUS AND GREED

_____

_____

_____

The inner door of Intake 2 crumps with the sound of metal bending. It's not, though. It's just the lock being released.

Our escort, a tall corporal, motions us forward. There are six of us, all orange-clad inmates. We are returning from court. My court appearance was one of my many preliminary restitution hearings. It was continued. We know the routine. Walking three feet off the corporal's left shoulder, we troop to the podium in single file. The corporal stops halfway to the podium.

"Be sure you check in," he says, then turns back the way he came.

One by one, each inmate gives his name and cell number to the COs at the podium. The COs check us in on their computer. I am next to last. It is my turn.

"Name and cell number?" says the Asian CO.

"Radic, Cell 52."

The other CO gives me a strange look. "Hold up, Radic," he says.

I step to the side and wait.

After the last inmate has left, the CO motions me to the podium. I stare straight ahead, not meeting his eyes, not glancing at anything on the podium.

"Yes, sir?" I say.

"Radic, we have some information about you." His voice is mannered, professional.

A knot of fear tightens in my stomach. Information? What does that mean? I ask myself. I dart a look at his gold name tag. Moore.

"I want to talk to you about the information we received," he says, seating himself in his chair behind the podium.

"Yes, sir." I stare at the wall.

Looking to his left, Officer Moore sees Todd, the trustee, approaching the podium. "We'll talk later," he says. "You can go back to your cell."

I leave. As I climb the stairs, I wonder what is going on. In jail, any time you are singled out for attention is an ill omen.

When I enter the cell, Josh is huffing and puffing from his exercise routine. I climb up into my bunk to stay out of his way.

"How was court?" Josh says.

"Freezing," I say. "I get to stand in the tank for hours. Then, when I finally go in, they continue it. I was in the courtroom for all of three minutes."

"Sucks, I know," Josh says, running in place.

"Yeah. When I checked in at the podium just now, the CO says he wants to talk to me about — and I quote — some information they received about me. What the hell does that mean?"

"I don't know," Josh says.

"Well, it's got me worried. Did I do something?"

"Fuck, Radic," Josh says, "don't worry about it. If it was some big fucking deal, they'd have asked you about it right away."

I think about that. He's probably right. But then the knot in my stomach becomes a double-hitch knot, squirming tighter and tighter. "Well, I don't know," I say. "That's the first time that ever happened." Even I can hear the whine in my voice.

"Fuck," puffs Josh, doing dips on the desk. "You're such a pussy. It's nothing."

"Yeah, well, all I know is it's got me worried."

"There's nothing you can do about it," Josh says. "So fucking leave it alone. They'll let you know soon enough."

"Yeah," I agree. But I am not convinced. "You eat?" I ask, changing the subject.

"If you want to call it eating," says Josh. He is at the sink, marking the wall with his pencil.

"What was it?" Since being jailed, I put a premium upon food, which I now consider high among human virtues, probably because the food in jail is so abominable.

"Those spicy hot dogs," says Josh. "Good shit, those." He smacks his lips with relish.

My face squinches up. "I hate those."

"I know," Josh says, "but you don't know shit either. Dumb fucknuts pastor tries to sell his church, buy a BMW." He laughs with fat pleasure.

I do too. It sounds funny when it's put like that, when you think about it. "We should get rec pretty soon, huh?" I say, still smiling.

"Any time now." He looks at me. "How come you guys are so late?"

"I don't know. The bus was late. Some junk about having to go to Tracy first or something."

Josh laughs. "Means one of the buses is broke down."

"I guess."

Twenty minutes later the cell doors pop.

"Fully dressed, beds made, T-shirts tucked in, IDs on," bellows a voice. "And keep the noise down."

Rather than immediately cleaning, I go down the stairs to the podium. I want to get this over with, find out what's going on. I walk to within ten feet of the podium, stand at attention, wait to be noticed. Officer Moore glances up from his newspaper, nods to me. I approach the podium, careful not to gaze directly at anything or anybody.

"You wanted to speak with me, sir," I say. My arms behind me, my hands clasped on my butt.

"Yeah," says Officer Moore. He glances at his partner, a

handsome Asian CO with a tonsure cut.

"Yes, sir?"

"We received some information on you," he says, looking directly at me. There's a "You've been a bad boy" undertone in his voice. "You used to be a pastor, right?"

"Yes, sir." I continue to stare at the wall.

"Which church?"

"A Congregational Church in Ripon," I say.

"Then you sold it, right?"

"Yes, sir. And the parsonage." I don't want him to think I'm lying to him. Besides, it's been on the front page of the newspapers and on the television newscasts.

"Yeah," he nods. "Why'd you do that?"

"Greed is the simple answer, sir."

Officer Moore turns to his partner, gives him an "Are you listening to this shit?" look. "Greed. Yeah," he says. "My dad and my granddad were both pastors." He stares at me. "I'm a Christian."

"Yes, sir."

"Tell me about this greed," he says, nodding to his partner, who appears half asleep, uninterested. His nod is a tacit "You ought to listen to this, it might save your soul."

"Yes, sir," I say. "Well, sir — I got tired of watching other people have all the stuff I wanted. Cars, nice clothes, furniture, vacations, all that stuff. So I gave in to greed."

"Yeah," he nods. Then turns to his partner. "Greed is a horrible sin. Gets you every time." He looks at me, his eyebrows up where his hairline would be if he didn't shave his head. "Have you learned your lesson?"

"Yes, sir. The hard way."

"And what'd you get? Sixteen months, I read?"

"Yes, sir."

"That's not too long," says the Asian CO.

"No, sir," I say. "In fact, I got off kind of easy."

"What'll you do when you get out?" says the Asian CO.

"Well, sir, I doubt I'll go back into the ministry." I smile.
They both laugh.

"Me too," Officer Moore says.

"I don't know what I'll do. Something totally different, I
guess," I say, shrugging.

"They take everything?" says the Asian CO.

"Yes, sir. I have no house, no car, no job, and no money."

"So you'll be homeless, pretty much," says the Asian CO.

"Yes, sir."

"You got any family around here?" Officer Moore asks.

"No, sir. Only my fiancée."

"So you'll have someplace to stay, then?"

"Yes, sir."

Officer Moore nods as if in confirmation. "Okay, Radic,"
he says. "Thanks for being so open about it."

"Thanks for being interested, sir."

He lifts his right hand, makes a brushing motion, as if
there's a fly on it. The gesture indicates "end of conversation."
"I was just curious," he says.

As I back away from the podium, he adds, "Good luck to
you."

I nod. "Thank you, sir."

I go back up the stairs to clean the cell. I feel somehow a little
bit cleaner than I did ten minutes ago.

I'm coming out of the storage room, carrying a broom, a
mop, agent orange, and a thick wad of paper towels, when I
run into Ed Ventura, cell 63. He is leaning on the steel railing
outside his cell, hunched over like someone shot him in the
back, talking to his cell mate, Mike, and Tommy Covey.

"Hey, OG," Ed says.

I nod to Ed and Mike. I do not acknowledge Tommy
Covey. I look through him, as if he is not there.

"Saw you down at the podium," Ed says, slumped over the
steel railing. "What was that all about?"

Ed is thirty-something, dark hair, dark brown eyes, which are placid, like those of a cow. He is so handsome he is almost pretty. A former marine, he learned to cut hair while in the military. This skill puts him in high demand here in jail.

"Nothing much," I say. "They were asking me about my crime, talking to me about greed. The one CO is a Christian."

This pleases Ed as he professes Christianity. In fact, it is all he talks about: how he lost his way, turned his back on Jesus, which in his mind explains why he is here — because he backslid. Ed oozes contrition.

Ed is here for indecent exposure. This is his second time in jail. The first time was for being a peeping Tom. Jesus has nothing to do with it to my way of thinking.

"Jesus is the only answer," says Ed. "Without him, according to scripture, we can do nothing."

"That's what it says," I say.

Mike nods and smiles. He is always smiling, always happy, as if he's the evergreen tree of happiness.

"I know he's the only one that helps me," Tommy Covey chimes.

I pay no attention to Tommy's blithering idiocies. Tommy is a chomo. He is a disease in a petrie dish, probably insane, definitely disgusting.

"Yes," Ed says, nodding in affirmation. "Jesus is the way, the truth, the life. And by praying to him, you and I, all of us, can be forgiven of our sins." Ed drops his head all pious-like, looks down at the carpet. Inspired, he staples on a devotion, "And he can do with us as he will. Like Joseph, we, too, will be released when we have seen the rightness of God's way."

These superspiritual emanations strain my tolerance level. So I decide to vacate the premises. "Well," I say, "I gotta go clean." I hold the mop out as evidence, just in case they missed it.

I start to turn away when Ed says, "Hey, Radic. How about joining us at Bible study tonight? As a former pastor, your insights would be welcome."

"No, thanks."

"Okay," Ed says, smiling. "You're always welcome, though."

"I'll keep it in mind." I leave.

Chomo Church, as I call it, meets every evening rec. All the recently converted Christians gather at one of the tables in the quad. They read their Bibles, discuss ways to manipulate God and each other. It's bullshit is what it is.

Ninety-nine point nine percent of the attendees of Chomo Church are sex-related offenders. None of the attendees has more than a high school education, if that. And in my opinion, they, to a man, are fakers. They didn't attend church before jail and won't attend church after their release. It's a front, a ruse, to impress others. At the least, it is a clumsy attempt to "use" God as a way out of jail. As if by being goodie-goodies for a month or two they can bribe God into effecting their early release. They're even trying to scam God.

I have walked by Chomo Church as they read from their Bibles. One of them reads a passage out loud. After the reading, the leader asks, "What does that mean to you?" Whereupon each orange-clad, felonious Saint Augustine gives his interpretation of the passage. Everyone listens rapturously, nodding his head supportively.

What a joke!

Josh is already in the cell, rolling more cigarettes, as I enter with my cleaning arsenal.

"You almost done?" I ask, setting down my weapons of sterilization.

"Yeah," Josh says. He blows tobacco all over the floor.

"Ed Ventura just invited me to Bible study." I snort as if I'm trying to get a booger out of my nose.

"Fuck that shit," Josh says. Then he looks at me as if he's Torquemada and this is the Spanish Inquisition. "You're not going, are you?"

"No way."

I lift the toilet seat, point my spray bottle, depress the trigger, and atomize it with agent orange. Germs, infectious microbes, and bacteria die by the quadrillions. I feel clean.

"Good answer," Josh says. "I don't want no Jesus freaking motherfucker as a cellie." He zips toward the door. "Later, dog."

"Yeah, later," I say to his contrail.

INTAKE 3

Day Two, Thursday

Five more days to go. I can do this.

After breaking fast with corn flakes and some kind of muffin, which looks, tastes, and feels like a four-inch square of two-by-four wood, all of which is flushed down the toilet with high ceremony, I exercise. Then I read. Then I nap.

Neither side of the unit receives any morning rec. Lunch comes, delivered by my waitress, the beautiful, black priestess of girth. I don't know her name. But she is kind.

A blond co unlocks my cell door. I recognize him from Intake 2. He is cool, not an asshole. "Lunch," he says as he swings the cell door open. He hands me my mail: two *San Francisco Chronicles* and a letter from my fiancée. "These came over from Intake 2," he says, a quizzical furrow in his brow, as if he wants to know why I'm here. But he does not pursue the subject.

"Excuse me, sir," I say. "May I ask a question, sir?"

"Sure."

The priestess hands me my tray. On it is balanced a white Styrofoam cup of cold water. Next to the cup is a small white packet of "kool-aid." It's not really Kool-Aid, but that's what it is called by the inmates. It's vitamin-C-enriched, safe-for-diabetics, artificially sweetened powder, which comes in two flavors: yellow and red.

"Thank you," I say to the trustee.

"You're welcome." Her smile is rich and wide.

I look at the CO. "Will the classification officer see me sometime today, sir?"

"I would think so," he says. "This unit is very efficient. So I'm sure he'll be around."

"Yes, sir. I hope so, sir. I'd like to get out for rec with the others."

"I'm sure you will," says the CO.

"Excuse me," says the trustee. "When you finish with those" — she points at my newspapers — "could I see them?" Her voice is tawny and gooey, like warm Velveeta.

"Sure. I'll give them to you at dinner."

She nods, smiles at me, turns to her silver cart.

The cell door slams shut.

Three hours later my cell door pops. I leap up from my bunk, press the door open. The blond CO is standing there.

"Radic," says the CO. "You've got one hour and one hour only to take care of your business."

"Yes, sir."

I walk across the quad, snag two rolls of toilet paper, put them on the floor of my cell, next to the toilet. Then I shower quickly.

At the phones, I call Sharla but cannot get through. I feel abandoned.

I return to my cell to get my tumbler. As I approach my cell door, the guy in cell 24 shouts something at me. I can't make it out. "What?" I say, standing at his cell door.

"Hey, man, make a call for me?" A slip of paper, like a white tongue darting out of a mouth, thrusts out between the cell door and the doorjamb. "Make a call for me, man," he says.

I can see him through his window. He is tall, black, and thin. "What?" I repeat, not because I don't understand but because I don't want to waste my rec time on him and his phone call.

"Make a call for me, man. The number's on the paper."

I take the paper, look at it. On it is a phone number and a woman's name. Theresa.

"Call Theresa. That's my wife," he says. "Tell her to call my brother so's he can bail me out."

"Fuck," I say. "Okay, okay."

"Tell her Steve called. That's me."

Back at the phones, I dial, wait for the recorded prompt: "Please state your name."

"Stephen," I say. I wait.

"Hello?" says a thick female voice.

"Hello," I say. "I'm calling for Steve. Is this Theresa?"

"Who is this?" She sounds angry, suspicious.

"I'm calling for Steve," I repeat. "I'm in the cell next to his in jail."

"What's that asshole want?" she says. "He call me last night already."

"He wants you to call his brother, tell him to bail Steve out."

"Shit asshole call me last night," she yells. "I call his brother. He ain't home. Ain't going to bail his ass."

"Okay, I'll tell him. He just told me to call for him."

"You tell him don't be callin' here no more. Motherfuck," she shouts.

"Okay. I'll tell him."

"Tell that asshole don't be —"

I hang up. Fuck Steve, I think to myself. I walk back to my cell.

Steve is at his cell door window, waiting. "You call, man?" he shouts.

"Yeah, I called."

"You give her the message?"

"Yeah." I slip the paper back in to him.

"Wha' she say?"

"She said she called your brother last night."

"And?"

"I don't think anyone's going to bail you out, man."

I walk into my cell, snag my tumbler. As I leave the cell, I can hear Steve yammering to me still. I don't even turn to acknowledge him. I've already wasted too much time on him.

I fill my tumbler with hot water, drop in a tea bag. I head for the yard door, checking the sole clock in the unit, which hangs above the yard door. The clock is placed so only the COs behind the podium can see it.

I have thirty minutes left. I walk around the outer edge of the yard, counterclockwise. I sip my tea. Its bitterness bites at my tongue.

Twenty minutes later the yard door opens. The blond CO enters the yard. I stop walking.

"Radic?" he says.

"Yes, sir."

"Did you make a phone call?"

"Yes, sir."

"To whom?"

"My fiancée."

He nods, turns to leave. Then turns back to me. "Did you make any other phone calls?"

"Yes, sir. For the guy in cell 24."

"No can do." He frowns at me.

"I thought phone calls were permitted, sir."

"Not for other inmates."

"Yes, sir."

"Okay, lock it down," he says.

"Yes, sir." Fucking Steve can't keep his mouth shut, I tell myself.

The CO holds the yard door open for me.

"I apologize, sir," I say as I exit the yard. "It won't happen again."

He stares at me. "I could write you up."

"It won't happen again, sir," I repeat.

"Okay," he says.

As I approach my cell door, Steve starts shouting at me again, or maybe he never stopped. I don't know. I just walk into my cell, shut the door.

Lying on my bunk, I reflect on my status, the reason I am here. For my crime, of course, but *here* because of Roy G. Smith. Twice-convicted child molester, alleged murderer. A red man.

BEAUTY AND THE BEAST

_____

_____

_____

She is slim, with dark hair arching over average features, not quite pretty but not plain either. Nice enough might describe her. Her gestures are shy, her voice tentative. Mary Morino-Starkey, forty-six years old.

Baton twirler, drum majorette, dancer — her feeble claim to fame, but that was thirty years ago. Right now she's just trying to sell her boat, which hunkers out front on a white trailer. It's a nice-enough boat. A sign divulges the boat's plight to passing cars: FOR SALE.

It is mid-June in California, dry and all but hot. A good time to sell a boat because water sports are popular and the season is just under way. A man called and made inquiries about the boat, his voice low toned and whispery over the phone.

When he arrives, Mary greets him, and they walk to the boat. His rounded shoulders slope to heaviness, with black swirls of hair poking out of his shirt collar, like untended ivy on a wall.

An odd couple, they examine the boat. A car pulls into the driveway. Mary's eighty-two-year-old mother, Olivia, uncrates herself from the cockpit of the automobile. Olivia joins them. Mary introduces her mother to the man, who is gracious and presses the old lady's hand.

The boat meets his approval, so he makes an offer, which Mary accepts. He will pay cash. However, he explains, it would be silly and unsafe to carry that amount of cash on his person, so would it be all right if she follows him to the bank? Once there, he will withdraw the cash, and they can complete the transaction.

Mary agrees. They shake hands on the deal. She follows him in her car, waving to Olivia as she leaves the driveway.

Mary never returns.

The police are contacted by Mary's family members. A search is instituted but is fruitless.

Embarrassing questions are asked. Could Mary have run off? Was she having an affair and departed with her lover? Could she have gone on vacation? Did she often disappear for days without explanation?

No.

Mary's family, distraught, plasters the surrounding area with flyers. Each flyer carries Mary's photograph and announces a $15,000 reward for information leading to the arrest and conviction of the guilty person or persons.

A few days later, the old lady's nephew, Vito Vavaro, is driving past the Franzia Winery, going east on rural Highway 120. Vito glances at the ugly structure as he passes: poop-colored two-and-three-story buildings, tiled waste towers, capacious tanks covered with pipes and valves, and a vast docking area for the trucks. It is the weekend, and the parking lot of the winery is empty, save for one car. It is Mary's car. Why in God's name would Mary's car be here?

Vito notifies the police. The police examine the car, request a forensics team. Tapes from Franzia Winery's surveillance cameras are viewed, revealing a dark-haired, middle-aged man driving Mary's car into the winery's parking lot.

Inquiries by the police reveal that the man is an employee of Franzia Winery. He works in maintenance.

The suspect suffers a common human malaise: information dissemination. Translation: he can't keep his mouth shut. He cannot resist sharing his brutality with others. Lust for approbation, unbridled exhibitionism drive him. To that end, he brags to a coworker, relates the tale: how he strangled the woman, stole her car, her cell phone, and $327 in cash from her purse.

Police detectives question the frightened coworker, who reveals what he knows and agrees to testify against the man.

The suspect is Roy Gerald Smith. Smith is a registered sex offender with two prior convictions. Both convictions were violent in nature.

Smith lives in an apartment in Manteca, which advertises itself as a growing bedroom community. In fact, the city is a low-rent, dismal Sodom and Gomorrah.

Smith has a wife and two children, ages two and four. Police surround the apartment, arrest Smith. Taking his wife into another part of the apartment, they question her while other officers transport Smith to the police station for interrogation.

At the police station, Smith is surly, using coarse language. *Fuck* is his noun, verb, and adjective of choice. He refuses to answer any questions, demands legal representation.

Meanwhile, at the apartment, Smith's wife tells police investigators she saw a woman's body in their bathroom, in the tub. One arm and a naked shoulder were peeking out from behind the shower curtain. When she saw the body, she screamed at her husband, "I hate you! I hate you!"

"Take the kids and get out of here," Smith commanded. He closed the bathroom door.

She called to her children, got in her car, and left. When she returned a few hours later, the body was gone.

Smith is transferred to San Joaquin County Jail, where he is booked, placed in the Hole for his own protection. The San Joaquin County Public Defender's Office appoints Keith Arthur as Smith's attorney.

Smith remains in the Hole for five months. Then he is transferred to Protective Custody, Intake 2.

• • •

Based upon the coworker's information and that of other witnesses, investigators begin searching storm and sewer drain systems throughout Manteca. Commercial dumpsters are searched, and a two-day dig at the county landfill ensues. At the landfill, a high-tech ground-penetrating radar system is utilized in the search. Nothing is found.

One week before Christmas, friends and relatives of Mary Morino-Starkey gather in a rented building. They convene to remember the "sweet, tender, soft-spoken, caring, gentle" woman. Many individuals rise, come forward, speaking in broken voices as they recall Mary. The featured speaker is Les Weidman, Governor Schwarzenegger's public safety liaison. Weidman reads from a letter written by Olivia Morino: "Mr. Governor, I have only two daughters. Now that Mary is gone, I have one daughter left. My husband died two years ago, and I'm alone to bear the agony of the pain and loss of our younger daughter."

Mary's body has yet to be found.

INTAKE 3

Friday

No rec for the lockdowns today. So I read then exercise: twenty-five jumping jacks, fifty squats, ten push-ups, fifty side bounces, twenty tricep thrusts on the wall above the toilet. I repeat this sequence until incipient madness embraces me. I consider myself going mad: an animal becoming savage.

My only concern is the abatement of boredom leading to lunacy. I lie on my bunk, situating myself and my stopgap pillow, begin reading Orwell's *Essays*. In one of the essays, Orwell remarks on many individuals' languid attitude toward life because they never chance upon life's raw guts. This occasions thoughts of my life before jail and my life in jail. Languid certainly describes my life before jail. And life's raw guts is the perfect description of life in jail — like living in bleeding intestines.

INTAKE 3

The two female COs are back, the older one and the short, dark-haired one. I approve of both of them even though they are quick to yell and are strict. There is an intricate pattern of humanity, of kindness, spreading through them. Somehow they avoid malice, hate, cruelty. Most of the guards do, for a fact.

As the young co unlocks my cell door, I look at the face of the black female trustee. She smiles as always.

The cell door opens. Proffering the plastic tray, she gazes at my hands expectantly. I give her yesterday's papers as she gives me my tray.

"Thanks," she says. "You wan' 'em back?"

"No," I say. "Pass 'em on to whomever you like."

"How come they don' let you out?" the trustee asks.

"I don't know," I lie. "But I'm being released on Tuesday."

She smiles at me, like the sun appearing at night. "Ya have anythin' you don' wan', you give it to me, yes?"

"Sure. I'll be sure you get it."

The CO, listening, smiles.

"Okay," she says, "enough small talk. We've got other lockdowns to feed."

The cell door slams shut.

I eat the two synthetic sausages, drink the coffee before it gets cold. I flush the rehydrated eggs and the watery oatmeal down the toilet; in the disposal of the orange juice and milk,

I pour it in my stainless steel sink.

It is freezing in my cell, so I climb under my two sheets and thin, blue coverlet, prop my head on my rolled-up towel, and read. Soon I catch myself reading the same sentence over and over and still not comprehending what I just read.

On the one hand, I am too excited by my impending release to concentrate. And Sharla will visit me tonight. I can hardly wait to see her. On the other hand, boredom is sucking the life from me. In jail, you go along with what is demanded of you, and pretty soon you don't even think about it anymore. You become used to it. Constant vigilance is the only remedy.

Rising from my bunk, I doff my sweatshirt, begin exercising. Fifty squats, then ten push-ups. Then back on the bunk for fifty sit-ups, followed by twenty tricep presses on the wall above my stainless steel toilet. Then seventy-five shoulder bounces between the walls. Repeat, repeat, repeat, repeat, repeat, repeat.

Finally, I finish. I am warm for the moment. Doffing my T-shirt, I stand in front of my six-inch by nine-inch mirror, which, unlike the one I had in Intake 2, is not a real mirror. Here, in Intake 3, it is highly polished stainless steel.

Thin. Auschwitz thin is the body looking back at me. I could count my ribs if necessary. At a guess, I now weigh 140 pounds. I do the math. Down twenty-five pounds in twenty-three weeks. Just over one pound per week.

Putting on my T-shirt, my sweatshirt, I sit on my bunk with the sheets and blanket on my legs. I will be released in three days, not counting today. On the day I am released, I will have been two days short of six months in here.

My cell door opens. The black female trustee stands there. I hand her my empty dinner tray.

"Thank you," I say.

CO Moore stands beside her, his hand on my cell door.

She grins at me. "They ever gonna let you out?"

"I don't know," I say, shrugging.

"Thanks." She gives me another grin. "I'll say a prayer for you."

"Thanks," I say. "I need all the prayers I can get."

She moves off. CO Moore steps into the doorway. "We're still shopping a cop with the story that you went to DVI."

"Thank you."

"Gay seems to be okay with it," he says, glancing over his shoulder. "But Roy Smith is acting pretty weird."

"You think he knows already?" I ask. The icy fingers of fear poke my intestines. My sphincter loosens, but I clamp down on it.

"I don't know." He shakes his head. He looks at me. "He's a strange guy."

"He scares me," I admit. I look down at my white socks on the cold cement floor.

"Anything you need?" asks CO Moore.

"No, sir," I reply. "But thanks for asking. And thanks for what you're doing. I appreciate it."

"No problem," he says. He shuts the door, locks it.

INTAKE 3

Sunday

At two in the afternoon, my cell door pops. I step out in my socks.

"Radic!" shouts a female voice from the podium.

"Yes, ma'am."

"You got one half hour to do your business," she yells. It is the older female CO from a few days ago. She's back. Her partner, the young one, stands with her at the podium.

"Yes, ma'am," I reply. I think about this because it is unexpected, unscheduled. Lockdowns receive one hour of rec time every other day or a minimum of three hours per week. This is my third rec time in four days. Do the guards know? I wonder. Are they being nice to me because I'm a snitch?

Placing my soap dish, towel, and shampoo on my red plastic chair, I hustle to the shower. My shower thongs slap, slap, slap as I walk. Muffled shouts cause me to look up. On the second tier, in cell 65, some whacko supreme white power dude is screaming at me, flipping me off. He stands with his face beveled in his cell door window. Spittle flies out of his mouth as he shouts at me, grinning like a maniac. I listen. "Welcome to PC! Asshole! Welcome to PC! Motherfucker!"

I smile up at him. "Fuck off," I enunciate silently, carefully, as if I'm speaking to a deaf person.

He understands me because he begins pounding his cell door, screaming even louder.

I laugh to myself as I enter the shower. As I wash my hair, feeling the white foam pappy between my fingers, I think about how stupid supreme white power dudes are.

INTAKE 3

Monday

Today and tomorrow. Two days to go. Maybe less, depending on when they release me.

After breakfast, the shift change takes place. CO Palmer is on duty for the day. His partner is female, young and blonde; she has power-lifter thighs and baby-got-back buns of steel.

Lunch comes and goes. I wonder if I will get rec time this afternoon. I decide to ask CO Palmer the next time he makes his rounds. Most of the COs alternate hourly with their partners.

One hour later, Palmer, walking slowly, peering into each cell, approaches cell 23.

"Excuse me, sir," I say, standing at my cell door window.

Palmer stops, looks at me through the window. His blond hair looks freshly cut, neat. "Yeah, Radic?" he asks.

"Will I be getting out for rec today, sir?"

He shakes his head. "No. Tuesday, Thursday, and Saturday this week." He turns to walk away, pauses, and adds, "It's on the schedule."

"Thank you, sir," I respond, machine-like.

I think about this. Being locked down forty-seven out of every forty-eight hours is leaving me breathless with incipient claustrophobia, especially since I know I get out tomorrow. Especially since I know I have a deal to testify, and I don't know why I just can't go home now.

In an effort to void my claustrophobia, I recline on my

bunk, think about Bob and his trial. I wonder how his trial is going, how he is feeling. What he is doing. Is he still walking without me? If he is, it seems a kind of vague betrayal because it's what *we* did.

I think back to our discussion of the color orange and the psychological implications of incarceration. When I recall that the environment of jail — all of it — is designed to brainwash its inmates, it reminds me not to allow it to take place. It also informs me that I am not going insane. Rather, I am responding to neuro-programming, to cultural cues, to stimuli deprivation, to the subconscious suggestions of color.

OMNIPOTENT ORANGE

January 2006

Afternoon rec time, from 1:30 p.m. until 4:30 p.m.

Bob and I walk rapidly. As we dodge orange-clad bodies, my eyes begin to hurt, as if they're going to bleed, from all the orange.

Jailhouse haute couture is orange, blaze orange. Cunt orange, I call it, because it's like a woman you despise but are chained to. You can't get away. Orange pants, the ones with spandex waists, sans fly, and orange short-sleeved V-necked pullover tops. The left pant leg has JAIL stenciled on it in black paint, in four-inch uncials. On the back of the pullover top the same thing: JAIL in six-inch letters. Even the white T-shirt worn under the orange top has JAIL stenciled across its back.

"Bob," I say. "What's with all this orange? I mean, couldn't they have picked something like blue or green or even gray? Something a little more restful? Something not quite so visually unsettling? So, so garish?" I ask because Bob knows shit. Lots of shit. He holds an MBA from Ohio State University.

Bob laughs. His laugh is deep, like his voice. It's the kind of laugh a whale would have, deep, slow, and extreme. "A salient and pertinent question," Bob says.

This makes me laugh. "Bob," I state matter of factly, "that's why I like you so much. You use words like *salient* and *pertinent*. No one else in here would ever use them."

His smile is large. "I know," he says. "And I'm willing to

298

bet no one else in here has even *heard* of them, much less used them."

"You're probably right," I agree, staying on his heels as we walk.

"Back to your question," says Bob, "the answer is simple. Because it's psychological. The orange color is specifically designed to make you not only feel like a megaloser but also to make you believe that you are a Malthusian twee-pop inside an orange Judas-hole."

"Okay," I say slowly, thinking about this. "You're going to have to explain that."

"Well," says Bob, "I've thought about it at length. The psychological implication of orange is retrograde, which is jazzy lingo meaning it causes you to revert to an inferior and interior state."

"Slow down, Dr. Freud," I say. "Pretend you're talking to someone who doesn't know what the fuck you're talking about — only don't pretend."

"Okay," says Bob, flopping his hands out, as if he's holding two melons. "Orange is the color of warning and emergency signs along the highways and byways of America. It's used for visibility enhancement. It is the contrasting color of blue and therefore is clearly visible against a clear sky." He looks over his shoulder at me. "You getting this so far?" he asks.

"Yeah." I cut the corner to keep up with him.

"Good. Now the color orange occurs between red and yellow in the visible spectrum. Actually at a wavelength of about 585 to 620 nanometers, if you want to get technical about it."

I laugh at my own ignorance. "Okay, Mr. Wizard, that does not compute. Or try it this way: it doesn't mean diddle to me."

Bob laughs easily. "Okay. Think of it like this: it's instantly recognizable. It means you're one of the bad guys, one of the criminal types, a radical weirdo that society has to be warned about and protected from."

I nod. "I'm with you so far."

"It all boils down to perception control," explains Bob, "which equals emotional control, which translates to behavior control. Which is what jail is all about. Coercive persuasion and the loss of identity. No more individuation. No more you. No more me."

"So what you're saying is this, if I'm following you," I offer, "they're using the color orange to make us all the same, which makes it easier to maintain control of us?"

"Correct," Bob says, like a teacher in class. "Orange is what is called a 'stimulating' color, because it's the bastard child of red and yellow. Your eyes see it and react to it both physically and emotionally."

"Kinda like blue is used in hospitals and dentists' offices?"

"Right," pronounces Bob. "Orange focuses the mind on issues of comfort, like food, warmth, and shelter, which explains why mealtime is so important in here. Everything revolves around breakfast, lunch, and dinner. Our whole daily schedule is molded around food."

"Where'd you get all this stuff?" I ask, impressed.

"Books from the jail library," Bob replies.

"You're kidding me?" I blurt out. "You mean they came right out and said that?"

"Not in so many words," Bob says, looking back at me. "This is my interpretation of what I read."

"Well, it sounds good so far," I say, giving a little shrug.

"A lot of orange, like we have in here," he waves his hand at our surroundings, "suggests frivolity and precludes serious intellectual pursuits. Which is precisely what they don't want you to do. They don't want you to think." Bob slows as we approach the stairs up to the quad area. "I need to get some tea and take a bathroom break," he says.

"Me, too," I say. I look up at the clock. "I'll meet you back here in ten minutes."

"Okay."

I walk across the quad to the stairs, mount them, and turn the corners to cell 52.

Ten minutes later I return. Bob is walking, sipping his presweetened lemon tea from a plastic tumbler.

Falling in behind him, I say, "Okay. Back to what you were saying about orange and behavior control."

"Where was I?" he asks.

"You had just said that a lot of orange makes for a lack of intellectual pursuit," I reply.

"Yeah," he says, nodding. He takes another sip of tea then places his tumbler on a counter by the phones.

We walk, and for a few moments Bob is silent. "Okay," he says, turning to look at me over his shoulder, "who wears black in here?"

"The cos," I respond, wondering what this has to do with orange.

"The color black," explains Bob, "signifies menace. It also denotes moral and physical excellence and authority. And, most importantly, black expresses threat and aggression."

"Shit," I say, awed by what I am hearing. "So it's like a whole system of brainwashing."

"Bingo!" whoops Bob, glancing back over his shoulder. "Give the man a cigar. You see, color is just light. And light is processed through your eyes, and thus it — the light — affects hormonal levels in your body. In fact, it affects your entire endocrine system." Turning left, Bob looks at me. "I got the hormone stuff from my son," he explains.

"He's a doctor, right?"

"Yeah," Bob says. "Anyway, it is brainwashing. Pure and simple." He keeps walking but stops talking. Then he says, "Do you know what brainwashing is?"

"Not really," I reply. "Just that somehow somebody gets you to think differently."

"Almost," says Bob. "What it is not is someone force-feeding you instructions, like a dog being obedience trained.

Obedience-training your dog is not brainwashing. Because the dog is still a dog and still thinks like a dog."

I laugh at his analogy. I don't know why. It strikes me as funny because all the inmates refer to each other as "dog."

"So that is not brainwashing," continues Bob, making a negative motion with his hands. "Brainwashing is a systematically imposed formula, or system if you prefer, designed to alter your core values and beliefs. And that's what they're trying to do to us in here — brainwash us."

"Whaddaya mean?" I ask, my voice rising upward in ignorance.

"Forget about rehabilitation," growls Bob, "that's just lip service." He holds his hands out in front of his face, making three-quarters of a marquee. "California Department of Corrections and Rehabilitation." He drops his hands. "That's balderdash! You know why?"

"No, but I think you're going to tell me."

"Because rehabilitation would assume psychoanalysis, therapy, and healing. Along with education or at the very least vocational training. But that takes too long and costs too much. Whereas brainwashing is faster, cheaper, and more effective."

"Okay," I nod as we continue tacking to port, like two sailboats with puffy orange spinnakers. "I get what you're saying about rehabilitation not being cost effective, but I don't see what orange has to do with brainwashing." I shrug. "It just makes my eyes hurt. And it's pretty ugly."

"Look," explains Bob, "what happens to you when you first come in here? You are isolated, right? You have no contact with anyone — loved ones, friends, family members. That's why you only get two visits a week and then only for forty-five minutes each."

"Now what?" I ask. I am not getting it.

"They want you to feel isolated and helpless," emphasizes Bob, making his voice even deeper than normal. "But they feed you regularly and on a very strict schedule. The isolation reactivates instinctual behaviors. In other words, the isolation takes you back to being a baby. And what do babies want? Their mommies, right?"

I nod.

"And food? All that is called nurturing." Bob stops talking, marshaling his thoughts. "So in here you are isolated from love and affection, you feel helpless, you are disoriented, and you are scared shitless. All that takes you back to raw, basic instincts." He turns and gives me a significant look. "But they feed you. The fact that they feed you, that is, they act as your mommy, causes you to imprint the institution — jail — as your maternal, nurturing entity."

"You mean jail becomes my surrogate mother?" I ask.

"Bingo!" exclaims Bob. "Another cigar for the man in orange."

"Wow," I mutter. I think about this. "That's pretty scary but pretty ingenious too. I mean, somebody put some thought into all this."

"Darn right they did," Bob agrees. "It didn't just happen. Some very smart psychologists and psychiatrists were consulted." He shakes his head disgustedly. "It's all been programmed."

"Gives me the heebeejeebies," I say, looking around, as if expecting to see a bunch of mad scientists with clipboards peering at us.

"I know," harmonizes Bob. He leans forward a little as he walks, as if he's trying to move closer to something he wants to analyze. "The brutal environment —"

"Like a goddamn zoo," I interrupt.

Bob nods, continuing, "Along with dependence upon jail — the institution — triggers the biological survival instinct."

"The limbic system," I blurt out. "I've been reading about the limbic system — the primordial brain, as it were — in pattern recognition. You know, that book by Gibson."

"Oh, yeah," recalls Bob. "You loaned it to me. I remember that now."

I nod.

"Okay," Bob says. "Now. The next stage of brainwashing involves humiliation and ridicule. This is where the COs come in — although I doubt they are conscious participants."

My face pinches. "Whaddaya mean not conscious participants?"

"They're not actively, consciously trying to brainwash us," says Bob, a sneer in his voice. "They're too stupid and uneducated to be involved at any sophisticated level."

"I don't know about that," I disagree. "Some of 'em are pretty smart."

"Pffftth," snorts Bob. "Uneducated, illiterate, petty bullies! If it wasn't for the county, they'd all be out picking cotton in some field."

"I know what you think of them," I say, "but I disagree. They're the good guys, and we're the bad guys."

"Yeah," says Bob, sarcasm dripping from his words, "except some of us" — he taps his chest — "shouldn't be in here in the first place."

I don't say anything because I don't want to argue with Bob. He's my friend.

After eight more left turns, I say, "Tell me about the ridicule and humiliation part of brainwashing."

"You know how it is," Bob insists. "No matter what you say or do, the COs ridicule it and you. All your ideas, habits, even the way you wear your hair — all of it — is scorned and made fun of."

"Okay," I say, "but how does that fit in with brainwashing?"

"It causes you to change your behavior," explains Bob. "You become more acceptable to the institution, to the COs. And that engages your ego, the basic 'you.'"

"So they're molding me?" I ask.

Bob nods vigorously. "Squeezing you right into it."

"Then what?"

"Then the last stage of brainwashing," Bob says. "Now that they've got you changing your behavior, the way you speak and think — now they put their words and ideas in. They replace your words and ideas with their words and ideas."

I think about this. After a few seconds, I realize it's true.

Bob looks back at me. "You've just been brainwashed," he concludes. "Reprogrammed."

"Yeah," I admit delicately.

"And all of this," Bob says, waving his hand to encompass the jail and its brainwashing processes, "is supported by the jail system of rewards and punishments. You know — if you're a good boy, we'll let you out longer or make you a trustee. But if you're a bad boy, we'll take away your commissary or throw you in the Hole."

We keep walking.

Finally, I say, "That's why Jimbo can't handle it on the outside, then, isn't it?"

"Yeah," Bob says, his voice echoing the sadness of his mind. "He's been brainwashed to the point of being institutionalized. Jimbo has reached the point where he not only has assumed the words and ideas of the mommy institution but also has faith in them. So he keeps coming back because he can't handle the real world anymore. This," Bob jabs his index finger toward the floor, "is his mommy."

"Shit," I utter without any emphasis.

"And, of course," adds Bob with a green flavor, as if he's biting into an unripe apple, "Jimbo's return to the womb of jail ensures the longevity of the institution, the financial fitness of the institution, and the job security of the COs."

I think about this. "So it's all about money," I state in a monotone.

"Yeah," Bob says.

INTAKE 3

Tuesday

May 2, 2006

The muffled thumps of kitchen dock doors and the creaking of tray carts wake me at 5:00 a.m. Instantly, I am alert, ready. I think about Sponge Bob Square Pants and his sidekick, Patrick Star. Like Sponge Bob, I want to run around my cell, waving my arms, dancing my feet, shouting, "I'm ready! I'm ready! I'm ready!"

Ready to go home. Today's the day.

The jail releases prisoners at 8:00 a.m., 2:00 p.m., and 8:00 p.m. I doubt I will be released at 8:00 a.m. I don't know why, it's just a feeling I have.

Nevertheless, thirty minutes later, at 5:30 a.m., I am ready. A large brown commissary sack sits in the corner of my cell. The top is folded, neatly closed. Within the sack are my treasures, my personal belongings: letters from Sharla, letters from my mother and sister, letters from my daughter, photographs, my yellow tablet, one four-inch pencil, shower sandals, and four books: E.M. Cioran's *Tears and Saints*; Jack Vance's *To Live Forever*; Neal Stephenson's *The System of the World*; William Gibson's *Mona Lisa Overdrive*.

Everything else I am either leaving in the cell or giving to the black female trustee, whose name I don't even know. But because of her smile and her kindness, I am giving all my commissary food to her.

In the metal drawers of my bunk, I abandon a number of

306

personal books, a half-used tube of red Colgate toothpaste, two four-inch toothbrushes (one used, one new and still in the cellophane wrapper), a plastic soap dish, one bar of soap, one bottle of shaving gel, one plastic comb (black), eight four-inch pencils, three erasers, two disposable razors.

Maybe the next guy can use them, some poor slob without any money on his books. Besides, I don't want any of it. I want "real world" stuff. Real stuff, not shit from commissary.

One paper bag of stuff, one pair of white tackies, and the clothes I had on when I was arrested. That's what I will leave with. It's not much, but it's mine. And, truth to tell, it's all I have.

Hearing the rattle of keys in my cell door, I move to the door. As it swings open, I see the expansive black female trustee. Her smile is effusive as she says, "Good morning. Breakfast."

"Thank you," I say, smiling back at her. She wears a plastic apron, plastic gloves, and a funky plastic cap on her hair. All for reasons of hygiene. She looks like something out of *Alice in Wonderland*.

"Ya leaving today?" she asks, holding the tray out toward me.

"That's what my attorney says," I reply, taking the tray. Glancing at it, I note dry cereal, three pieces of spongy wheat bread, and an orange.

The trustee places a cup of coffee and a carton of milk on the edge of my tray. "Leave me anything you don' wan'," she says.

"Yes, I will."

She smiles at me again. "Thanks."

The co, a short, beefy female with a Dutch girl haircut, shuts the cell door. I do not recognize her. I set the tray down on the floor by the cell door.

I sip the lukewarm coffee, eat a bag of peanuts.

To kill time, I sit on my bunk with three *San Francisco Chronicles* stacked neatly in front of me. I browse through them section by section, noting each and every article on each and every page. If an article sounds even remotely interesting, I read it slowly. I even look at the advertisements. After I finish, I meticulously fold and stack the newspapers in order then place them by the cell door.

Through my cell door, I hear the COs shouting out names. I distinctly hear the words "Roll up your stuff!" Walking to the cell door window, I peer out.

Three female and two male inmates, carrying plastic bags of personal property and their bedrolls, are moving near the podium. A black-clad officer stands by the cross-barred intake door, a piece of paper in his hand. He will escort the inmates to the release center; there they will be processed out of the jail.

One of those about to be released is the white male trustee — the slender, muscular one with the goatee and shaved head. He walks to the other trustees, who are standing idly in the kitchen area. A smile on his face, he hugs and shakes hands with each of the trustees.

The escort CO barks, "Let's go! I ain't got all day!"

The lucky five — those to be released — line up in front of the CO, clasping their plastic baggies, which contain their worldly goods. The heavy door pops, the CO swings it open, and they march out.

Obviously, I won't be leaving at 8:00 a.m.

Back on my bunk, I try to read but can't. The words don't register. My mind, like my body, is fidgety, vibrating like a stretched-tight wire that was just plucked.

Lying back on my bunk, I put my feet up on the end rail, fold my hands on my chest, and stare at the ceiling. Thoughts, like whirling dervishes, spin through my head. As they emerge, I attempt to annihilate them, but it doesn't work. More appear, then more, then more, until an army of jumbled musings looms on my mental horizon. It's like looking into a jar of worms, a slithering, twisting, distorted mess.

I just wanna go home. But I have to wait.

I wonder about the five who just left. According to Bob,

during our daily walking-talking festivals, three of the five will be back in jail within two years. Sixty percent is the rate of recidivism. I don't want to participate in that statistic. Everyone who leaves this place says, "I'm never coming back!" Yet six out of ten do.

Keys grind in my cell door. Lunch is here, which means it's somewhere between 11:00 a.m. and 12:00 p.m. Which means in two to three hours I might be released.

I jump up from my bunk, take three steps to the cell door. It swings open, heavy on its hinges. In the doorway stands the beefy female CO. Like a miniature Clydesdale, she moves with powerful gestures.

"Lunch," she says and sidles aside to make room for the trustee — my big-bang black baby.

"Man, they keepin' you locked down a long time," says the trustee, presenting me with my tray.

"Yeah," I reply. "Maybe I'll get out for an hour this afternoon." I glance at the CO, looking for some indication. Uninterested, she is in a valley of her own thoughts.

"Maybe," says the trustee. Her eyes peer at me expectantly.

"Excuse me, ma'am," I say to the CO. "May I give the trustee my newspapers?"

The CO looks at me, nods.

I hand the stack of *Chronicles* to the trustee.

"Thanks."

"You are most welcome," I reply.

The cell door closes. As the CO and the trustee walk away, I stand looking out the window of my cell at them, enjoying the aftermath, the waning substance of human intercourse. A few words, a smile, a nod; it's not much, but it's my social time.

Without even looking to see what it is, I place my lunch tray on the floor next to the cell door. I'm too nervous to eat.

Back on my bunk, I lie down, trying, by force of will, to make time pass faster. It doesn't. In fact, the effort seems to have the opposite effect. Time's passage wallows in its own currents, turns back on itself, bobbles, and begins to sink. It's a kind of dying. Waiting.

Like in a bizarre horror movie, my body diffuses into billions of tiny particles, almost like minute bubbles. The bubbles float slowly away, curling and bunching to the whims of unseen eddies. From above, I look down upon myself and see only crystal-clear bubbles, like silver pearls. From below, I look up and see the bubbles that used to be me.

After a while, sounds from outside my cell cause all the billions of bubbles to collapse together, splashing and popping as they come together. I look around. I'm still in my cell, still waiting.

Rising from my bunk, I walk in my white-socked feet to my cell door window. The gray cement is cold through my socks. Peering out, I see that the quad is full of orange-clad female bodies. The other side of the unit, the female side, is out on rec. Which explains the sounds I heard.

They look like a gaggle of pigeons in orange jackets, milling about aimlessly. A few gather cleaning supplies, others walk with towels over their shoulders, going to the showers, and there is a constant shuttle of smokers coming and going from the yard. But most of them wander, like zombies searching for victims. Mindless, bored, semi-sentient organisms seeking something to satisfy the empty hunger inside. It's not a hungry hunger, as in needing food. Rather, it's a psychological hunger, maybe even a spiritual hunger. A quest for peace, love, happiness — something to fill the big hole in the middle of their being. And it's a desperate quest, for if they do not find some type of matter to fill their hollowness all they will have is despair.

Just watching them makes me wretchedly bored too. And depressed.

Back on my bunk, I attempt to slay time by reading. Picking up my novel, I force my mind to forge into the sentences. My premeditated murder methodology works for about two hours, I figure. By then, my eyes are merely sliding across the words, like a child going down a slide in a park, there is no comprehension, just abandonment to the passage.

Two o'clock release occurs. I peer out my cell door window, watching a lone female inmate drop her bedding into a laundry barrel, the coarse white sheets mixed with the blue blankets. Later they will be taken to the laundry, washed in hot water bubbling with detergent and antibacterial solutions. From there, they will travel back to the intakes, where the trustees fold them.

The about-to-be-released woman is a very short, very plump, very Hispanic chick. She looks to be twenty-something; there is a storminess to her face, as if there's a tornado brewing inside. Her hair, like a wild horse's mane, is untamed and long.

As the escort CO examines her ID tag, she stares straight ahead. And when the two of them walk to the door, she waves to no one — no cell mate, no acquaintance.

I wonder what she was in here for. Probably drugs.

My name is not called. So now I will tarry six more hours and trust they have not forgotten me.

Back on my bunk, staring at the jail-white ceiling. Jail white is different from hospital white, which is genuine white, sincere in its radiance, clean and bright. Jail white contains two dollops of gray and one dollop of blue, just enough so the white is not healthy. Rather, it's an ailing white, like looking at the complexion of a cancer patient. The patient is alive but sick. Jail white is infected white.

Clack, clack, clack. The door locks rattle like firecrackers.

"Rec time!" shouts a voice from the podium. "Be sure you're fully dressed, T-shirts tucked in, beds made, ID tags on!"

I walk to my cell door, push against it. Locked, of course, but hope springs eternal.

Peering out, I see the two COs at the podium. They are conferring. The younger of the two turns, shouts, "Be sure your cells are clean! We'll be checking on our rounds. Any cell not clean, you will be locked down!"

Orange-clad male bodies move deliberately. Some walk rapidly toward the tables, roll them out, unfold them, grab chairs, sit down. These are the card players. The two most popular card games in jail are poker, of course, in all its variations, and hearts. Gin rummy is a close third.

Others sit down in front of the televisions. They watch *Little House on the Prairie* with the same avidity as *COPS*. Most, though, move out into the yard for a smoke and conversation. Those who have tobacco are followed closely by their groupies, those who have no tobacco but hang around acting pitiably, on the chance that someone will give them a few drags or, even better, a whole cigarette. The haves and the have-nots.

I can't see them, but I know there are three or four snipe hunters. Those who scavenge the used cigarette butts, hoarding the bits of tobacco until they have enough to roll a cigarette. These are the never-haves. Never have any family. Never have any friends on the outside. Never have any money on their books, which means no commissary, which means no tobacco, no soups, no sweets, no nothing. Even jail has panhandlers.

The television near my cell is showing a movie. *Willy Wonka and the Chocolate Factory*. The six seats in front of the television are already full. Other inmates drag gray plastic chairs over, sit down behind the front row. Behind them, others stand, arms crossed over their chests. I've never seen it, but I have heard it numerous times.

I decide to try to take a nap. Tapping on my cell door window, I attract the attention of an inmate seated in the front row before the television. He looks at me, gives me a "Whaddaya want?" look.

"Hit my lights, will ya?" I ask.

"What?" he says, leaning closer to my cell. He's twenty-something, long dark hair.

"Hit my lights, please?"

"Your lights?" he asks.

"Yeah. Hit my lights, please?"

He starts to rise to hit my light switches, but the inmate seated next to him puts his hand out, touches his arm. He says something to twenty-something. They both stare at the television, pretending I don't exist.

I tap on my cell door window again, this time more insistently. They sit like rock statues, motionless.

"Hey!" I shout through the cell door, tapping.

The other one, the touchy dude, looks over at me. "Get outta the window," he snarls at me.

"What?" I shout.

"Get outta the window, ya fucking chomo! Go sit down!" he rebukes in a loud voice.

I recoil at the verbal spanking. "I'm not a chomo," I protest.

"Go sit down," he repeats.

Retreating to my bunk, I lie down. They think I'm a child molestor because I'm locked down. But I'm not! Making them understand this becomes important all at once. I'm a snitch but not a child molestor.

Angry and hurt, I brood on the insult for a minute or two. Fury energizes me. I want to defend myself. I want to yell and scream that I'm not a chomo. I want to punch my accuser in the face, kick his ass, beat him senseless, stand over his prostrate body, and proclaim to everyone, "I am not a chomo!"

Futile. Even if I could tell him, he would not believe me. I would think the same thing if I were him. More than that, I tell myself, why do I care what another felon thinks of me?

Rolling under my sheet and blue blanket, I lie on my bunk, feeling numb and cold on the inside, as if my organs are packed in ice. I do not sleep. I float in a world where my senses are muffled, where only I exist. That's all — just exist. I don't think. I don't feel.

I lie there wrapped in my blue cocoon, my mind like petrified wood, impenetrable and heavy, until a voice yells out, "Lock it down! Lock it down! Rec time is over! Lock it down, people!" The words power up my brain.

Getting up from my bunk, I note it must be late afternoon, for darkness is beginning its rise, eating up the light. I look out the back window of my cell. Manicured green lawns stretch fifty yards to a lonely parking lot, with only one customer — a white Ford Taurus — parked by the curb. Two hundred yards away stands the chain link that surrounds the jail. Three strands of barbed wire form a prickly dorsal fin at the fence's top. A white truck meanders into view on the service road leading to the parking lot. It stops, and three inmates clamber out of the cab. By their white jail-issue clothes, I know they are kitchen workers.

Dinner has arrived. But it will sit in the dock area for at least an hour, until the shift change. The outgoing guards don't like to mess with dinner when they're ready to go home. More often than not, they postpone it until the new shift arrives.

Back on my bunk, I read one of the books I'm leaving here. Taking a book out of my neatly folded, meticulously ready brown paper bag would make it seem as if I'm not really leaving. I know that is nonsense; it's just me being superstitious, but it grips me and tasks me, so I refuse to do it. It would be like breaking a magic spell or something. You have to be careful, or it (luck, God, chance?) could backfire on you.

Heavy thuds, the opening of the intake doors, announce the arrival of the new guards. I walk to the window to see who they are.

One is male, the tall corporal, mid-thirties, dark hair combed straight back. I like him. He is strict but fair and will answer questions, converse with the inmates. His partner tonight is female. She is five feet five inches or so in height, medium build, short, severe hair. I like her too. Her bark is worse than her bite, and she will answer questions as long as she doesn't think you are bullshitting her.

The trustees do their thing: pull in the tray cart, set up the coffee and water dispensers, put on their plastic gloves, caps, and aprons, set out the crates of milk cartons and two crates of oranges.

Big-bang black baby raises her right hand with its plastic glove, speaks to the tall corporal. "We're ready when you are."

The tall corporal, standing next to the podium, arms crossed across his chest, nods to his partner. She stands behind the podium, in front of the control panel on the back wall. The control panel shows a red or green light for each cell. Red means the cell door is locked, green indicates it is open. Each cell has a flicker switch just above the indicator light. She palms a row of flicker switches and flips them rapidly. A rapid clatter ensues as half the locks on cells on the other side, the female side of the unit, respond to electronic commands.

"Dinner!" shouts the tall corporal. "T-shirts tucked in and ID tags on!"

Orange-clad harridans emerge from their eighty-four-square-foot cells. Although recently the guards, at the direction of some memo, probably, refer to them as "rooms." The crones line up in front of the kitchen, shuffle forward, receive their trays. Then they walk to their table of choice and eat.

When the line of female inmates shortens, the CO palms another row of switches, pops them quickly. The other half of the other side comes out.

As they sup, the female CO accompanies big-bang black baby as she delivers trays to the lockdowns.

My cell door opens. "Radic?" says the female CO.

"Yes, ma'am."

"You're being released tonight. So have your stuff ready. When we pop the door locks, just come on out," she instructs me.

At the word *release*, tension drains from my shoulders, I

can actually feel it slide down my back. "Yes ma'am. Thank you for telling me, ma'am."

Big-bang black baby hands me my tray and coffee cup. She smiles. "Lucky you. Goin' home."

I just smile back. Jailhouse etiquette prohibits gloating at such times.

Taking my tray, I turn to the CO. "Excuse me, ma'am. May I make a request?"

The CO gives me a look as old as time.

"What?"

"When it's convenient, ma'am, could I get a plastic bag for my commissary? I would like to give it to the trustee before I leave." I nod at big-bang black baby.

"For her?" the CO inquires.

"Yes, ma'am."

She pauses. Nods. "Okay, when I have time," she states in a tone of approval.

"Thank you, ma'am," I say, looking at big-bang black baby, who exposes a wide grin.

"Enough talk," declares the CO, "we've got other lock-downs to feed." She closes my cell door with a boom.

I'm going home! I can't believe it. The guard confirmed it.

Setting my tray by the cell door, I sip my coffee, which is actually hot. It tastes divine. In celebration, I sit on my bunk and slowly eat one package of Planter's roasted and salted peanuts, 105 calories per serving, according to the nutritional panel on the back of the package.

Glancing at my tray by the cell door, I see what I am missing: beans, one flour tortilla, iceberg lettuce, one orange, and a square of tiger cake. Tiger cake is chocolate and vanilla cake with swirls of each, so it looks like a bleached-out tiger. I chuckle out loud. No more slop.

Opening my steel drawers, I slowly remove all commissary food, placing it in neat stacks on the cement floor. Three boxes of saltine crackers; one jar of peanut butter; fifteen tea bags; three boxes of Little Debbie Crunchie Bars; three boxes of Star Crunches; ten packages of maple oatmeal; ten packages of regular oatmeal; two pouches of rice; one bar of Dial soap; two yellow legal tablets; five four-inch pencils; one tube of red Colgate toothpaste; one new toothbrush in its plastic wrapper.

The sum total of my wealth. It now belongs to big-bang black baby. A poor payment for all her kindness. But since it is all I have, it will have to do.

My side eats next. Like explosive dominoes, the door locks ripple and pop. Certain as I am that my cell door remains locked, nevertheless I test it, pushing against it. Locked. So I stand looking out my cell door window as orange automatons form a line; like ants, they know their function, the routine. Take a cup, choose either coffee or water, fill the cup; take a tray, turn to the right, and one trustee places an orange on the edge of the tray; take a step to the right, another trustee places a carton of milk on your tray, move to your table.

Ten minutes later, a command lashes through the air. "Wrap it up, gentlemen! Chow is over!"

Back on my bunk, I hear the trays thump against the inside of the trash barrels as the slop is pounded from them. The voices are vague, as if wearing little coats, and sound like seagulls squawking as they swap books, search for a secret light for a cigarette, tell jokes, gripe. Cell doors pound shut. Hydraulic locks snap home.

A dark shadow flits by my cell — the tall corporal making his rounds.

Silence. The after-dinner hush of jail.

I read George Orwell's *Essays*, a jail library book. My heart keeps beating, time keeps passing, yet I feel stuck in oblivion, the twilight zone of now. Eight o'clock should be here. I should be processed out.

A key turns in my cell door. Jumping up, I walk three paces to the door. The female CO swings it open, hands me two large plastic bags, the kind that line the trash barrels. They are thick and hold fifty gallons of whatever.

"For your commissary," she says.

"Thank you, ma'am," I reply, accepting them. I am touched by her kindness, that she remembered.

"Excuse me, ma'am?" I add.

"What is it, Radic?" she asks.

"Could you tell me the time, ma'am?"

Glancing at her watch, she says, "Seven o'clock."

"Thank you, ma'am."

She shuts the cell door in my face. As she turns her key in the lock, she looks at me through the window. "Don't worry. We won't forget you."

"Thank you, ma'am," I shout as she moves away.

Kneeling on the floor next to my bunk, I open one of the bags, place my gift — my possessions — into it. One at a time, like eggs that might crack or break, I insert them with care. Boxes of saltine crackers first, at the bottom. Then the Little Debbies, then the Star Crunches, then the smaller articles.

Finished, I tie a knot in the neck of the bag and place it on my red plastic chair so I won't forget it. For it holds religious significance, more like it's an atonement offering than a bag of foodstuffs from commissary.

I look around my cell to make sure I miss nothing. Opening the steel drawers, I check them. Like a dog, I drop to all fours, look under my bunk. I don't want to overlook anything.

Back on my bunk, I laugh at myself. How much can I miss in eighty-four square feet?

Lying back, I cover myself with my sheet and my blue blanket. My head rests on my orange sweatshirt. Five minutes pass. I can't lie still. Getting up, I slip on my rubber sandals and pace. Five steps to the door, turn 180 degrees to the left, five paces back to the desk, turn 180 degrees to the right. Repeat.

Hundreds of turns later, I hear the intake door crunch. Standing at my cell door window, I see a black-clad CO enter.

In his right hand, he holds a white computer printout. Eight o'clock. It must be! The tall corporal accepts the printout, reads it. Saying something to his partner, he yells out four names.

But not Radic.

"Roll up your stuff!" he shouts. Then repeats the names. I hear locks pop. Four women walk to the podium. They leave with their escort.

Wait! Wait! I want to scream. What about me?

About ten minutes later, another CO enters through the heavy steel intake door. Another computer printout is tendered to the tall corporal as he stands near the podium, his dark hair swept back, his arms folded across his chest, one booted sole pressed against the wall at his back. Again he shouts out the names.

And again Radic is not one of the names.

Five inmates from my side of the unit, the "male" side, roll up their stuff and hustle up to the podium. Their escort officer leads them out the intake door.

My limbs grow cold with a numb anguish, my mind is hollow with a blank worry that fills every synapse. I'm not getting out. Something's gone wrong. The DA changed his mind.

Standing at my cell door window, motionless, I stare at the podium. I try to cause the tall corporal to shout my name, pop my door locks, through sheer force of will, prayer, mental power. It fails.

I would scream. I would cry. But no one would care.

The other CO, the raven-haired female, makes her rounds and surprises me as she approaches my cell door. I didn't see her coming. She gazes directly at me as she strides by. Three paces past she stops, turns back to my cell door window. Looking through the narrow window, she says, "Don't worry, Radic. You're getting out. They're just running slow tonight."

"You're sure?" I ask.

"Yeah, I'm sure," she states. She smiles at me, then, as she turns to finish her rounds, says, "We won't forget you."

My brain sighs, a puff of fear-laced breath.

Back on my bunk, I lie supine, staring at the bluish-white ceiling with its curious black marks. I feel each second of each minute as it passes. Rising from my bunk, I move to the cell door window; it is time for nine o'clock rounds. I see the tall corporal striding along the second tier. He descends the stairs, makes a left, then a right, and doubles back to cell 16.

Arriving at cell 23, my cell, he pauses, peers in. Reaching for his key, he unlocks my cell door. I step back two paces as the cell door opens.

"Radic?"

"Yes, sir."

"My partner told me you're all stressed out." A smile plays about his lips.

"Yes, sir," I admit.

"Don't be. They've got 250 prisoners to release tonight, so it's taking a while. You'll probably be called in another thirty to forty minutes."

"Yes, sir. Thank you for telling me, sir."

"Be ready," he says, shutting my cell door. The door locks pop into place as he turns his key.

Back on my bunk, I wait.

Thirty minutes later the distant rattle of door locks popping informs me that the other side, the female side, is getting out for evening rec.

"Fully dressed, IDs on, cells clean, and beds made," sounds the voice of the tall corporal.

Moving to my cell door window, I see the female inmates exit their cells. The female CO stands at cell 16, the door open. She passes something to the occupant, shuts the door with a dull boom.

Glancing my way, she sees me. "You're getting out soon," she shouts at me. "But you're last."

"Thank you," I yell.

She moves off.

Last. Why am I last? Because I'm a level six? Or because they don't want anyone to see me being released? Or sheer happenstance? I don't know.

Moving back to my bunk, I grab my bedroll, drape the three sheets and the blue blanket over my shoulder. Then I move my brown paper bag of personal belongings next to the cell door. Next to it I place the plastic bag of goodies for big-bang baby. Standing at the cell door window, I wait.

Minutes pass, then pop, pop, pop. The door locks snap, startling me.

"Radic!" yells the tall corporal from the podium. "Roll up your stuff!"

Pushing the cell door open, I pick up my brown paper bag and the plastic bag full of commissary. I step out. As I walk toward the podium, the female co strides toward me. She stops as we meet.

"Dump your bedroll," she says.

"Yes, ma'am."

I walk to the cart, dump my bedroll in it. She follows me. Turning, I hold up the plastic bag. "Excuse me, ma'am, may I give this to the female trustee?" I ask.

"Okay," she nods. "Follow me."

She leads me to cell 15, the first of two trustee cells on the female side of the unit. Knocking on the cell door, she swings it open. The interior of the cell is dark. I see movement on the bunk.

"Yeah?" says a sleepy voice.

The co gives me a look.

"I've got my commissary for you," I say.

Big-bang baby, the trustee, stands in the doorway. "Oh, thanks." She gives me a tired smile.

"Here," I say, thrusting the bag toward her.

She grasps the bag, looks at it. "All this?"

"I don't need it where I'm going," I tell her. I smile. "Thanks for everything."

"Wow!" exclaims big-bang baby. "Thanks. Thanks a lot. Today's my birthday."

"Happy birthday!" I exclaim, surprised.

"Thanks. And good luck. Say a prayer for me, will ya?"

"Count on it."

The female CO points toward a round table on the female side of the unit. "Have a seat," she says. "They'll be here in a few minutes."

Moving to the table, I pull out a gray plastic chair and sit down. My brown paper bag sits next to my feet. The CO stands nearby, watching me, looking around. Female inmates roam around. A pretty one walks near my chair on her way to the podium. She is tall and slender, with long dark hair cascading down over her shoulders to the middle of her back. As she passes me, she tilts her head to one side, pulls the cascade of hair to the side and forward, so it all flows over her left shoulder onto her breast. I stare at her face. With the tasteful application of cosmetics, I decide, she would be gorgeous. But that's not why she is striking. Her protuberant belly precedes her. Even the cunt orange of boxy jail couture cannot hide her pregnancy. This stirs me. We are both in jail. I am waiting to be released, she is waiting to give birth.

I feel sorry for her. But I don't know why. I think about it for a few seconds and realize it's not her I feel sorry for. I feel pity for the child.

The female CO moves closer to me. "You're the preacher, right?" she says. A statement as well as a question.

"Yes, ma'am." I look at my white tackies, my orange pants, my brown paper bag. Then I look up at the CO.

"I read about you," she says. "I thought you got sixteen months?"

For an instant, I wonder how much to reveal. I shrug to myself: if you can't trust a CO, then something is definitely wrong. "I did, but the judge ORed me," I reply.

Her brow furrows a bit. "How come?"

I cock my head, give her a quizzical look. "I made a deal with the DA. If I provide testimony, they let me out early."

She uncovers her face to me, turning off her professional demeanor for a second. "Someone in here, in jail?"

"Roy Smith. Over in Intake 2."

She nods. "I know who he is." Glancing around, then over at the tall corporal behind the podium, she asks, "Aren't you scared?"

"Yes, ma'am, I am." I bend forward, placing my elbows on my knees, interlacing my fingers.

She stares at me, then nods. "I'm a Christian," she informs me.

I nod, not knowing what to say.

"Maybe this is a way for you to redeem yourself," she declares.

Not wanting to debate the doctrine of redemption with her, I nod. "Perhaps it is."

Walking around to my right, she arranges two of the gray plastic chairs circling the table. "I was on duty in the Hole when Smith was in there," she tells me. She glances around, looks over her shoulder. "He's a scary guy," she says in a quiet voice.

"Yes, ma'am," I agree.

Moving another plastic chair closer to the table, she looks at me. "Good luck to you."

"Thank you, ma'am."

She walks briskly toward the podium.

The intake door renders a heavy thunk, then opens. A well-built, very erect, middle-aged CO enters. He carries a computer printout in his hand. Seeing me at the table, he glances toward the tall corporal behind the podium. The corporal nods.

"Okay, Radic," says my escort CO, "let's go."

We walk down the long green hall, suffering in its own color scheme. Hugging my brown paper grocery bag to my chest, I feel like I'm dreaming.

My CO waves his left hand, which carries the white printout, at a heavy steel door on our left. The printout complains as it flaps with a shirring noise in the environmentally controlled, machine-cleaned air.

Turning left, I follow the CO to the door. Above it, in three-inch black letters, RELEASE.

A camera, like an electronic cyclops, inspects us as we near the door. Two heavy pops as the hydraulic locks are emancipated. The CO pulls the door open, waits as I pass through. "Check in at the window," he instructs me. The door booms closed behind me.

I'm in a long, narrow lobby. It is white with a gray linoleum floor. Along one wall are four numbered doors. The doors are shut. Two glass windows with pass holes on a wall face six black plastic chairs on the opposite wall.

Walking to the first window, I see a young blond CO on the other side of the glass. I recognize him from Intake 2. Aggressive and arrogant, he is not to be trifled with. Careful, I warn myself. Respect and submission.

"Name?" he asks in a curt voice.

"Radic."

"ID," he commands, thrusting his hand out the pass hole. Both his hands wear white latex gloves.

I unclip my ID, place it in his open hand.

He reads it, makes a notation on a clipboard in front of him. "Have a seat," he commands, not looking at me.

Turning, I take a seat, still hugging my brown paper bag to my chest. Three other orange-clad figures are already seated. One is black and very young; two are Hispanic, probably gang members.

Another CO appears at the other window. Fifty-something, stocky, walrus mustache. I recognize him too. He is cool, patient.

"All right, gentlemen," says the older CO. "Each of you will enter one of the dressing rooms. You will take off your orange, your T-shirts, your shorts, your socks, and your rubber sandals. Place them in the plastic bag you will find in your room.

"You will find your personal property in a green bag in the room. Dress in your personal property — the clothes you had on when you were booked. Leave the green bag and the plastic bag in the room."

He pauses then, dropping his chin, gives us a stern expression. "Do not, gentlemen, please do not attempt to hang on to any souvenirs — such as a jail T-shirt. These items are the property of San Joaquin County Jail. If you do take anything — and are caught — you will be charged with a felony." His voice is chiding, as if he knows he's wasting his breath and someone's going to try anyway.

I glance at the two gangbangers. They are looking at each other, grinning like skunks eating shit. To me, they look dumb enough to still try it.

"Radic!" snarls the young blond co.

"Yes, sir," I respond automatically.

"Over here," he snaps, indicating his window with the pen in his hand.

"Yes, sir," I say respectfully, standing in front of the window.

"I got your property list here." He taps his clipboard with the pen. "One black T-shirt, one pair of socks, one pair of athletic shoes, one pair blue gym shorts, one pair black boxers, one blue jacket, one wallet — brown — and one cell phone — blue." He jabs the point of his pen into the paper on the clipboard, looks directly at me. "If that's correct, put your signature there" — he points with the pen — "and today's date there." Spinning the clipboard on its axis, he extends the pen through the pass hole.

I take it, sign off on my property. Carefully and respectfully, I hand him back his pen.

He squints at me through the filthy windowpane. "Room 4," he commands me. "Now."

"Yes, sir. Thank you, sir."

Eight feet by eight feet, room 4 has dirty walls, a disgustingly filthy, unpainted gray cement floor, and a slide-open window, which is open. On the other side of the window is the older CO, holding a green mesh bag. My clothes, the ones I had on when I was arrested.

"Radic," he says.

"Yes, sir."

"Here's your property." He hands me the green bag. "Be sure to place your orange in this plastic bag. Leave it on the floor, in the corner. When you're dressed, go back outside and have a seat."

"Yes, sir."

Setting down my brown paper bag, I strip quickly, placing each article of jail clothing in the plastic bag. The CO remains at the window watching me. Six months before, I would have felt self-conscious and humiliated. Now I stand stark naked in the middle of a holding tank, more barren due to its very filthiness, a black-clad corrections officer scrutinizing my every move. And I don't care.

Tossing the plastic bag into the far corner, I open the green mesh bag, withdraw my clothes. A dry odor comes from them, like old dust on a hot day in a famine. As I don them, they feel strange, foreign. Their material holds a different texture, softer, smoother. I feel ridiculous but good too.

Sitting on the cement floor, I pull on my athletic shoes. I don't untie them, just pull them on. When I stand up, my feet feel like they're floating on a cushion of air. The shoes support my feet rather than my feet supporting the shoes. Looking down at my shoes, I wriggle my toes inside them.

"Radic," says the CO standing at the open window.

"Yes, sir?"

"How's it feel to be getting out?"

I think about that for a second. "It feels great, sir." I smile at him.

"How long were you here?"

"Six months, sir."

He gazes at me, as if he's weighing me with his eyes. "Did you learn your lesson?"

I don't need to think about that because I've thought about it for six months. "Yes sir, I did."

He grins at me. "Good. Go have a seat."

Back outside, hugging my brown paper bag, I take a seat on a black plastic chair.

The other three are there already. And already they look the part — gangbangers. They wear loose, sagging jeans, too-large formless shirts, and white Nike athletic shoes. Their jeans look brand new: dark blue, stiff, with a kind of sheen to them. Their white shoes are antiseptically clean.

"Okay," snarls the young CO from behind his windowpane. "Come get your release forms."

The others jump up, jostling each other to get to the window. I stay in my chair.

"One at a goddamned time!" bellows the CO. He points aggressively at the black plastic chairs. "Sit back down!" He glares at them, shaking his head.

They move slowly back to their chairs, smiling at each other. Their attitudes, their gestures, their stances denote their insolence.

"You know," the CO states, "I can add time right now if you punks want me to." He glares at them. "Another week or ten days. All I have to do is call the sergeant in, and it'll happen."

The gangbangers grin at each other, nudge each other with hands and elbows.

"Naw, sir," says the young black dude, "we don' want that."

The CO continues to scowl at them then, finally, nods stiffly.

"Okay, now, when I call your name, come get your release form. Then out that door." He indicates the exit door with his head. "Once you're outside, take your form to the window. If you have any money left on your books, they will give it to you. If not, then you're free to leave."

"Radic," calls the CO.

I rise and accept my form. Walking to the exit door, I turn the knob, fully expecting it to be locked. I step out into a large waiting room, like a doctor's office. Padded seats, plants, blue walls. Off to the right is a caged window.

Sharla appears in front of me. She smiles. I try to swallow and almost start to cry. We move toward one another. Putting her arms around my neck, she kisses me. Still hugging my brown paper bag to my chest, it gets in the way. But I won't put it down. It's all I own in the world.

"Finally," says Sharla, an oozing balm in her voice. "I came at 7:30 and waited. Then they told me that you wouldn't be out till after 9:00."

"What time is it now?" I ask, hugging my brown paper bag to my chest with one arm, my other hand holding Sharla's hand.

Glancing at her wristwatch, she says, "It's ten after ten."

"Jesus," I tell her. "I've been waiting and waiting. I didn't think I was going to get out at all."

"I knew you'd get out," she assures me. "*When* was worrying me."

"You've been here since 7:30?"

"No, when they told me it would be later, I left. Got something to eat, picked up a coffee at Starbucks."

I look to my right, see the caged window. Ten feet in front of the window a red line is painted on the floor. Next to the line is a free-standing sign with a white placard that says "Remain behind the line until called."

"I guess I need to get in line," I tell Sharla, pointing at the caged window.

The two gangbangers are already in line, posturing — that undulating, jerky thing they do with their heads, upper torsos, and gestures. Gang pose. Means they're bad and supercool.

Holding up my release form so Sharla can see it, I add, "I give them this, and they give me the money left on my books."

"Okay," she says. "Here, give me your stuff, and I'll hold it for you."

I give her my brown paper bag, move into place behind the red line. One of the gangbangers is in front of me, the other at the caged window. The one in front of me says something in Spanish to his homie at the window. The homie turns to look, flashes a shit-eating grin and a gang sign with his right hand. A sarcastic laugh issues from the lips of the one in front of me. He sways, pumping his head a little like a chicken.

At the window, the homie scoops up his money and walks back toward his buddy. Holding up two twenty-dollar bills, he grins, sticks out his tongue, does a little gang jig: shuffles his feet with stiff knees, pumps his head, lurches his arms. In a high falsetto, he sings, "Money, money, money."

The homeboy in front of me gurgles a laugh, moves to the window. A few minutes later he has his money, and the two depart with a little gangbanger groupie, a fashionista dressed in spotless white Nike trainers, blue jeans rolled up to capri level, and a white tanktop over a red bra.

Walking up to the window, I see a woman with gray hair pulled into a tight bun; her dress is gray with black diamonds on it. Her skin is gray too, but her eyes are alert and friendly. She sits in a pale green secretary's chair in front of a huge electric typewriter, which is piggybacked to a CPU. A flat-screen monitor roosts to her right; beside it rests a keyboard.

I shove my release form through the pass hole. She reads it, then dances her fingers over the computer keyboard. She turns to look at me. "You have $630," she announces.

"Yes, ma'am."

"I can give you up to $200 in cash now, if you like. The rest, though, will have to be as a check, which will be mailed to you." She gazes at me expectantly.

"That will be fine," I reply.

"Okay," she says and turns to her keyboard. Thirty seconds later she counts out ten twenty-dollar bills, puts them in an envelope, hands it to me.

"Thank you."

"You're welcome," she replies. Her expression tells me she doesn't hear "thank you" very often.

A computer printout slides out the pass hole to me.

"Signature and date at the bottom, please," she says. As I sign my name, she adds, "Your check should arrive in three to six weeks."

"Thank you very much." I slide the form back to her.

"That's it," she says.

"Thank you."

I walk back to Sharla, who is holding my brown paper bag. Taking the bag, I hand her the envelope. "Put that in your purse, would you?" I ask.

"Sure. What is it?"

"Two hundred dollars. The rest will be sent to me. I guess they can't give out more than that in cash."

"Ready?" she asks, zipping her purse shut.

"Boy, am I!"

We walk out the doors of the jail into the cool of the night. A vast cement quadrangle with a naked flagpole extends before us. Beyond, a vast parking lot with dim flowered light poles spaced every twenty-five yards. Sharla examines the area.

"What?" I ask.

"It's dark," she explains, "and they've been releasing inmates all night. Just makes me nervous. I mean, most of them are real scuzzy looking. They could wait out here and jump people, take their money."

"In front of the jail?"

"You never know," she says, squeezing my hand.

"Well, you'd have to be really stupid to do that right in front of the jail." I think about this for a moment. "You're right, though," I nod. "Most of them are that stupid."

I glance around but see no one. The red brake lights of a car turning out of the lot burn brightly. Probably the two homies and their designated fashionista.

At her car, I place my brown paper bag on the back seat

then settle into the passenger's seat. Sharla starts the car, hits a switch. Two white beams of light lance out from the front of her car. Positioning her purse on the floor in front of her seat, she says, "Look in the glove box."

I do. In it is a small plastic baggie holding five cigars. Three are ocher in color, indicating natural wrappers; the other two glint a coffee brown color, maduros. Opening the baggie, I shove my nose into it, inhale. The piquant stench of tobacco adheres to my nostrils, like aromatic velcro.

"Ahhhh!" I breathe.

Sharla laughs. "I thought you'd want some."

"Can I smoke one now, in your car?" I ask.

"Sure," she says. "I put your cutter in there too." She cracks her window, pulls out a lighter and a Marlboro Ultra Light One Hundred. Flicking her Bic, she ignites the cigarette. She inhales deeply, lets the smoke curl out of her mouth.

There's a box of stick matches along with the guillotine in the baggie. Decapitating the end of a light brown Hoya with the guillotine, I slide its length under my nose, inhaling its musty bouquet. I light up. A haze of stinky blue smoke inflates the cockpit of the car.

Sharla coughs, laughs, waving her hand in front of her face. "I forgot how strong those things are."

I laugh too. A grand, happy laugh. Then I crack my window.

"Man, that tastes good," I sigh. I lean over and give her a kiss. "Thanks, sweet girl."

"You're welcome," she says. Putting the car in gear, she drives into the night, away from the jail.

I don't have to look at the cement buildings as they slide into the distance behind us. I can feel them. For they have left their marks on me, like brands on the flanks of cattle. Only mine are more like inner stigmata, a kind of soul scar. They can't be distinguished, but they are there.

Just like jail is there. Waiting.

Puffing on my cigar, I hold Sharla's hand as she steers through the streets toward I-5. A surge of emotions grips me, overwhelms me; tears leak out of my eyes, trickle down my cheeks. It's the little things I missed: holding hands; smoking a cigar; riding in a car, going somewhere.

I sniff, and Sharla glances over at me. "You okay?" she asks.

"Yeah," I reply, squeezing her hand. "It's so different out here, ya know? Six months in jail is a long time, more like six years in real time."

"I guess so." She brings my hand to her mouth, kisses the back of my hand oh-so-lightly, like a brief encounter with a dove's wing. "I'm just glad you're out."

"Me, too," I laugh, wiping my eyes with the sleeve of my jacket.

"I was going to take you to Tony Roma's for dinner," she tells me. "But it's too late now. We'll go tomorrow, for sure."

"Yeah, that would be great."

"Are you hungry?"

"No, not really. But I'd like a glass of wine. I missed wine too."

"I've got a bottle at home," she says, looking at me. She smiles. "McManus Cabernet, your favorite."

"Cool."

We arrive at her house at around 11 p.m. She leads me into the kitchen, opens the bottle of wine, pours its maroon contents into a long-stemmed wine glass. No more Styrofoam cups. She pours herself a beer: Coors Light in a tall, slender, frozen glass, which she removes from her freezer.

Sitting in the dark on her patio, I sense the oddities around me: the texture of the air, the sounds of cars driving by, the cuckoo of a crosswalk signal.

Taking a sip of wine, feeling it dance on my taste buds, I ask, "Are we still getting married?"

"That's right!" she exclaims. "I forgot to show you. It's on my computer — the place I rented for us in San Francisco." She jumps up, walks into the house.

Sixty seconds later she says, "C'mere. You have to see it."

In the house, I stand behind her as she sits before her computer screen.

"There," she points. "That's it."

As she scrolls through the interior shots of the apartment, I feel distracted, as if something is wrong. It's as if I'm Moses in the Bible, a stranger in a strange land. "It looks wonderful," I tell her. "You did good!"

"I hope it's as nice as it looks," she says. "We have it for a whole week. In San Francisco! I can hardly wait."

Back on her patio, we speak of jail, the people I met in there, the way they act, the addiction of environment, of Bob's trial, of Roy's case and my testimony. We discuss many things.

Later, lying on her bed, staring up at the vaulted ceiling, I wonder if I can sleep on a real bed. I wonder if I will dream of jail or awake to find that I am still in jail, dreaming about being out.